# jMonkeyEngine 3.0 Beginner's Guide

Develop professional 3D games for desktop, web, and mobile, all in the familiar Java programming language

**Ruth Kusterer**

[ PACKT ] open source ✿
PUBLISHING      community experience distilled

BIRMINGHAM - MUMBAI

# jMonkeyEngine 3.0 Beginner's Guide

First published: June 2013

Production Reference: 1180613

Published by Packt Publishing Ltd.
Livery Place
35 Livery Street
Birmingham B3 2PB, UK.

ISBN 978-1-84951-646-4

www.packtpub.com

Cover Image by Girish Suryawanshi (girish.suryawanshi@gmail.com)

# Credits

**Author**
Ruth Kusterer

**Reviewers**
Peter Backx

T. Joseph Duchesne

Jens Hohmuth

Dany Rioux

Glauco Márdano

**Acquisition Editor**
Antony Lowe

**Lead Technical Editor**
Mayur Hule

**Technical Editors**
Prasad Dalvi

Pushpak Poddar

Kirti Pujari

**Project Coordinator**
Michelle Quadros

**Proofreaders**
Aaron Nash

Jonathan Todd

**Indexer**
Tejal Soni

**Production Coordinator**
Nitesh Thakur

**Cover Work**
Nitesh Thakur

# About the Author

**Ruth Kusterer** became intrigued by Java and open source software while completing her degree in computational linguistics. In 2005, she joined Sun Microsystems, Inc. as a technical writer for netbeans.org where she wrote *100 NetBeans IDE Tips & Tricks*. Since 2010, she has been working for CA Technologies, Inc. where she's a senior technical writer for security software. In her spare time, she hangs out on jMonkeyEngine.org and strives eternally to write the ultimate Java game.

I would like to thank the jMonkeyEngine core team for answering a BigInteger of newbie questions and helping out with non-trivial code samples. I would also like to thank all the jMonkeys posting inspiring videos of completed games, and a big shout-out to the NetBeans community whose NetBeans platform is the base of the jMonkeyEngine SDK.

# About the Reviewers

**Peter Backx** is a software developer and architect. He has used Java for more than a decade to shape unique user experiences and build rock-solid scalable software. He received a PhD in Computer Sciences from Ghent University, Belgium. Peter maintains a technical blog at `http://www.streamhead.com`.

**T. Joseph Duchesne** holds a Computer Engineering degree from Dalhousie University and works in software-as-a-service web applications, primarily in backend infrastructure using a wide variety of technologies. In his free time, he enjoys video game development and has competed in open source/independent game development competitions.

Joseph is currently Sr. Infrastructure and Software Engineer at SimplyCast (`www.simplycast.com`), an online software-as-a-service marketing platform.

**Jens Hohmuth** graduated in Computer Science in 1998 from the University of Applied Sciences of Zwickau, Germany. Jens has been working for more than 10 years as a professional Software Developer. At his day job at a German company, he works for banks and financial services providers applying e-banking solutions on a wide range of different platforms. Jens has expertise in analysis, design, implementation, and support of software projects from small to large scale. He is an gile software development follower and a natural born problem solver.

Jens has outstanding training and presentation skills, and created a popular Intel Protected Mode and MMX Tutorial series as his internship back in college. This tutorial is still one of the top references for Intel Protected Mode today.

At night time, he is a wannabe game developer and the founder of the open source Java GUI Framework "Nifty GUI". Besides "Nifty GUI" he has contributed to many other open source projects. When he's not coding he enjoys creating 2D and 3D art as well as playing his guitar and piano. In the summertime, you can find him outside on his mountain bike (probably with his Macbook Air in the backpack).

I'd like to thank all the jMonkeyEngine core members for being extremely friendly and a great joy to work with. And of course all the "Nifty GUI" users (and critics) in the world for their continuing support.

**Dany Rioux** received his programmer/analyst diploma more than 15 years ago at the Herzing College in Montreal, Canada.

Although he left the programming side of things for numerous years to work in user support, he has come back to his first love and has been actively working on Disenthral, an RPG space game, based on the jMonkeyEngine3, for the past two years.

# www.PacktPub.com

## Support files, eBooks, discount offers and more

You might want to visit www.PacktPub.com for support files and downloads related to your book.

Did you know that Packt offers eBook versions of every book published, with PDF and ePub files available? You can upgrade to the eBook version at www.PacktPub.com and as a print book customer, you are entitled to a discount on the eBook copy. Get in touch with us at service@packtpub.com for more details.

At www.PacktPub.com, you can also read a collection of free technical articles, sign up for a range of free newsletters and receive exclusive discounts and offers on Packt books and eBooks.

http://PacktLib.PacktPub.com

Do you need instant solutions to your IT questions? PacktLib is Packt's online digital book library. Here, you can access, read and search across Packt's entire library of books.

### Why Subscribe?

- Fully searchable across every book published by Packt
- Copy and paste, print and bookmark content
- On demand and accessible via web browser

### Free Access for Packt account holders

If you have an account with Packt Publishing at www.PacktPub.com, you can use this to access PacktLib today and view nine entirely free books. Simply use your login credentials for immediate access.

# Table of Contents

# Preface

*"You, my brave hero, are about to embark on an adventure full of challenges and risks, but the reward at the end of your journey will be plentiful and will restore peace on earth. Are you ready?"*

You have probably played many games before reading this book, and gladly accepted challenges such as this one! Now you will face a new adventure. You will create your own video game. There too will be challenges, but jMonkeyEngine gives you the tools to overcome them. This book introduces Java developers to 3D game development and shows how jMonkeyEngine can make a game developer's life easier.

Note that this book does not cover 3D model or sound design, nor the creative process of coming up with an original game concept—read the appendix for some related resources. By the end of this book, you will be ready to develop a 3D game, and have fun doing it!

## What this book covers

*Chapter 1, Installing jMonkeyEngine*, helps you install the software and run a sample application.

*Chapter 2, Creating Your First 3D Scene*, teaches you how to add objects and transform them.

*Chapter 3, Interacting with the User*, reveals how to control game mechanics in the main loop.

*Chapter 4, Adding Character to Your Game*, shows how to load and convert models.

*Chapter 5, Creating Materials*, demonstrates how to manipulate the surface of objects.

*Chapter 6, Having Fun with Physics*, teaches you how to make objects act solid or heavy.

*Chapter 7, Adding Spark to the Game*, shows basic types of decorative effects.

*Chapter 8, Creating Landscapes*, introduces terrains and environmental effects.

*Chapter 9, Making Yourself Heard*, teaches how to integrate sounds and music.

*Chapter 10, Showing Your Game to the World*, shows how to save, load, build, and distribute games.

*Appendix A, What's Next?*, reveals how to make your games fun and challenging.

*Appendix B, Additional Resources for Fellow jMonkeys*, introduces you to more advanced user interfaces.

*Free Download Chapter, Playing on the Network*, explains network communication in multiplayer games. This chapter is available as a free download chapter at `http://www.packtpub.com/sites/default/files/downloads/6464OS_Free_Download_Chapter_Playing_on_the_Network.pdf`

# Get a head start

Game development involves a wide range of abilities. Mathematics, software programming, graphic design, musical arts, and writing skills. Like a member of a World of Warcraft guild, you need a firm grasp of the tools of your trade before you set out for your quest. Intermediate or advanced Java skills are a must, as is a basic grasp of multimedia design and 3D modeling.

Thanks to 3D engines, however, you do not have to reinvent the mathematical wheel for every 3D game that you write. 3D engines such as jMonkeyEngine handle the following tasks for you:

+ **Transformation**: Rotating, scaling, and moving 3D objects
+ **Projection**: Automatic conversion of 3D scene data to 2D images on the screen
+ **Rendering**: State-of the-art shading and lighting of object surfaces

The sunlit ocean bay in this screenshot is just one of many examples of what can be achieved when a collection of advanced 3D rendering techniques come together:

In addition to transformation, projection, and rendering, there is a lot of internal functionality that is the same in every 3D game. By reusing proven implementations, you spare yourself the need to handcode standard algorithms. jMonkeyEngine includes many features that are otherwise only found in commercial game engines:

◆ A 3D scene graph: A data structure that is optimized to store objects of a 3D scene

◆ A main event loop: A modular component that controls game mechanics and interactions

◆ Support for loading and displaying multimedia assets

◆ Support for handling user input and graphical user interfaces

◆ An intuitive camera object that marks the point of view of the player

◆ Physics simulation, special effects, multiplayer networking, and more

jMonkeyEngine gives you a head start, so you have more time for coding the parts that make your game unique.

# Who this book is for

To set expectations right, jMonkeyEngine is not one of these drag-and-drop tools that mass-produces games with just a few clicks. To create a truly original game, you have to be able to write Java code. Let's have a look at an example:

This screenshot shows a scene from Hostile Sector, a browser-based multiplayer strategy game created with the jMonkeyEngine (`http://www.mindemia.com/hostilesector/`). In this game, two armed teams fight each other in an abandoned town. To be able to create such a basic game scene, you need to be familiar with the following mathematical concepts:

- **The Cartesian coordinate system**: You use coordinates every time you position a character or building into the scene.

- **Vectors**: You use vectors to specify angles and directions every time you make a computer-controlled enemy turn around. You use vectors when calculating distances and speeds every time an enemy follows a player character.

This book will walk you through these mathematical concepts where necessary, and introduce you to the appropriate built-in methods and classes that get these tasks done.

# Getting things done

It is often that successful games such as Minecraft that inspire players to become game developers themselves. An example of a game that was inspired by Minecraft is Mythruna (`http://mythruna.com/`), an open-world game developed with the jMonkeyEngine.

For its creator, Mythruna was not the first game he ever wrote. Successful developers achieved their level of skill by starting small. Begin your developer career by creating a portfolio of solid mini-games to gain experience. Equipped with this knowledge, you can work your way up to the "MMORPG of your dreams".

The key to success is to stick to one idea and dare to strip off everything unnecessary. Don't aimlessly attempt to top every best-selling game of the last decade in your first release. And don't water down your game by adding tons of distracting effects just because everyone else is doing it.

Everyone else can start a game, but you want to finish it, too. A good feasibility test is to sum up your concept in one line. An example catchline for a Minecraft-like idea could be, "Build by day, survive by night". If you can't convey your idea in one straightforward line, it's too complicated to implement. Start with a clearly cut-out idea, and soon you will have something cool to show.

Do you already have a game idea? Let's have a quick look at the process of breaking down a complex idea into the building blocks of game development.

# The building blocks of game development

Let's say you are creating something similar to Hostile Sector, basically an arena with two fighters. One is a player-controlled character, the other a hostile non-player character (NPC).

How does the computer-controlled NPC "see" where the player is? How does the enemy approach the player without stupidly bumping into walls? At first, any game concept may seem like an undertaking of real-life complexity. But when you think about it for a minute, you notice that even a complex game scene is composed of only a handful of basic actions.

- You attach 3D objects to the scene to make them appear, and detach them to make them disappear. Examples include terrains, buildings, players, enemies, cars, obstacles, traps, and so on.
- You transform 3D objects. **Transformation** means that you make the game engine translate (position), rotate (turn), or scale (resize) objects in the scene.
- You modify physical properties of 3D objects. Examples include lighting and shading, materials and colors, mass, speed, bounciness, or solidity.
- You detect user input from the keyboard, the mouse, or a joystick, and respond to it. For example, the player clicks to shoot.

♦ You specify a rule how the game acts and causes state changes for the player. This includes automatic game mechanics such as intelligent computer-controlled enemies who attack when the player approaches their secret lair.

♦ You specify a rule how the game reacts to state changes. You repeatedly get and set object properties (such as current location, direction, or points) and use them in specific conditions. This includes game mechanics such as "if health equals zero, then game over" or "if distance between player and enemy is less than one meter, then attack".

♦ You play audio, video, animations, and special effects. These are only decorations, but they add a lot to the immersion, if used right.

Now that you are aware of the basic atoms, a seemingly intricate scene turns into a manageable pattern of smaller pieces. Just like building blocks, you can use these elements in any order or number that fulfills your game's purpose. The only limits are the capabilities of your PC.

## Listening to the heartbeat of your game

How do you apply what you just learned in context? Let's look at the overall structure of computer games. Obviously, you will have to write code to initialize the scene, and also to shut down the game cleanly. Between the beginning and the end, every interactive 3D application constantly loops through three stages: listen, update, and render.

♦ **Initialize**: The game loads objects and brings them in their starting positions. The loop starts:

   ❑ **Listen**: The engine detects user input and responds according to your input handlers

   ❑ **Update**: Your game code polls and updates its state, and acts and reacts according to your game mechanics

   ❑ **Render**: The engine draws the scene to the screen

♦ **End**: The player has won, lost, paused, or quit the game. The loop ends.

In each stage of the game loop, you can make use of all basic elements described here. Let's look at an example of how to put the pieces together.

# Putting the pieces together

Our example is of two fighters in an arena. In simple terms, you can break this scene down as follows:

1. **Initialization**: You load the landscape, player, and enemy models, attach them to the scene, and position them. The loop starts.

2. **Listen**: The game listens for keyboard input in case the player moves his character. The game listens for mouse input in case the player clicks to attack the enemy.

3. **Update**: The game checks for obstacles between the two opponents, and rotates the computer-controlled enemy to approach the player's location. If certain conditions are met, the enemy attacks the player and plays a sound. The game polls location, armor, and health of the opponents, and calculates the outcome of every attack. The game updates location, armor, and health values according to the outcome.

4. **Render**: The game draws the updated state to the screen and the loop repeats.

5. **End**: A test checks if one of the fighters has reached zero health points. If yes, then the loop ends and a winner is declared.

Looks more manageable now, doesn't it?

# Sources of information

In the preceding example, you saw how a game scene comes together. As you read on, your understanding of the application structure will improve. The book includes a lot of hands-on sample code and fun challenges, because writing code and trying it out is the best (and most interesting) way to learn.

As additional sources, you should bookmark the following two pages:

◆ `http://jMonkeyEngine.org/wiki/doku.php/=jme3`: Visit the wiki to get the latest sample code, beginner tutorials, intermediate articles, and advanced documentation.

◆ `http://jMonkeyEngine.org/forums-index`: Search the forums for answers to the most common questions, or chat with like-minded developers about different approaches.

# Conventions

In this book, you will find several headings appearing frequently.

To give clear instructions on how to complete a procedure or task, we use:

# Time for action – heading

1. Action 1
2. Action 2
3. Action 3

Instructions often need some extra explanation so that they make sense, so they are followed with:

## What just happened?

This heading explains the working of tasks or instructions that you have just completed.

You will also find some other learning aids in the book, including:

# Pop quiz – heading

These are short multiple choice questions intended to help you test your own understanding.

# Have a go hero – heading

These set practical challenges and give you ideas for experimenting with what you have learned.

You will also find a number of styles of text that distinguish between different kinds of information. Here are some examples of these styles, and an explanation of their meaning.

Code words in text are shown as follows: "Browse to the jMonkeyProjects/BasicGame/dist/ folder in your user home."

A block of code is set as follows:

```
import com.jme3.app.SimpleApplication;
import com.jme3.material.Material;
import com.jme3.math.ColorRGBA;
import com.jme3.math.Vector3f;
import com.jme3.renderer.RenderManager;
import com.jme3.scene.Geometry;
import com.jme3.scene.shape.Box;
```

When we wish to draw your attention to a particular part of a code block, the relevant lines or items are set in bold:

```
SceneGraphVisitorAdapter myEmitterVisitor =
                        new SceneGraphVisitorAdapter() {
  @Override
  public void visit(Geometry geom) {
    super.visit(geom);
    searchForEmitter(geom); // trigger custom test
  }
  @Override
  public void visit(Node node) {
    super.visit(node);
```

**New terms** and **important words** are shown in bold. Words that you see on the screen, in menus or dialog boxes for example, appear in the text like this: "If you still need to install the JDK, click on the **Download JDK** button."

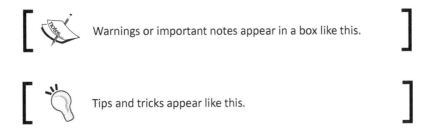

Warnings or important notes appear in a box like this.

Tips and tricks appear like this.

# Reader feedback

Feedback from our readers is always welcome. Let us know what you think about this book—what you liked or may have disliked. Reader feedback is important for us to develop titles that you really get the most out of.

To send us general feedback, simply send an e-mail to feedback@packtpub.com, and mention the book title through the subject of your message.

If there is a topic that you have expertise in and you are interested in either writing or contributing to a book, see our author guide on www.packtpub.com/authors.

# Customer support

Now that you are the proud owner of a Packt book, we have a number of things to help you to get the most from your purchase.

## Downloading the example code

You can download the example code files for all Packt books you have purchased from your account at http://www.packtpub.com. If you purchased this book elsewhere, you can visit http://www.packtpub.com/support and register to have the files e-mailed directly to you.

# Downloading the color images of this book

We also provide you a PDF file that has color images of the screenshots/diagrams used in this book. The color images will help you better understand the changes in the output. You can download this file from http://www.packtpub.com/sites/default/files/downloads/6464OS_ColoredImages.pdf.

# Errata

Although we have taken every care to ensure the accuracy of our content, mistakes do happen. If you find a mistake in one of our books—maybe a mistake in the text or the code—we would be grateful if you would report this to us. By doing so, you can save other readers from frustration and help us improve subsequent versions of this book. If you find any errata, please report them by visiting http://www.packtpub.com/support, selecting your book, clicking on the **errata submission form** link, and entering the details of your errata. Once your errata are verified, your submission will be accepted and the errata will be uploaded to our website, or added to any list of existing errata, under the Errata section of that title.

# Piracy

Piracy of copyright material on the Internet is an ongoing problem across all media. At Packt, we take the protection of our copyright and licenses very seriously. If you come across any illegal copies of our works, in any form, on the Internet, please provide us with the location address or website name immediately so that we can pursue a remedy.

Please contact us at copyright@packtpub.com with a link to the suspected pirated material.

We appreciate your help in protecting our authors and our ability to bring you valuable content.

# Questions

You can contact us at questions@packtpub.com if you are having a problem with any aspect of the book, and we will do our best to address it.

# 1
# Installing jMonkeyEngine

*When a group of heroes set out on a quest, they grab their armor and weapons—when you set out on a game development adventure, you grab the jMonkeyEngine SDK.*

The jMonkeyEngine Software Development Kit (SDK) contains everything that you need to get started quickly: the jMonkeyEngine libraries, Javadoc, sample code, and lots of nifty game development utilities. This bundle also includes all necessary native libraries, such as LightWeight Java Game Library (LWJGL). This means there is no second installation step, neither for the development team, nor for users of the games that we create.

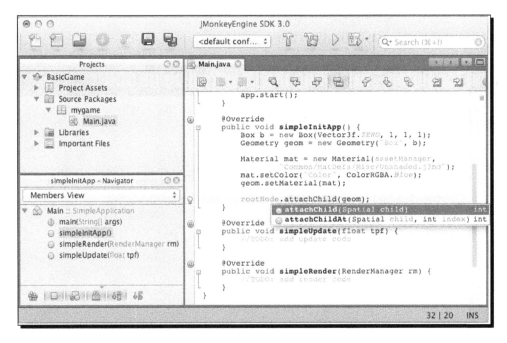

In this chapter you will learn:

- What the hardware and software requirements are
- How to install the jMonkeyEngine SDK
- How the tools in the jMonkeyEngine SDK make a developer's life easier
- How to create and distribute jMonkeyEngine games

# Installation requirements for game developers

At the time of printing, the jMonkeyEngine SDK needs 40 MB of memory, plus enough memory to load the particular game's assets. Your computer should have a minimum of 1 GHz CPU, and your graphic card must support OpenGL 2.0, or better. Suitable graphic cards include ATI Radeon 9500, NVIDIA GeForce 5 FX, Intel GMA 4500, and all newer ones.

You can use the jMonkeyEngine SDK on all operating systems that support the Java Development Kit 6 (JDK 6) or better. Currently this includes Windows XP/Windows Vista/Windows 7 or better, Mac OS X 10.5 or better, and Linux kernel 2.6 or better.

Enter the following command in your terminal to check whether you have the required Java Development Kit (JDK) installed:

```
javac -version
```

If this command returns `javac 1.6.x` or better, then your Java installation is set to go. If you still need to install the JDK, click on the **Download JDK** button at `http://www.oracle.com/technetwork/java/javase/downloads/index.html` and follow the installation instructions there.

## Time for action – installing the jMonkeyEngine SDK

The jMonkey team devised the jMonkeyEngine SDK to make the installation process as smooth as possible:

1. Go to `http://jmonkeyengine.org/downloads/`.
2. Download the **jME3 SDK** for your operating system and unzip it, if necessary.
3. Double-click on the installer and complete the installation wizard.

It's time for your first test run:

1.  Find the **jMonkeyEngine SDK** icon in your **Applications** folder or **Start** menu and double-click on it to run the SDK.

2.  When the jMonkeyEngine SDK opens for the first time, a dialog box asks you to specify a folder for storing your projects. Browse to your home directory, click on the **Create new folder** button, and name the folder jMonkeyProjects.

3.  With your new folder still selected, click on **Set Project Folder** to close the dialog box.

When the SDK opens, you will see the following application screen:

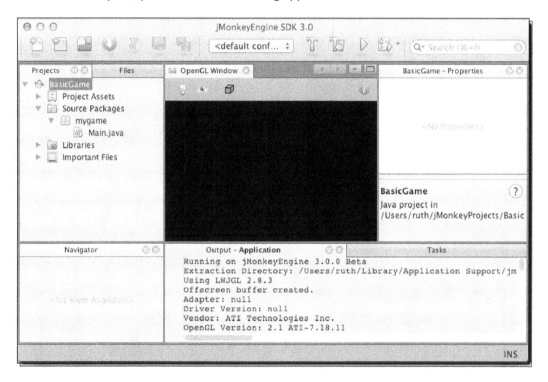

The **Projects** window, on the top left-hand side, is where you will browse Java files and manage Java packages, among other things. The SDK also contains an editor window for Java files, not visible here, that we will look at in a minute. At the bottom right-hand side of the screen, you see the **Output - Application** window; this is where build messages, runtime exceptions, warnings, and println() appear.

In the center, you see the **OpenGL Window**. We will use it later to preview the 3D scenes that we created using the **Properties**, **SceneExplorer**, and **SceneComposer** windows, not visible here.

The other two windows you can ignore for now. Later you may use the **FilterExplorer** window to configure special effects, and the **AssetPackBrowser** window to bundle up collections of 3D models.

Congrats, your tools are ready, and you have accomplished your first mission. Let's take a closer look at the jMonkeyEngine SDK.

# jMonkeyEngine SDK at your service

The jMonkeyEngine SDK is your graphical user interface for the jMonkeyEngine library. The jMonkey team devised this integrated development environment (IDE) especially for 3D game development with Java. The jMonkeyEngine SDK assists you from start to end, whether you write code, integrate game assets, lay out scenes, or deploy the finished application.

Creating your Java game projects with jMonkeyEngine SDK has the added value that they are already preconfigured:

- The jMonkeyEngine JAR files and native libraries are on the classpath
- Javadoc popups and code completion for jMonkeyEngine methods are set up in the source editor
- The provided Ant build script is ready to build, run, and deploy your application

At the same time, there is nothing proprietary about the projects that the SDK creates: you are looking at standard Java SE projects. The SDK's clean, build, and run actions are automated using standard Ant build scripts. The Apache Ant build tool is already included when you install the SDK.

**Did you know?**

jMonkeyEngine SDK is built on top of the NetBeans Platform. This means that you can install all kinds of NetBeans IDE plugins. The NetBeans plugins prepackaged in the jMonkeyEngine SDK include version control tools and a Java debugger. Open the jMonkeyEngine SDK and choose **Tools | Plugins** from the menu, then click on **Available Plugins** to browse and install other cool add-ons for free, such as a Java profiler.

# Can I work in other Java IDEs?

Although this book will repeatedly tell you how awesome the jMonkeyEngine SDK is, you are not forced to use it for coding. The jMonkeyEngine library is open source software: If you download the latest binary bundle from `http://www.jmonkeyengine.com/nightly/`, you can manually add the JAR files from the `lib` directory to your `CLASSPATH`, just like any other Java library. You can link these libraries in your favorite Java IDE, or do your Java development in a text editor on the command line if that's how you roll.

For now, let's continue using the SDK because it will get you started more swiftly. This book strives to keep code samples IDE-independent. If a shortcut or workflow only applies to the jMonkeyEngine SDK, it will be clearly pointed out as such.

Nonetheless you should give the jMonkeyEngine SDK a try. It contains many plugins that you will not find in generic IDEs: an asset pack manager and file converters for 3D models, a scene viewer and scene composer, a terrain editor, a procedural texture generator, a code snippet palette, and much more. Try it! If you are not convinced by the end of this book, you will find setup instructions for other IDEs in the appendix. Deal?

## Time for action – running a demo

In order to test whether everything was installed correctly, let's run a few demos. A set of demos comes bundled with the jMonkeyEngine SDK as one of the project templates.

1. Choose **File** | **New Project** from the menu to open the **New Project** wizard.
2. Select **JME3 Tests** from the **jME3** category.
3. Accept the defaults and complete the wizard.

The SDK unpacks the bundled demos and makes copies of the demo sources. The new **JME3 Tests** project appears in the **Projects** window.

To run a demo:

1. Right-click on **JME3 Tests** and click on **Build and Run**. Wait for the **TestChooser** window to open.
2. For example, select the **TestWalkingChar** demo and click on **OK**.

 Type **walking** into the filter box to find it more quickly.

**3.** Accept the default display settings and click on **OK**.

**4.** When the demo opens, use the *WASD* keys and drag the mouse to navigate the simple scene. Press the Space bar to shoot fireballs.

**5.** When you have seen enough of this demo, the press *Esc* key. Either select another demo, or click on **Cancel** to exit.

Now that you know how to use the **TestChooser**, run some demos to see what is possible with jMonkeyEngine.

## What just happened?

It's good to know that, during the development process, you can always return to the **JME3 Tests** demos for inspiration. Browse the demo's **Source Package** if you are looking for code samples that showcase particular features. Feel free to modify your copy of the code samples and experiment. In the unlikely case that you break the project, you can always recreate the **JME3 Tests** template from the **New Project** menu.

Restoring the demos is as easy as creating a fresh game project, which is what we will do next.

## Time for action – creating a project

The jMonkeyEngine SDK provides you with a preconfigured project template that gets you started at lightning speed.

This is how you create a new project:

**1.** Choose **File | New Project** from the menu

**2.** Select **BasicGame** from the **jME3** category.

**3.** You can rename the project here, but for now, accept the defaults and complete the wizard.

A new Java project named **BasicGame** appears in the **Projects** window, next to the **JME3 Tests** project.

The **BasicGame** project contains a simple `Main.java` template. Let's try to run this Java application:

**1.** Open the **BasicGame** project's **Source Packages**, and double-click on the `mygame/Main.java` file to open it. You see that the JDK contains a full-featured editor for Java files.

2. Right-click on the **BasicGame** project and click on **Build and Run**.

3. Accept the default display settings and click on **OK**.

4. The application window opens and shows a blue 3D cube on a black background. If this works, you know that your project is set up correctly.

5. Press the *Esc* key to quit the **BasicGame** project's window.

As you can see, it's easy to create and run fully preconfigured game projects in the jMonkeyEngine SDK.

## *What just happened?*

Let's open the **BasicGame** folder in the **Projects** window and look at the project structure that the SDK has just created for you.

You can see that the **Projects** window gives you access to three important areas: **Project Assets**, **Source Packages**, and **Libraries**, as well as the build script.

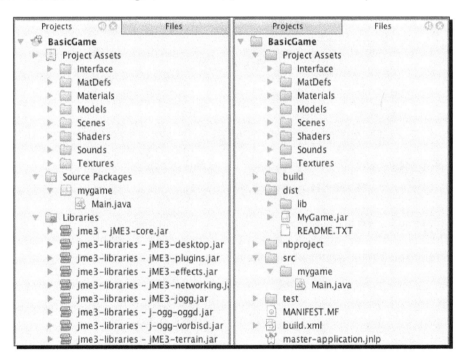

The **Projects** window shows the *logical* structure of a jMonkeyEngine project. This view only displays files that you need during development, and it filters out build folders and configuration files. For comparison, have a look at the project's *physical* structure, which lets you browse the actual files on your hard drive; choose **Window | Files** from the menu to open the **Files** window. Click the triangles to open the subsections and compare the two views, as shown in the previous screenshot.

Browse the **Libraries** section in the **Projects** window. You can see that it lists all the JAR files that are preconfigured on this project's CLASSPATH. Compare this to the physical dist/lib directory in the **Files** window.

If you know about Ant build scripts, you may want to open the **Important Files** node in the **Projects** window and browse the preconfigured Ant targets. Compare this to the physical build file, build.xml in the **Files** window.

You will see that a jMonkeyEngine-based application is a standard Java project made up of the following files and folders:

| Project folder | Usage |
| --- | --- |
| JMonkeyProjects/BasicGame/assets | You store multimedia assets here |
| jMonkeyProjects/BasicGame/build/ | The SDK generates build classes here |
| jMonkeyProjects/BasicGame/build.xml | You customize the Ant build script here |
| jMonkeyProjects/BasicGame/dist/ | The SDK generates executables here |
| jMonkeyProjects/BasicGame/nbproject/ | The SDK stores the default build script and metadata here |
| jMonkeyProjects/BasicGame/src/ | You store source code here |
| jMonkeyProjects/BasicGame/test/ | You store JUnit test classes here (optional) |

Certain files and folders are automatically created and maintained by the jMonkeyEngine SDK such as build, dist, and nbproject. The SDK recreates these files and folders when you build the application, so do not edit them.

The other folders, highlighted in yellow, contain your sources and assets. Using the test folder is optional; for now, just ignore it. As in any Java project, you have full control over the project's build.xml file, and your two main folders, assets and src.

Switch back to the **Projects** window. You see that the **Project Assets** folder corresponds to `jMonkeyProjects/BasicGame/assets/`, and the **Source Packages** folder corresponds to `jMonkeyProjects/BasicGame/src/`. You are free to set up subfolders and packages inside these two folders, as your project requires.

Your Java classes obviously go into **Source Packages**, but what does the **Project Assets** folder contain? Open the **Project Assets** folder and look inside: you will see subfolders for **Sounds**, **Textures**, and **Models**. This folder is where you store your multimedia content.

# Assets and the art pipeline

Every 3D game requires some multimedia assets, whether it's 3D models, image files, sound clips, video clips, or music. This book focuses on the development aspect—how to tie assets and code together and deploy the game. Being able to write source code only takes you halfway there: to develop games, you also need to go through the art pipeline.

By art pipeline we mean the creative process of creating 3D models, composing background music, and so on. The art pipeline runs in stages parallel to your coding milestones:

1. Lay out concept art, either digital or on paper, to get an idea of what you need; you do this in parallel to planning your Java object model.

2. Insert mock-up art in alpha builds: these sample files don't look and sound like the real thing yet. They are merely placeholders in the right size and format that help you debug your loading code.

3. Insert drafts in beta builds that are close to the final look and feel that you want; this helps you beta test and iron out the kinks.

4. Include the final artwork in the release builds. Typically, assets are converted to data formats that are optimized for the target platform.

Including sounds and images in your game means that you either need access to a multimedia library, or you need to create your assets using external tools.

The jMonkeyEngine SDK does not include any multimedia editors. This is because a game engine should not prescribe the artist's choice of design software. You are free to create assets in any third-party tools that you fancy and have access to. Just make certain that you can export the artwork in formats that jMonkeyEngine supports.

The following external file types are supported by jMonkeyEngine:

| Supported File Type | Usage |
| --- | --- |
| `.mesh.xml`, `.material`, `.skeleton.xml`, `.scene` | Ogre Mesh XML (3D models)<br>Ogre DotScene (3D scenes) |
| `.obj`, `.mtl` | Wavefront objects (3D models) |
| `.blend` | Blender files (3D models) |
| `.jpg`, `.png`, `.tga`, `.gif`, `.dds`, `.hdr`, `.pfm` | Images and textures |
| `.fnt` | Bitmap fonts |
| `.wav`, `.ogg` | Wave and OGG Vorbis audio |

If you have not chosen your multimedia tools yet, the following are some suggestions of popular editors that support the formats mentioned earlier:

- `http://Blender.org`: This is a full-featured mesh editor for 3D models and scenes
- `http://Gimp.org`: This is a graphic editor for images and textures
- `http://Audacity.sourceforge.net`: This is a sound editor for audio files

All of these are examples of software that is available for Windows, Mac OS, and Linux; all three are open source, and you can download and use them for free.

There are many more free and paid design tools available if you do a search. Whichever software you choose to create your assets, consult the respective manuals for details on how to use them. 3D modeling in particular is not a trivial task, but it's definitely worth learning.

Now that you have the design and development tools installed, you have everything you need to create your game.

But what do your users install to play your game?

# Time for action – distributing a game

During the development phase, you typically build and run your game right from the jMonkeyEngine SDK. Your users, however, neither have nor want the SDK. They expect to run the game by, for instance, executing a desktop application that runs on their Java Virtual Machine.

Switch to the **Files** window, and look into the `dist` folder. Every time you **Build** this project, the SDK generates an executable JAR file here. When you right-click on the project and choose **Clean**, the `dist` folder is deleted—so remember never to move any unique files there.

Let's go through the basic deployment process together:

1. Right-click on the **BasicGame** project in SDK, and open the project's **Properties** window.
2. Go to the **Application | Desktop** pane and select the checkboxes for your target operating systems, for example Windows, Mac, and Linux. Click on **OK**.
3. Right-click on the **BasicGame** project, and **Clean and Build** it.

Look into the **Output** window to follow the build process.

## What just happened?

When the build is finished, switch to your operating system's file explorer:

1. Browse to the `jMonkeyProjects/BasicGame/dist/` folder in your user home.
2. Unzip and run the **BasicGame** executable for your operating system.
3. The application window opens and displays the blue cube demo. Press the *Esc* key to quit.

This exercise shows you that the SDK generates distributable builds of your **BasicGame** project that runs fine on your desktop, outside the jMonkeyEngine SDK.

Impressive—you have just built a basic 3D application that runs on the three most widely used operating systems. Notice how you didn't have to configure any CLASSPATH or library paths.

# Can I sell my jMonkeyEngine game?

Yes, the jMonkeyEngine SDK is a free open source software released under the BSD license. To answer the most common questions right away:

◆ You do not pay any fees to use the jMonkeyEngine libraries or SDK

◆ You can use the jMonkeyEngine for hobby, educational, or commercial purposes

◆ You can include the jMonkeyEngine libraries in a Java application that you sell or give away for free

◆ You can offer your application that includes the jMonkeyEngine libraries as download, serve it over the network, or distribute it on digital media

◆ Using the jMonkeyEngine does not require you to open source your own code (but you can)

All that is required from you is that you adhere to the BSD license, and keep the license together with the jMonkeyEngine libraries included in your distribution. Simply copy the license from the jMonkeyHomepage. Don't worry, it's nice and short and can be found at http://jMonkeyEngine.org/wiki/doku.php/bsd_license.

# Summary

In this chapter you learned how to install the jMonkeyEngine SDK and run sample applications. You saw that it is easy to get started with game development using the jMonkeyEngine SDK, and how easy it is to distribute a game using the jMonkeyEngine SDK.

Come on over to the next chapter, where we write some actual code!

# 2
# Creating Your First 3D Scene

*Now that you have installed the engine and understood the physical file structure of a project, we will take a look inside to understand the flow of a jMonkeyEngine game.*

In this chapter, you will learn:

- ◆ How to initialize a scene
- ◆ How to refer to objects in the 3D scene
- ◆ How to position, rotate, and resize objects
- ◆ How to configure the way the scene is displayed
- ◆ How to navigate the scene using the keyboard and mouse

It's time to look at some code.

## A basic template to initialize scenes

From the previous chapter, you'll remember that we executed the `BasicGame` template to test whether the installation was successful. This project template demonstrates the structure of a typical jMonkeyEngine main class that initializes the scene and starts the application.

# Time for action – initializing a scene step by step

If you no longer have the `BasicGame` template open, open it again in the jMonkeyEngine SDK. Remember that you can always recreate this project template using the **New Project** wizard in the **File** menu.

Let's look at the main class of the `BasicGame` project:

1. Open the `BasicGame` project in the **Projects** window.

2. Double-click on the `mygame/Main.java` file in the `Source Packages` folder. `Main.java` opens in the source editor.

3. When you look at the `Main.java` template, you see a standard Java class that extends the `com.jme3.app.SimpleApplication` class. `SimpleApplication` is the base class that we use to write all our 3D games.

The basic code sample is short enough so that you can type it yourself—we just use the `BasicGame` template because it is quicker:

```java
import com.jme3.app.SimpleApplication;
import com.jme3.material.Material;
import com.jme3.math.ColorRGBA;
import com.jme3.math.Vector3f;
import com.jme3.renderer.RenderManager;
import com.jme3.scene.Geometry;
import com.jme3.scene.shape.Box;

/** Basic jMonkeyEngine game template. */
public class Main extends SimpleApplication {

    @Override
    /** initialize the scene here */
    public void simpleInitApp() {
        // create a cube-shaped mesh
        Box b = new Box(Vector3f.ZERO, 1, 1, 1);
        // create an object from the mesh
        Geometry geom = new Geometry("Box", b);

        // create a simple blue material
        Material mat = new Material(assetManager,
                "Common/MatDefs/Misc/Unshaded.j3md");
        mat.setColor("Color", ColorRGBA.Blue);
        // give the object the blue material
        geom.setMaterial(mat);
        // make the object appear in the scene
        rootNode.attachChild(geom);
    }

    @Override
    /** (optional) Interact with update loop here */
```

```
public void simpleUpdate(float tpf) {}

@Override
/** (optional) Advanced renderer/frameBuffer modifications */
public void simpleRender(RenderManager rm) {}

/** Start the jMonkeyEngine application */
public static void main(String[] args) {
    Main app = new Main();
    app.start();
}
}
```

**Downloading the example code**

You can download the example code files for all Packt books you have purchased from your account at http://www.packtpub.com. If you purchased this book elsewhere, you can visit http://www.packtpub.com/support and register to have the files e-mailed directly to you.

You can right-click on the file and click on **Run**, if you want to see the application again. The Main class generates a simple scene containing a blue cube. Let's take a closer look at the code template to learn how to structure a jMonkeyEngine application.

## What just happened?

The scene displayed by our BasicGame template only contains a blue cube, but this is enough to introduce you to the basic process that all scenes have in common, whether it's a haunted dungeon or an alien jungle. The cube, like any other scene object, is initialized in the simpleInitApp() method. Let's walk through the simpleInitApp() method line by line to understand what is happening.

The com.jme3.scene.shape.Box class provides us with a quick and simple box shape for testing. The Box() constructor expects a location, and three values defining the size of the box—we create the shape in the center of the scene, which we express in Java as Vector3f.ZERO. We choose to extend the box's size by 1 in every direction, which results in a 2x2x2 cube. We refer to our Box() object with the variable b. The Java code that creates the box looks as follows:

```
Box b = new Box(Vector3f.ZERO, 1, 1, 1);
```

Internally, a Box() object contains numbers specifying the corner points of the cube. The corners describe the shape (*mesh*) of the object. But a cube is not just corners, it also has faces. The faces are the surfaces that make the cube visible in the first place. In 3D graphics, you must specify a shape and a surface for every object.

jMonkeyEngine has a data type that combines the shape and surface information of an object. This data type is called geometry (com.jme3.scene.Geometry), and we will be using it a lot. Let's create a geometry geom for our cube shape b, and label the geometry Box. In larger scenes, you can use these labels to access geometries.

In code, this step looks as follows:

```
Geometry geom = new Geometry("Box", b);
```

Our geometry now has a cube shape; next, we must add the surface information for the cube's faces. In 3D graphics terms, the surface of a geometry has a *material* (com.jme3.material.Material). In this example, we use a type of material called Unshaded.j3md. This default material definition is built into the engine, and we access it using the assetManager object. You create the material using the following line of code:

```
Material mat = new Material(assetManager,
    "Common/MatDefs/Misc/Unshaded.j3md");
```

Every material has parameters that specify how the surface looks. Materials can be very intricate—you can make them look like wood, metal, rock, grass, skin, plastic, water, glass, and so on. The unshaded material that we use here is simple in comparison; for now, we only choose to set this material's Color parameter to Blue. To do that, we use the Blue constant from the com.jme3.math.ColorRGBA class:

```
mat.setColor("Color", ColorRGBA.Blue);
```

Now we have a geometry object geom, which contains the cube's shape, and a material object mat containing a plain blue material for the cube's surface. The next step is to combine the two in order to create a blue cube:

```
geom.setMaterial(mat);
```

The blue cube is ready, but its geometry only exists in memory. To actually make it visible, you have to attach the object to the scene. Remember that we made this class extend SimpleApplication? We did that so we would inherit a special object—the rootNode. SimpleApplication is preconfigured to draw all objects that are attached to the rootNode; that's just what we need! We add our blue cube geom to the 3D scene using the following command:

```
rootNode.attachChild(geom);
```

This short simpleInitApp() method demonstrates the typical initialization process. For each object that you add to the scene, remember to perform the following steps:

1. Create a shape.
2. Create a geometry from the shape.
3. Create a material.

4. Apply the material to the geometry.

5. Attach the geometry to the `rootNode`.

# Starting and stopping the application

After you have initialized the scene, you need to start the application.

## Time for action – starting the application

In the `main()` method of the class, you need to create a new instance of the application and call its `start()` method. In this case, the main class is called `Main`, but you can also name it MyGame or whatever you like:

```
public static void main(String[] args) {
  Main app = new Main();
  app.start();
}
```

When you run this code, the application window opens and the jMonkeyEngine starts rendering the scene.

### What just happened?

Every jMonkeyEngine application provides the following methods for starting and stopping the game:

| | |
|---|---|
| `app.start();` | This method starts a jME3 game, typically used from the `main()` class. It opens a window, initializes and draws the scene, and starts the event loop. |
| `app.restart();` | This method reloads the settings and makes them take effect. Use this when you change application settings, such as the resolution, at runtime. |
| `app.stop();` | This method stops the running jME3 game and closes the window. It is triggered by default when you press the *Esc* key. |

 When a user presses the *Alt + Tab shortcut* or clicks outside the game window, the running application loses focus. You can set `app.setPauseOnLostFocus` as `true,` to specify that your game should pause whenever the window loses focus. For real-time or online games, set `app.setPauseOnLostFocus as false` instead, to keep the game running.

Let's sum up what we just learned. When you write a jMonkeyEngine game, you have to:

- Extend `com.jme3.app.SimpleApplication`
- Implement abstract methods, such as `simpleInitApp()`, `simpleUpdate(float tpf)`, and `simpleRender(RenderManager rm)` (described later in the chapter)
- Call `app.start()` on your instance of `SimpleApplication`

The jMonkeyEngine runs the application even if you leave the three method bodies empty. If you run a `SimpleApplication` class without initializing any scene, the screen shows up empty.

# Orient yourself in 3D space

When you initialize your game world, you want to fill the empty scene. Maybe you add a ground with streets and some buildings, or a terrain with forests and caves. You strategically place your players and enemies, and you sprinkle some treasure and traps on the map. Now how exactly do you tell the jMonkeyEngine where to place an object? You need a way to orient yourself in 3D space—through a coordinate system.

The following figure is based on an image created by Sakurambo, and can be found at `http://de.wikipedia.org/w/index.php?title=Datei:3D_coordinate_system.svg`.

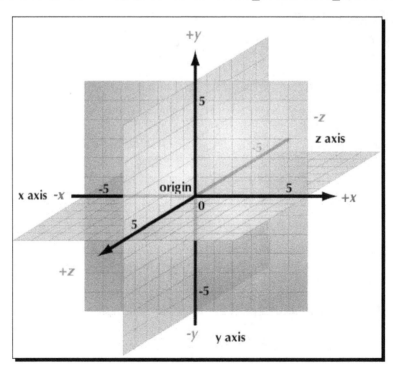

The jMonkeyEngine uses a right-handed coordinate system, just as the Open Graphics Library (OpenGL) does.

 If the concept of coordinates is new to you, you may want to start with a quick visual introduction on our web page, which can be found at:

`http://jmonkeyengine.org/wiki/doku.php/`
`jme3:scenegraph_for_dummies`

Let's have a look at the illustration and recapitulate the concepts behind the Cartesian coordinate system:

◆   The central point of the 3D scene is called the origin.

◆   The origin is always at coordinate (0,0,0).

◆   The three coordinate axes stand at 90 degree angles to one another, and meet in the origin. In the previous screenshot:

    ❑   The x axis goes from left to right

    ❑   The y axis goes from down to up

    ❑   The z axis starts away from you and goes towards you

This means that, if you see positive numbers, you follow the arrow along the axis. If you see negative numbers, you move in the direction against the arrow.

It's important to understand these concepts, since all distances, directions, and locations in a 3D scene are expressed in relation to this coordinate system. It's an easy principle, as you will see in the following example.

## Time for action – finding the spot

Using coordinates, we pinpoint a location in 3D space by specifying the distance from the origin along the three axes x, y, and z.

 Remember the order: (x,y,z) coordinates always go in the same rut (Right-Up-Towards you). You can use the word R.U.T. as a mnemonic.

So how do you go about locating a point? Let's try to find coordinate (2,3,-4):

1.   Always start at the origin.

2.   The first value of the (2,3,-4) coordinates tells you to go two steps right, following the arrow of the x axis.

3. The second value of the (2,3,-4) coordinates tells you to go three steps up, following the arrow of the y axis.

4. The third value of the (2,3,-4) coordinates tells you to go four steps away from you, against the arrow of the z axis.

## What just happened?

If you followed the description with your finger on the picture, you moved two steps right, three steps up, and four steps *into the page*—your finger is now at coordinate (2,3,-4).

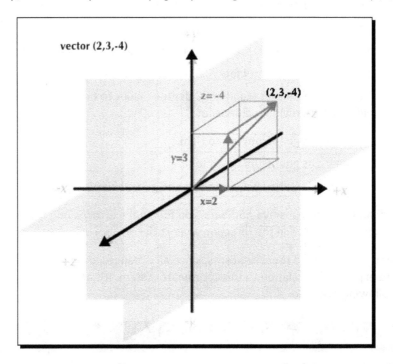

Try another example: the point (1,3,2) is one step right, three steps up, and two steps towards you. Here is one with negative numbers—the point (-3,-2,-1) is three steps left, two steps down, and one step away from you.

Using this coordinate system, you can pinpoint every spot in the 3D space.

In case you are wondering, *What's a step? A kilometer, an inch?*, our unit of measurement is the *world unit*, abbreviated as *WU*. In most games that are set in the human world, 1 WU is 1 meter. If your game is set in an ant hill, you can declare the WU to be 1 millimeter; if your game is set in outer space, you can declare it to be 1 lightyear. The important thing is that you tell your graphic designers which unit size they should work with, so that you do not have to worry about scaling models later.

Every time you create 3D models on a grid or use a method that expects float values, which represent a size, scale, or distance, then you are working in world units.

## Pop quiz – which way, vector?

Q1. List the three directions that the values in the coordinates stand for, in the correct order. Use the mnemonic you have learned.

1. Z = left, Y = up, X = go back (mnemonic L.U.G.)

2. X = right, Y = up, Z = towards you (mnemonic R.U.T.)

3. X = red, Y = green, Z = blue (mnemonic R.G.B.)

4. Z = north, Y = east, X = away from you (mnemonic N.E.W.)

# And how do I say that in Java?

Imagine an arrow pointing from the origin to an X-Y-Z coordinate. This arrow is called a *vector*. You will be using vectors to represent locations. Since a vector always starts at the origin, and the arrow points in the direction of the given (x,y,z) coordinates, a vector can also be used to specify a direction. Quite useful!

In your Java code, you use the `com.jme3.math.Vector3f` class for this data type. A `Vector3f` is an object with three float components, `x`, `y`, and `z`. For example:

```
Vector3f v = new Vector3f( 2.0f , 3.0f , -4.0f );
```

Remember when we created the blue cube earlier and placed it in the middle of the scene? We positioned it at the location `Vector3f.ZERO`. This built-in constant stands for a `Vector3f(0f,0f,0f)`. The (0,0,0) coordinates vector represents the origin of the coordinate system, the middle of the scene.

Now that you know how to orient yourself in 3D space, we can apply this knowledge and *transform* our blue cube; let's position, resize, and turn it. In terms of 3D graphics, we say that we *translate*, *scale*, and *rotate* the object. In the next three sections, we look at each of the three transformations in detail, and learn the appropriate Java syntax.

## Time for action – position it!

To practice positioning objects, we create a second cube and place it next to the first one. Open the `BasicGame` template and look at the `simpleInitApp()` method.

1. Create a `com.jme3.math.Vector3f` object. This is the target location for the second cube:

    ```
    Vector3f v = new Vector3f(2.0f , 1.0f , -3.0f);
    ```

2. Copy the code snippet that creates the blue cube and adjust it to create a second, yellow cube.

3. Name the `new Box` object `b2`, the geometry `geom2`, and the material `mat2`. (Make sure to rename all instances!)

4. Change the `Color` parameter in the material `mat2` to `ColorRGBA.Yellow`.

5. Move the second box to its new location `v`:

   ```
   geom2.setLocalTranslation(v);
   ```

6. Attach `geom2` to the `rootNode` to add it to the scene.

7. Clean and build the `BasicGame` template, and right-click the class to run this file.

You should see a yellow cube behind the blue cube, but positioned a bit higher (y=1), a bit to the right (x=2), and further in the back (z=-3).

## What just happened?

Positioning an object, such as our cubes in the 3D scene, is called *translation*. You create geometries at the origin, then translate them to their intended position, and then attach them to the `rootNode`.

 Typically, you never create `Box()` objects and so on with an offset in the constructor. The offset will just get you into trouble later when the geometry does not move as expected. Always start at the origin, as in `Box b = new Box(Vector3f.ZERO, 1, 1, 1);`.

In Java, you can choose between two methods when you position objects:

| | |
|---|---|
| `geom2.move(3.0f, -2.0f,1.0f);` | This specifies an offset relative to the current position. It is like saying *step forward!* in real life. |
| `geom.setLocalTranslation(3.0f,-2.0f,1.0f);` | This specifies an absolute target position. It is like a GPS coordinate in real life. |

If you start out with both boxes at the origin, both methods result in the same target location. If you use the `move()` method several times, the offsets add up. If you use the `setLocalTranslation()` method several times, you simply place the cube at a new absolute location. Try these methods several times on each cube, with different values, and try to predict what happens.

# Time for action – scale it!

Your freshly loaded fighter model appears as tall as the tavern next to it, while the dragon turns out to be as small as a lizard—what happened? It's possible that geometries do not come in the same scale; especially when you populate the scene with models from different sources, you have to resize them to fit the scene.

Resizing geometries is called *scaling*. Let's scale our translated cubes by adding the following to the `simpleInitApp()` method:

1. Shrink the blue cube down to half its size: `geom.setLocalScale(0.5f);`.
2. Grow the yellow cube to twice its size: `geom2.scale(2.0f);`.
3. Clean and build the `BasicGame` template, and right-click on it to run the file.

Compare the outcome. The yellow cube is twice as big (2.0f) and the blue cube is half as big (0.5f) as before.

What happens if you supply three different floats (positive and larger than zero) as arguments instead, and run the file again? For example:

```
geom.setLocalScale(0.5f,3f,0.75f);
geom2.scale(2.0f,.33f,2.0f);
```

Try various values and see what happens. Can you distort the blue cube to be thin and tall, and the yellow cube to be wide and short?

## What just happened?

Just like translation, there are two Java methods—one for absolute and one for relative scaling:

| | |
|---|---|
| `geom2.scale(2.0f);` | This specifies a scale relative to the current size. For example, it is twice as big as whatever it was before. |
| `geom.setLocalScale(0.5f);` | This specifies the absolute scale. For example, it is half the size of the freshly loaded model. |

There are also `scale(x,y,z)` and `setLocalScale(x,y,z)` methods that accept three float arguments instead of just one.

The x value controls the width, from the left to the right. The y value controls the height, from up to down. The z value controls the depth, towards you and away from you. Does this (x,y,z) pattern look familiar?

# Time for action – rotate it!

Your cubes are at the right location and have the right size. Now you want to turn them to face in a specific direction. In an actual game, for example, you may want to turn characters to face an interesting part of the scene. Again, you can either use absolute or relative rotation.

For every rotation, you have to specify three float values—x, y, and z, one for each axis, around which you want to rotate. In contrast to translation and scale, rotations are not expressed in world units, but in radians. Don't worry—to convert between the familiar 360 degrees to radians, simply multiply the degree value by the built-in `FastMath.DEG_TO_RAD` constant, or `FastMath.RAD_TO_DEG` to convert it back. You can find this constant in the `com.jme3.math.FastMath` package.

As an example, let's rotate the two cubes by 45 degrees around the x and y axes, respectively:

1. Convert 45 degrees to radians:

   ```
   float r = FastMath.DEG_TO_RAD * 45f;
   ```

2. To rotate `geom2` around the x axis, add the following call at the end of the `simpleInitApp()` method:

   ```
   geom2.rotate(r, 0.0f, 0.0f);
   ```

3. To rotate `geom` around the y axis, add the following call below:

   ```
   geom.rotate(0.0f, r, 0.0f);
   ```

4. Clean and build the `BasicGame` template, and right-click on it to run the file.

## What just happened?

The yellow cube should be pitched forward around the x axis, facing you with a horizontal edge. The blue cube should have turned around its y axis, facing you with one of its vertical edges. Using the x, y, and z axes for the three directions should look familiar to you by now.

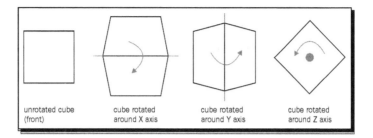

| unrotated cube (front) | cube rotated around X axis | cube rotated around Y axis | cube rotated around Z axis |

Use the method `rotate()` for relative rotation around the three axes.

Absolute rotation in 3D space, however, is a bit more sophisticated. Absolute rotations use a special data type called *quaternion*.

## Time for action – rotate it again, Sam

Think of a quaternion as a Java object capable of storing rotations, which you can then apply to a geometry. Don't worry, the 3D engine does the tough calculation work for you!

As an exercise, let's create a `Quaternion` object that accepts a 45-degree rotation around the x axis:

1. Create a `Quaternion` object:

   ```
   Quaternion roll045 = new Quaternion();
   ```

2. Supply the angle and the axis as arguments. The angle is `45*FastMath.DEG_TO_RAD`. The constant for the x axis is `Vector3f.UNIT_X`. This gives us:

   ```
   roll045.fromAngleAxis( 45*FastMath.DEG_TO_RAD , Vector3f.UNIT_X );
   ```

3. Replace the relative `rotate()` method from the previous exercises and apply this absolute rotation instead:

   ```
   geom2.setLocalRotation( roll045 );
   ```

4. Clean and build the `BasicGame` template, then right-click on it and run the file.

5. The yellow cube should be rotated by 45° as before.

## What just happened?

To store a rotation in a `com.jme3.math.Quaternion` object, you specify two values—the angle in radians, and the axis of the rotation.

The axis is defined by a type of vector called *unit vector*. A unit vector works just like any other vector; the only difference is that we do not care about its length (which is always 1 WU, hence the name). We only need the unit vector for its direction. Here are the most common examples of rotation axes:

| Rotate around | Use this vector! | Example |
| --- | --- | --- |
| x axis | `Vector3f.UNIT_X`<br>`= new Vector3f(1,0,0)` | Nodding your head |
| y axis | `Vector3f.UNIT_Y`<br>`= new Vector3f(0,1,0)` | Shaking your head |
| z axis | `Vector3f.UNIT_Z`<br>`= new Vector3f(0,0,1)` | Cocking your head |

Quaternions are worth knowing because they have many useful applications:

- You can concatenate several rotations into one `Quaternion` by using the `mult()` method, which is faster than doing transformations in several steps. Note that the order of rotations is non-commutative, so the order in which you multiply the quaternions makes a difference.

  `Quaternion pitchAndRoll = pitch180.mult(roll180);`

- Re-use `Quaternion` constants; give them meaningful names, such as roll90, pitch45, or yaw180, that remind you of what they do.

You can interpolate rotations between two quaternions using spherical linear interpolation (**slerp**). An interpolation lets you precisely fast-forward and rewind a complex rotation between its start and end points. Create two quaternions q1 and q2, for example, for a 40 degrees and a 50 degrees rotation around the x axis. Apply them with different interpolation values between 0.0f and 1.0f:

```
Quaternion q3 = new Quaternion();
q3.slerp(q1, q2, 0.5f);
geom2.setLocalRotation(q3);
```

# Where am I?

If all these transformations are starting to make you dizzy, you probably feel an urge to know where you are in the scene. Remember that you always look into the scene through the eye of a camera object.

By default, the camera is:

1. Located at the coordinate (0.0f , 0.0f , 10.0f).

2. Rotated to look in the direction (0.0f , 0.0f , -1.0f).

In other words, your default point of view is on the positive side of the z axis, from a spot that is 10 WU away from the origin. You are looking back down along the z axis, towards the origin.

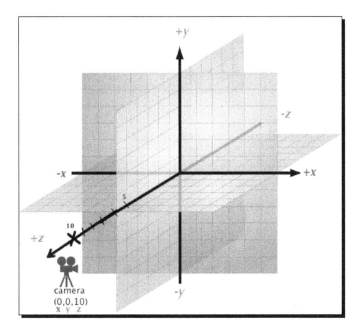

## Time for action – navigating the scene

Let's look at things from a different perspective:

1. Run the BasicGame template once more.

2. Press the **W**, **A**, **S**, and **D** keys to move forward, left, backwards, and right. Move the mouse to turn around. This navigates your camera away from the default location.

3. Press the *C* key while the application is running to print the current camera location and rotation to the console.

In your Java code, you can access the current camera location, which is also the location of the player in a first-person game, using getters on the cam object:

```
Vector3f    loc = cam.getLocation();
Quaternion rot = cam.getRotation();
```

If you want the camera to start out at a different location in the scene, position it using the following:

```
cam.setLocation(x,y,z);
cam.setRotation(q);
```

The default navigational keys in the included samples are optimized for QWERTY keyboards. Every game has its unique navigation that you will have to define yourself, including a way to let your users with a non-QWERTY keyboard customize the keys.

Note that `cam.setRotation(q)` is one of the rotation methods that accepts the `Quaternion` data type, which we just learned about, as an argument.

## Pop quiz - spinning around

Q2. How far does `geom.rotate(0.0f, 2.1f, 0.0f);` rotate the geometry around the y axis?

1. 2.1 times = 2.1 * 360° = 756° = 36°
2. 2.1 degrees
3. 2.1 radians = 120°
4. 2.1 world units

# Populating the scene

Now you know where you are, and how to position and transform 3D objects. When you start populating the scene, you face the issue of handling possibly hundreds of objects. In order to keep track of all your stuff, the jMonkeyEngine provides you with a special data structure—the **scene graph**. The scene graph manages all elements in a 3D scene. We call the elements in the 3D scene **spatials**.

Spatials are attached to one another in a parent-child relationship. When we speak of *attaching a spatial*, we mean that we add the spatial to the scene. When we speak of *detaching a spatial*, we remove it from the scene.

One specific parent spatial in every game is the root node of the scene. Every spatial that is attached to this one root node, directly or indirectly, is part of the scene graph.

JMonkeyEngine speeds up large scenes by ignoring spatials that are out of view or behind the camera. This feature is called *culling*. To make a spatial disappear temporarily without detaching it from the scene, tell the engine to cull it by setting `geom.setCullHint(CullHint.Always);`; similarly, you can use `CullHint.Never` to keep a spatial, such as a sky box, always visible. To reset the culling behavior back to its default, set it to `CullHint.Inherit`.

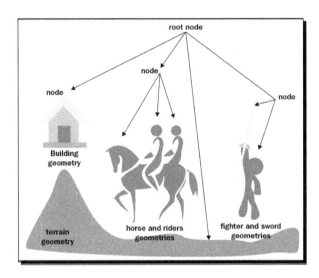

Let's have a look at the `BasicGame` template. We extend all our games from `SimpleApplication` because we want to inherit a certain class field: spatial called `rootNode`. This `rootNode` object gives us access to the scene graph. You remember the `rootNode` from `Main.java` when we added the blue cube `geom` to the scene?

```
rootNode.attachChild(geom);
```

In the examples here, you have now encountered a **geometry** (the blue cube) and a **node**, the `rootNode` object. Both are derived from com.jme3.scene.Spatial, and both are elements of the scene graph. What is the difference between a geometry and a node?

# Time for action – node versus geometry

Geometries are the objects in your scene. They represent loaded models, characters, terrains, and all kinds of other visible objects.

Nodes are a typical means of grouping other nodes and geometries. The typical use case for nodes is transformation, where they are used as handles for groups of spatials. If you group a driver geometry and a car geometry by attaching them to a common vehicle node, you can move both of them by simply translating the vehicle node.

Another use case for nodes is rotation. Do you intend to rotate around the geometry's center, or around another point? If you intend to rotate around a non-central point, create an invisible pivot node and attach the geometry to it. Then, apply the rotation to the pivot node and not to the geometry itself.

The following example shows two geometries rotated around a common, invisible center node, pivot:

1. Add the following lines at the end of your simpleInitApp() method:

```
Node pivot = new Node("pivot node");
pivot.attachChild(geom);
pivot.attachChild(geom2);
pivot.rotate(00, 0, FastMath.DEG_TO_RAD * 45);
rootNode.attachChild(pivot);
```

2. Attaching geom and geom2 to a new parent node implicitly detaches them from their previous parent node.

3. Clean and build the BasicGame template, and run the file.

Both geom and geom2 are now attached to the pivot node, and the pivot node is attached to the rootNode. The rotation affects both the nodes that are grouped under the pivot node.

## What just happened?

Spatials are Java objects that are used to load and save information about elements of the scene graph. There are two distinct types of spatials in the jMonkeyEngine—**nodes** and **geometries**.

|  | **Geometry** | **Node** |
| --- | --- | --- |
| Visibility | A visible 3D object. | An invisible handle for a group of objects. |
| Purpose | You use a geometry to represent the *look* of an object—its shape, color, material, texture, and transparency. | You attach spatials, geometries, and nodes to group them. When you transform the parent node, the transformation affects all child spatials, geometries, and nodes. |
| Content | Transformations, mesh (shape), material. | Transformations; no mesh, no material. |
| Examples | A box, a sphere, a player, a building, a terrain, a vehicle, missiles, NPCs, and so on. | The `rootNode`, an audio node, custom groups (for example, a driver and car, doors and buildings), and so on. |

Remember that you never create a `new Spatial()` instance—spatials are abstract. You only use the `Spatial` data type in methods that return either nodes and geometries (for example, the `load()` method), or in methods that accept either nodes and geometries as arguments (for example, the `save()` method). In these cases, you create a `Node` or `Geometry` object, and the method implicitly casts it to the `Spatial` data type.

## Pop quiz – the truth about spatials

Q1. Combine the following sentence fragments to form six true statements:

a. A node ...      b. A geometry ...      c. A spatial ...

1.   ... is an element of the scene graph.
2.   ... groups nodes and geometries.
3.   ... contains a mesh (shape) and a material.
4.   ... can be loaded and saved.
5.   ... is a visible object in the scene.
6.   ... is used as an invisible handle.

# Extending SimpleApplication

Although the class is called `SimpleApplication`, you base all your jMonkeyEngine games on this class, including very large projects. Don't think that only simple applications can be built with it; the name means that this class is already a simple application by itself. You make it *non-simple* by extending it. For example, you will override methods and modify the default properties, and add whatever your game requires.

When you look back on this chapter, you notice that we have already got a lot of default functionality just by extending `com.jme3.app.SimpleApplication`.

Even an application as simple as the `BasicGame` template already has access to the following features:

| Class field or method | Description |
| --- | --- |
| `rootNode` | The scene graph lets us manage the objects that we want to render. |
| `simpleInitApp()` `simpleUpdate()` `simpleRender()` | These are the three, main overridable methods of every game. You initialize scenes with code in the `simpleInitApp()` method, and you define interactions in the `simpleUpdate()` method. Advanced users can override the `simpleRender()` method for advanced modifications of the `frameBuffer` object and scene graph. |
| `cam` | The default camera uses perspective projection, has a 45-degree field of view, and it shows everything between 1 and 1000 WU. |
| `flyCam` | A first-person camera controller with preconfigured navigation inputs. |
| `assetManager` | The `AssetManager` object helps you load models, textures, materials, sounds, and so on. |
| `getAudioRenderer()`, `getListener()` | The 3D audio system. |
| `keyInput,` `mouseInput,` `joyInput` | JME3 handles keyboard, mouse, and input. |
| `getInputManager()` | Here you configure custom key, mouse, and joystick input handling. |
| `renderManager.` `getRenderer()` | Gives advanced users access to the rendering interface. |
| `viewPort` | This is the rectangular part of the screen that represents what the camera sees. It has scene processors for visual effects, and it also controls the background color. |
| `Application settings` | Configures display properties of your scene, such as screen resolution and anti-aliasing. |

We will look at these features throughout this book. Let's start looking at the application settings so that you can configure the way your scene is displayed.

# Make a big scene

The `SimpleApplication` object's default settings let you start with your first scene even without configuring display details. But you can configure the window size and the display quality if you want to.

## Time for action – configuring display settings

In order to control the display settings yourself, you need to create an `AppSettings` object in your application's `main()` method. Set the Boolean in the `AppSettings` constructor to true, if you want to keep the default settings for every value that you do not specify. You can set this parameter to false if you want to specify each property yourself. The engine will then raise an exception if you miss a setting.

```
public static void main(String[] args) {
  settings.setTitle("My Cool Game");
  // specify your settings here
  Main app = new Main();
  app.setSettings(settings); // apply settings to app
  app.start();                // use settings and run
}
```

The following application settings are available:

◆ **Dialog image**: If you choose to show the default display settings dialog, the window includes a splash screen. By default, the dialog box shows the jMonkeyEngine logo from the built-in `com/jme3/app/Monkey.png`. To reassure your users that this dialog box is already part of your game, you should specify a branded image from your `assets/interface` folder:

```
settings.setSettingsDialogImage("Interface/splashscreen.png")
```

◆ **Fullscreen mode**: By default, the application runs in a window of its own. Alternatively, you can switch to fullscreen mode and make the application window fill the whole screen. If you activate this mode, users will not be able to move the window or access any menus. By default, pressing the *Esc* key stops the application and helps exit the fullscreen mode gracefully.

```
GraphicsDevice device = GraphicsEnvironment.
  getLocalGraphicsEnvironment().getDefaultScreenDevice();
DisplayMode[] modes = device.getDisplayModes();
settings.setResolution(modes[0].getWidth(),modes[0].getHeight());
settings.setFrequency(modes[0].getRefreshRate());
settings.setDepthBits(modes[0].getBitDepth());
settings.setFullscreen(device.isFullScreenSupported());
```

◆ **Resolution**: The default resolution of a jMonkeyEngine window is 640 × 480 pixels. There are two equivalent ways to set the display resolution. You can set the width and height separately:

```
settings.setHeight(480); settings.setWidth(640);
```

Or both resolution values in one step:

```
settings.setResolution(640,480);
```

◆ **Anti-aliasing**: If you want your scene rendered more smoothly, you can choose to activate anti-aliasing. Depending on the graphics card, the user can set the anti-aliasing feature to use 2, 4, 8, 16, or 32 samples. With anti-aliasing activated, the scenes will render with softer edges, but the game may run slower on older hardware.

```
settings.setSamples(2);
```

To switch off anti-aliasing, leave multisampling at its default value 0. The scenes will render with harder edges, but the game may run faster.

◆ **Input handling**: You can choose whether the running application listens to user input, such as a mouse and keyboard. Input handling is active (true) by default. You can deactivate input handling for use cases, where you only play a 3D scene without any user interaction. You would do that, for example, when playing a non-interactive simulation.

```
settings.useInput(false);
```

◆ **Window title**: The window title of a jMonkeyEngine application is set to jMonkey Engine 3.0, by default. This is where you display your game's name. The window title is not visible when the game runs in fullscreen mode.

```
settings.setTitle("My Cool Game").
```

◆ **Saving settings**: A user-friendly application will ask you to specify display settings only once, and will then load them every time without asking again. In a jMonkeyEngine game, you load and save AppSettings objects using standard java.io serialization.

```
settings.save("MyGame.prefs");
settings.load("MyGame.prefs");
```

Typically, you use save() and load() methods together with a try-catch statement. You can copy an AppSettings object from oldSettings into newSettings using the following command:

```
newSettings.copyFrom(oldSettings)
```

## What just happened?

Specify the settings and apply them to the application before calling the `app.start()` method in the `main()` method. If you change the settings while the application is already running, use the `app.restart();` method instead, to load the new `AppSettings` object!

As you see, you can either specify the display settings yourself, or let users set their own options:

- Use the previous methods to specify the display settings yourself, in the `main()` method. Typically, you would create your own user interface to let users modify the settings on a custom options screen. In these cases, you should disable the default settings window at startup:

  ```
  app.setShowSettings(false);
  ```

- If you expect users with widely different hardware, you can let them choose the rendering options, such as the resolution, anti-aliasing, and color depth, to their liking. In this case, you can configure your application to open a **Display Settings** dialog box at start-up:

  ```
  app.setShowSettings(true);
  ```

- Add this setter after the creation of the `app` object, but before calling the `app.start()` method.

# Keeping an eye on your FPS

You may have noticed that a running `SimpleApplication` automatically displays a **head-up display (HUD)** with some statistics. How do you read them?

## Time for action – checking vital stats

The `com.jme3.app.StatsView` UI element provides various counts, which it gathers using `com.jme3.renderer.Statistics`:

1. Run the `BasicGame` template once more.
2. Look at the statistics on the bottom left-hand side; they display the object counts for the various elements.
3. Have a look at the bottom number in the HUD. It displays the **frames per second (FPS)**.

To interpret the numbers correctly, consider that the 14 lines of text themselves already count as 14 objects with 914 vertices.

## *What just happened?*

The StatsView window displays internal info about Textures, FrameBuffers (rendering surfaces), and Shaders (effects). The three values tell you how many are in memory (M), how many were used in the last frame (F), and how many were switched during the last frame (S).

During the development phase, keep an eye on these statistics because they can warn you about performance issues:

◆ If Textures (S) is significantly higher than Textures (F), you know you are using textures inefficiently (for example, there are too many transparent ones).

◆ If any (M) value is significantly higher than its (F) counterpart, then you have more objects of this type in memory than you are actually using. Determine which ones to deallocate.

◆ If a small scene with a few models has tens of thousands of triangles, you need to get rid of some high-polygon objects in the scene. The hard limit for the slowest current graphics card is around 100,000 vertices per scene. 10,000 to 50,000 vertices is a typical value.

◆ If your FPS stays below 30 frames or any counts are steadily increasing, you are looking at, for example, suboptimal loops or a memory leak. This should never happen in the final release.

In general, verify that the numbers are plausible for your scene.

For releases, or when you take screenshots, you will want to deactivate these StatView HUDs. To switch off the statistics and FPS views, use the following commands:

```
setDisplayFps(false);
setDisplayStatView(false);
```

## Navigating the scene with a mouse and a keyboard

If the settings.useInput() property is true, the flyCam camera becomes active, and you can navigate using the **W**, **A**, **S**, and **D** keys. The WASD navigation method is named after the four keys used on a QWERTY keyboard to mimic the layout of the arrow keys. WASD navigation is typically used in combination with a mouselook rotation.

# Time for action – move it!

Here's an overview of the default key bindings; try them!

| Camera Motion | User Input |
| --- | --- |
| Move forward | *W* key |
| Move left (Strafe) | *A* key |
| Move backward | *S* key |
| Move right (Strafe) | *D* key |
| Move up | *Q* key |
| Move down | *Z* key |
| Rotate left | Left arrow key, or move mouse left |
| Rotate right | Right arrow key, or move mouse right |
| Rotate up | Up arrow key, or move mouse forward |
| Rotate down | Down arrow key, or move mouse backward |
| Zoom in | Scroll mouse wheel backward |
| Zoom out | Scroll mouse wheel forward |
| Rotate drag | Hold left mouse button and move |

The `SimpleApplication` class offers a few additional key bindings that developers commonly use during the development phase. Even if you deactivate WASD navigation, the following three keys are still available:

| | |
| --- | --- |
| Print the camera position and rotation to the console (for debugging) | *C* key |
| Print memory usage to the console (for debugging) | *M* key |
| Stop the application and close the window | *Esc* key |

## What just happened?

As you can see, the default input settings go a long way in your first `SimpleApplication` class. As your own game grows, you will want to be able to have more fine-grained control over navigation and input handling. You may want to configure the *Esc* key to pause the game, or take users back to the settings screen of your application. You will implement custom game actions and want to set up keys that trigger them. For the final release, you will also want to deactivate the two default bindings that print debug information to the console.

In the next chapter, you learn how to interact with the user by setting up your own input handlers.

## Have a go hero – tower defense

Over the course of this book, we want to build up a little tower defense game. In a tower defense game, the player defends his (immobile) base against incoming (mobile) baddies—the creeps. During the game, players position armed towers around their base. While the computer-controlled creeps storm in and try to break through the barrier, the players face the challenge of keeping the automatic defense system charged with *ammo*. The game is played from a third-person perspective; this means that players look down on the terrain from above and click towers to assign ammo depending on their budget.

In our little demo, we want to set the player base at the end of a valley. This means that the creeps can only approach from one side, and it only makes sense to place the towers along the valley. As a simplification, the game automatically positions the towers for the player in each level.

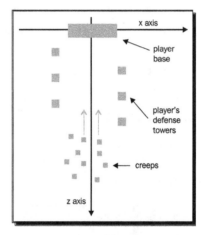

Create a new project from the `BasicGame` template. Extend the `SimpleApplication` class and amend the `main()` method and the `simpleInitApp()` method to initialize your scene. Use what you learned in this chapter!

1.  Modify the `settings` object in the `main()` method and specify an image of your choice as a splash screen. Set the name of the game to, for example, *My Tower Defense Demo*.

2.  Keep the default `flyCam` method active for now, so you can look at the scene while you create it. Remember that you will navigate using the mouse and the **W**, **A**, **S**, and **D** keys.

3.  Create a flat, 33-WU wide, orange `Box()` as the floor.

4.  Create a `playerNode`, a `towerNode`, and a `creepNode`, and attach them to the `rootNode`. Remember that nodes are invisible handles.

5.  Write code that creates (visible) geometries; one lying yellow `Box()` representing the player base, one tall green `Box()` representing one tower, and one black, small cube that represents one creep. Optimally, these are three reusable helper methods that accept a location (`Vector3f`) as an argument.

6.  Attach the geometries to the `playerNode`, the `towerNode`, and the `creepNode`, respectively. Since these nodes are attached to the `rootNode`, your geometries are visible parts of the scene now.

7.  Position the player base geometry at the origin. Placing a box at the origin is a good practice for orientation in the otherwise empty scene.

8.  Position one tower to the left and one to the right in front of the base, and some smaller creep cubes further down along the z axis. You will notice that the location is relative to the center of the box—if you don't want a box that is stuck halfway *underground*, move it up by half its height.

9.  Copy the code that deactivates the `StatsView` object and FPS to the beginning of the `simpleInitApp()` method, but leave it commented out for now. Watch how the statistics change when you add one box.

You can find an example implementation in the `mygame` package.

# Summary

After having read this chapter, you will have learned how to create scenes and configure application features. Now, you know how to orient yourself using the coordinate system. We also saw how to manage spatials in the scene graph and learned how to transform spatials. We studied the difference between nodes and geometries. Finally, we tried to navigate a scene using a keyboard and mouse.

In the next chapter, we will learn how to add action and interaction to your scene.

# 3
# Interacting with the User

*The main loop is your game's Dungeon Master, referee, and director: it listens for user input, updates the game state, and renders the output. In a game of Blockout, the loop drops blocks and clears finished layers. In a car racer, the loop calculates friction and acceleration. In a first-person shooter, the loop respawns enemies. The loop is where you make sure everyone sticks to the rules, and where you determine whether the player has won or lost.*

In the previous chapter, we learnt how to initialize a 3D scene using the `simpleInitApp()` method from the `SimpleApplication` class. You can translate, scale, and rotate objects into their start positions, and navigate the scene using the mouse and **W**, **A**, **S**, and **D** keys. But the scene is still static—we need some interaction!

In this chapter you will learn:

- How to respond to user input
- How to determine the target of a user action
- How to trigger game actions
- How to steer game characters

Let's make the application come alive.

# The digital Dungeon Master

Have you ever played a **role-playing game** (**RPG**) such as Dungeons & Dragons? In a pen-and-paper RPG, one of the players takes the role of the storyteller or **Dungeon Master** (**DM**). The DM keeps track of the score and describes the scene in words. The DM controls all **non-player characters** (**NPCs**), enemies as well as extras. The DM is also the referee who interprets rules.

In a computer game, the listen-update-render loop takes the role of the Dungeon Master. Instead of players moving pieces on the table, Java input listeners trigger game actions. Instead of players rolling dice and looking up rules, the update loop manages game mechanics. Instead of the DM deciding on random encounters, the update loop controls NPC behavior. Instead of the DM describing the scene in words, the renderer draws the scene in 3D.

## Time for action – from input to output in slow motion

Each game world has certain properties: the level, the score, players and enemies, position and speed of objects and characters, inventories and skills, maybe a countdown timer, and so on. These properties together are the **game state**.

Each game world also offers some actions: the player can decide to walk, jump, drive, fight, use equipment, take or drop items, change game options, and so on. There are also events that happen without user input: traps are reset, power-ups respawn, automatic doors open or close, and so on. We call these incidents **game actions**. Game actions are triggered either by the player (in response to input), or by NPCs and objects, as part of the main loop.

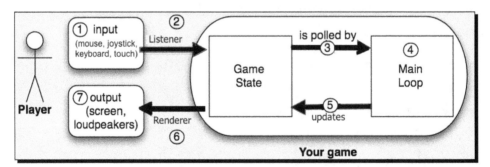

Let's zoom in on *one day in the life* of the average event-driven video game:

1.   The player's *input* triggers a *game action*. For example, the user clicks to attack an enemy, the user presses the *W*, *A*, *S*, and *D* keys to walk, and so on.

2. The *game action* updates the *game state*. For example: a successful attack decreases the enemy's health, walking changes the player's location, pushing a ball increases its momentum, and so on.

3. The *update loop* polls the *game state*. For example: what are the current locations of characters relative to any traps? What is the location and momentum of the rolling ball?

4. The *update loop* performs tests and decides which *game action* it should trigger. For example: if the enemy's health is zero, it dies and the player gets points; if the player is close, the trap goes off; as long as there are no obstacles, the ball keeps rolling, and so on.

5. The *game action* updates the *game state*. For example: the dead character is removed from the scene and the player's score increases, the trap inflicts damage on the player, the location and momentum of the rolling ball have changed a bit, and so on.

6. The game *outputs* the new *game state*. The output includes audio and video that communicate the updated game state to the player. For example: the scene is rendered in 3D and displayed on the user's screen, sounds and animations play, the score display is updated, and so on.

7. The player watches the new *game state*.

The listen-update-render loop continues running even if there is no player input—this means steps 1 and 2 are optional. The driving force is the main event loop, not the player.

## *What just happened?*

The listen-update-render loop is the heartbeat of your game and brings action and interaction to an otherwise static scene. You understand that game actions update the game state.

| Step | What happens? | What's that in Java? |
|------|---------------|----------------------|
| Listen | **Listeners** receive input from the player and handle events. | Java event handling |
| Update | **Game actions** update the **game state.** | Java methods (game actions) change Java objects (game state) |
| Render | The **renderer** outputs graphics and sound for the player. | Java video and audio libraries (LWJGL) |

The whole event loop is made up of familiar pieces: for the *Listen* step, you use Java event handling. You represent the game state as Java objects, and implement game actions as Java methods. In the *update* loop, you work with standard conditionals, timers, and randomizers, to advance the game by rules that you specify. The loop is the mastermind that pulls strings in the background for you.

As an example, let's implement a simple game action that changes the game state.

## Time for action – pushing the right buttons

Remember our friend, the blue cube from the template? Let's write some code that changes the cube state: the cube has a color, a scale, a location, and a rotation. So just for fun, let's make the cube rotate when we left-click on it, and change its color every time we press the Space bar.

**1.** Make another copy of the `BasicGame` project's `Main.java` template and name the class `UserInput.java`. Remember to also refactor the first line of the `main()` method to the following:

```
UserInput app = new UserInput();.
```

**2.** Define class constants that represent the Space bar and left-click of the mouse. Import the necessary classes from the `com.jme3.input.*` and `com.jme3.input.controls.*` packages.

```
private final static Trigger TRIGGER_COLOR =
    new KeyTrigger(KeyInput.KEY_SPACE);
private final static Trigger TRIGGER_ROTATE =
    new MouseButtonTrigger(MouseInput.BUTTON_LEFT);
```

**3.** Define two String class constants. We use these Strings to identify the two actions later: rotating the cube and toggling its color.

```
private final static String MAPPING_COLOR  = "Toggle Color";
private final static String MAPPING_ROTATE = "Rotate";
```

 In the jMonkeyEngine SDK, place the insertion point behind the period after `KeyInput.` or `MouseInput.`, and so on. Then press *Ctrl* + Space bar to select constants from the code-completion pop-up. You also find a list of input triggers for mouse, keyboard, touch, and joystick events in the appendix.

You now have two **triggers**, `TRIGGER_COLOR` and `TRIGGER_ROTATE`, and two **mappings**, `MAPPING_COLOR` and `MAPPING_ROTATE`.

## What just happened?

Each physical input, such as the Space bar or left-click of the mouse , is represented by a `Trigger` object. You create a `KeyTrigger` object for a key. You create `MouseButtonTrigger` objects for mouse clicks, and `MouseAxisTrigger` objects for mouse movement. Similarly, you create `JoyAxisTrigger` objects and `JoyButtonTrigger` objects for joystick buttons and movements. Android devices also support `TouchTrigger` objects that act similarly to `MouseButtonTrigger` objects.

The two action names that you prepared here, `MAPPING_COLOR` and `MAPPING_ROTATE`, are **mappings**. The mappings are case-sensitive Strings, and must be unique, one for each action. For mappings, always choose meaningful names that reflect the action, not the trigger. This way they still make sense even if you change the assigned triggers later.

Using String constants instead of Strings has the advantage that the compiler warns you if you misspell the mapping (as opposed to silently ignoring your input). Using String constants also makes it possible to use IDE features, such as refactoring or finding usages.

## Time for action – trigger meets mapping

The `SimpleApplication` class provides you with a handy `inputManager` object that you can configure.

1. Go to the `simpleInitApp()` method. Leave the template code that creates the blue cube as it is.

2. Register your mappings and triggers with the `inputManager`. At the beginning of the method, add the following two lines:

```
public void simpleInitApp(){
   inputManager.addMapping(MAPPING_COLOR,   TRIGGER_COLOR);
   inputManager.addMapping(MAPPING_ROTATE,  TRIGGER_ROTATE);
   // …
}
```

3. But what if half of your users think the Space bar is unintuitive for toggling color, and prefer the *C* key instead? You can easily allow several variants in one mapping; define a trigger object for the *C* key on the class level, as you did for the Space bar key:

```
private final static Trigger TRIGGER_COLOR2 =
    new KeyTrigger(KeyInput.KEY_C);
```

**4.** Register the alternative trigger to the mapping, with a comma as separator. Change the existing `MAPPING_COLOR` line as follows:

```
inputManager.addMapping(MAPPING_COLOR, TRIGGER_COLOR,
    TRIGGER_COLOR2);
```

You now have defined your input mappings.

## What just happened?

The `inputManager` object uses mappings to associate action names and triggers. You use mappings because the implementation of the action may change, and the assignment of keys or mouse clicks may change—but the mapping always remains the same. You can map one unique action name, such as `MAPPING_COLOR` to several triggers, such as `TRIGGER_COLOR`/Space bar and `TRIGGER_COLOR2`/C key. You can use each trigger only once (in one mapping) at the same time.

Now you have triggers, action names, and input mappings, but they don't do anything yet. Your mapping needs to be registered to the appropriate listener.

## Time for action – mapping meets listeners

To activate the mappings, you have to register them to an `InputListener` object. The jMonkeyEngine offers several `InputListener` objects in the `com.jme3.input. controls.*` package. Let's create instances of the two most common `InputListener` objects and compare what they do.

**1.** On class level, below the closing curly braces of the `simpleInitApp()` method, add the following code snippet:

```
private ActionListener actionListener = new ActionListener() {
  public void onAction(String name, boolean isPressed, float tpf)
{
    System.out.println("You triggered: "+name);
  }
};
private AnalogListener analogListener = new AnalogListener() {
  public void onAnalog(String name, float intensity, float tpf) {
    System.out.println("You triggered: "+name);
  }
};
```

When you paste code in the jMonkeyEngine SDK's editor, unknown symbols are underlined in red. Whenever you see yellow warnings next to lines, click on the lightbulb icon and execute the hint to resolve the problem, in this case, *Add import for...* Alternatively, you can also press the *Ctrl + Shift + I* shortcut keys to fix all import statements in one go.

**2.** Register each mapping to one of the `InputListener` objects. Paste the following two lines of code below the `addMapping()` code lines in the `simpleInitApp()` method:

```
inputManager.addListener(actionListener,
    new String[]{MAPPING_COLOR});
inputManager.addListener(analogListener,
    new String[]{MAPPING_ROTATE});
```

If you run the code sample now, and then click, or press the *C* key or Space bar, you should see some output in the console.

## What just happened?

jMonkeyEngine comes with three preconfigured `InputListener` objects: `ActionListener`, `AnalogListener`, and `TouchListener`. Each responds differently to `com.jme3.input.event.InputEvents`.

♦ `ActionListener` is optimized for discrete *either/or* `InputEvents`. Use it if you want to detect whether a key is either pressed or released, or the mouse button is either up or down, and so on.

♦ `AnalogListener` is optimized for continuous `InputEvents` with an intensity. This includes mouse or joystick movements, (for example, when looking around with the camera), or long-lasting key presses (for example, when walking by pressing the *W*, *A*, *S*, and *D* keys), or long mouse clicks (for example, when the player shoots an automatic weapon).

♦ `TouchListener` is optimized for `InputEvents` on touchscreen devices. It supports events, such as tap, double-tap, long pressed tap, fling, and two-finger gestures.

In the previous example, you registered `MAPPING_COLOR` to the `actionListener` object, because toggling a color is a discrete *either/or* decision. You have registered the `MAPPING_ROTATE` mapping to the `analogListener` object, because rotation is a continuous action. Make this decision for every mapping that you register. It's common to use both `InputListener` objects in one game, and to register all analog actions to one and all discrete actions to the other listener.

Note that the second argument of the `addListener()` method is a String array. This means that you can add several comma-separated mappings to one `InputListener` object in one go. It is also perfectly fine to call the `inputManager.addListener()` method more than once in the same application, and to add a few mappings per line. This keeps the code more readable. Adding more mappings to an `InputListener` object does not overwrite existing mappings.

## Time for action – listeners meet actions

Look at the inner methods of the `InputListener` objects:

◆ `onAction(String name, boolean isPressed, float tpf)` in `actionListener`

◆ `onAnalog(String name, float intensity, float tpf)` in `analogListener`

◆ `onTouch(String name, TouchEvent event, float tpf)` in `touchListener` (not depicted)

When you implement the actual actions, you write a series of conditionals in these inner methods. When you want to detect several triggers (the most common scenario), add several `else if` conditionals. You test for each mapping by `name`, and then execute the desired action. In our example, we want the action to affect the blue cube (`geom`).

1. Make `geom` accessible as a class field. Remember to adjust the `geom` object's constructor call in `simpleInitApp()` method accordingly.

```
private Geometry geom;
...
geom = new Geometry("Box", mesh);
```

Now the `InputListener` objects in your class have access to the cube geometry.

2. Let's handle `MAPPING_COLOR` first. In the inner `onAction()` method of the `actionListener` object, test whether `name` equals to `MAPPING_COLOR`. To execute the action when the trigger is released (that is, the key or mouse button is up again), test whether the Boolean is `!isPressed`:

```
private ActionListener actionListener = new ActionListener() {
    public void onAction(String name, boolean isPressed, float
tpf) {
        if (name.equals(MAPPING_COLOR) && !isPressed) {
            // implement action here
        }
    }
};
```

**3.** Implement the color toggle action for `geom`: get the cube's material, and set the `Color` property using the return value of the static `randomColor()` method. Replace the *implement action here* comment with the following line:

```
geom.getMaterial().setColor("Color", ColorRGBA.randomColor());
```

**4.** Let's handle `MAPPING_ROTATE`. In the inner `onAnalog()` method of the `analogListener`, test whether `name` equals `MAPPING_ROTATE`.

```
private AnalogListener analogListener = new AnalogListener() {
  public void onAnalog(String name, float intensity, float tpf) {
    if (name.equals(MAPPING_ROTATE)) {
      // implement action here
    }
  }
};
```

**5.** Implement the rotation action for `geom`. To execute the action continuously as long as the trigger is pressed, use the provided `intensity` value as a factor in your continuous rotation action. Replace the *implement action here* comment with the following line:

```
geom.rotate(0, intensity, 0); // rotate around Y axis
```

When you run `UserInput.java` now, you see the blue cube. Press the Space bar and the cube changes its color. Keep the left mouse button pressed and the cube rotates around its y axis. You can even do both at the same time. When you press the *C* key, however, you notice that the color changes, but the application also prints camera information to the console. Strange! Didn't you just declare the *C* key as an alternative to the Space bar? You did, but you did not consider the existing default mappings.

`SimpleApplication` internally maps the *C* key to a diagnostic output action. You will notice a similar issue if you map anything to the *M* (prints memory diagnostics) or *Esc* keys (stops the game), which are also internally registered by `SimpleApplication`. If necessary, you can remove any of the three existing mappings as follows:

```
inputManager.deleteMapping(INPUT_MAPPING_EXIT);       // Key_ESCAPE
inputManager.deleteMapping(INPUT_MAPPING_CAMERA_POS); // Key_C
inputManager.deleteMapping(INPUT_MAPPING_MEMORY);     // Key_M
```

You can call the `inputManager.clearMappings()` method and define all mappings from scratch. But clearing also removes the preconfigured *W*, *A*, *S*, and *D* key navigation, which we would like to keep as long as we're looking at examples. So don't clear the mappings for now—until you develop your own game.

## What just happened?

Congrats! You now know how to set up individual keys and mouse buttons, and so on to trigger custom game actions that change the game state.

1. Start by deciding on a list of actions and default triggers in your game.

2. Define triggers and give them unique names that describe the action, not the key.

3. Register each name—trigger pair as a mapping to the `inputManager` object.

4. Create `InputListener` instances for discrete and analog events, and register each mapping to one of them.

5. Finally, test for each mapping in its `InputListener` object's `onAction()`, `onAnalog()`, or `onTouch()` method, and implement its action.

# Click me if you can

Now you know how to trigger simple game actions such as rotating a cube. Since the cube is the only object in the scene, the user does not have any choice which spatial to interact with. But as soon as you have several objects in a scene, you need to find out what the user was *looking at* when he or she pressed an action key.

There are several possible targets of game actions: the target of navigational actions is typically the player character or vehicle—no explicit target selection is necessary. The target of a *take* action is, in contrast, one of many items lying around. The target of an attack can be a subset of enemy characters, while the target of a magic spell can be pretty much anything, depending on the spell: the player, an ally, an enemy, an item, or even the floor.

These seemingly different game actions are very similar from an implementation point of view: the player selects a target in the 3D scene, and then triggers an action on it. We call the process of identifying the target **picking**.

If the *hot spot* for clicks is the center of the screen, some games mark it with crosshairs. Alternatively, a game can offer a visible mouse cursor. In either case, you need to determine what 3D object the player was aiming at.

## Time for action – pick a brick (using crosshairs)

To learn about picking a target in the scene, let's add a second cube to the scene. Again we want to click to rotate a cube, but this time, we want to pick the cube that will be the target of the action.

1. Make a copy of the previous exercise, `UserInput.java`. Keep the mouse click and the key press actions for inspiration.

2. Rename the copy of the class to `TargetPickCenter.java`. Remember to also refactor the first line of the `main()` method to the following:

```
TargetPickCenter app = new TargetPickCenter();.
```

3. Let's write a simple cube generator so that we can generate sample content more easily: move the code block that creates the blue cube from the `simpleInitApp()` method into a custom method called `myCube()`. Turn the `Box` mesh object into a static class field so that you can reuse it. Your method should use three arguments: `String name`, `Vector3f loc`, and `ColorRGBA color`. The method should return a new colored and named cube `Geometry` at the specified location.

```
private static Box mesh = new Box(Vector3f.ZERO, 1, 1, 1);

public Geometry myBox(String name, Vector3f loc, ColorRGBA color)
{
    Geometry geom = new Geometry(name, mesh);
    Material mat = new Material(assetManager,
        "Common/MatDefs/Misc/Unshaded.j3md");
    mat.setColor("Color", color);
    geom.setMaterial(mat);
    geom.setLocalTranslation(loc);
    return geom;
}
```

4. Use your `myBox()` method to attach two cubes to the `rootNode` object, a red one and a blue one. Space them apart a little bit so that they don't overlap sitting at the origin: move the red one up 1.5f WU, and the blue one down 1.5f WU, along the y axis.

```
rootNode.attachChild(myBox("Red Cube",
    new Vector3f(0,  1.5f, 0), ColorRGBA.Red));
rootNode.attachChild(myBox("Blue Cube",
    new Vector3f(0, -1.5f, 0), ColorRGBA.Blue));
```

5. Reuse the class constants `MAPPING_ROTATE` and `TRIGGER_ROTATE` that you created previously, and register the left-click mapping in the `simpleInitApp()` method as before.

```
private static final String MAPPING_ROTATE = "Rotate";
private static final Trigger TRIGGER_ROTATE = new
MouseButtonTrigger(MouseInput.BUTTON_LEFT);
...
public void simpleInitApp() {
    inputManager.addMapping(MAPPING_ROTATE, TRIGGER_ROTATE);
    inputManager.addListener(analogListener,
    new String[]{MAPPING_ROTATE});
```

**6.** To make aiming easier, let's mark the center of the screen with a little white cube. Since a mark is 2D, we attach it to the 2D user interface (guiNode), and not to the 3D scene (rootNode)! Call the `attachCenterMark()` method from the `simpleInitApp()` method.

```
private void attachCenterMark() {
    Geometry c = myBox("center mark",
        Vector3f.ZERO, ColorRGBA.White);
    c.scale(4);
    c.setLocalTranslation( settings.getWidth()/2,
        settings.getHeight()/2, 0 );
    guiNode.attachChild(c); // attach to 2D user interface
}
```

Run the `TargetPickCenter` method to see the intermediate result, the red cube above the blue cube.

## What just happened?

Whenever you need to *mass produce* geometries, consider writing a convenience method, such as the `myBox()` method with parameters to decrease clutter in the `simpleInitApp()` method.

Between the two cubes you see a tiny white cube—this is our center mark. When you look around by moving the mouse, or navigate to the sides by pressing the *A* or *D* keys, you notice that the center mark stays put. This mark is not attached to the `rootNode` object—and, therefore, is not part of the projected 3D scene. It is attached to a special `guiNode` object, and is therefore part of the 2D graphical user interface (GUI). Just as with the `rootNode` object, you inherited the `guiNode` object from the `SimpleApplication` class.

We added the center mark because you may have noticed that the mouse pointer is invisible in a running game. It would be hard to click and select a target without some visual feedback. For a sample application, our white mark is enough—in a real game, you would attach a crosshairs graphic of higher artistic value.

## Time for action – pick a brick (crosshairs with ray casting)

You want the player to aim and click one of the cubes. You want to identify the selected cube, and make it rotate.

**1.** Start by implementing the `AnalogListener` object on the `Analog()` method to test for our left-click action, `MAPPING_ROTATE`. Remember, we chose the `AnalogListener` object because rotation is a continuous motion.

```
private AnalogListener analogListener = new AnalogListener() {
```

```
        public void onAnalog(String name, float intensity, float tpf)
    {

        if (name.equals(MAPPING_ROTATE)) {
            // implement action here
        }

    }
};
```

2.  To identify what was clicked, we use methods from the `com.jme3.collision` package. Replace the *implement action here* comment with the following code; first we create an empty results list.

    ```
    CollisionResults results = new CollisionResults();
    ```

3.  We aim at an invisible line (a so called `com.jme3.math.ray`) straight from the camera location forward in the camera direction.

    ```
    Ray ray = new Ray(cam.getLocation(), cam.getDirection());
    ```

4.  We calculate intersections between this line-of-sight ray and all geometries attached to the `rootNode` object, and collect them in the results list.

    ```
    rootNode.collideWith(ray, results);
    ```

5.  Let's print the intermediate result, so that we can see what is going on. For each *hit*, we know the distance from the camera, the impact point, and the geometry.

    ```
    for (int i = 0; i < results.size(); i++) {
        float    dist  = results.getCollision(i).getDistance();
        Vector3f pt    = results.getCollision(i).getContactPoint();
        String   target = results.getCollision(i).getGeometry().
    getName();
        System.out.println("Selection: #" + i + ": " + target +
            " at " + pt + ", " + dist + " WU away.");
    }
    ```

6.  If the user has clicked anything, the results list is not empty. In this case we identify the selected geometry; the closest item must be the target that the player picked! If the results list is empty, we just print some feedback to the console.

    ```
    if (results.size() > 0) {
        Geometry target = results.getClosestCollision().getGeometry();
        // implement action here
    } else {
        System.out.println("Selection: Nothing" );
    }
    ```

**7.** Replace the *implement action here* comment with the actual code that rotates the cubes around their y axes. You can use the `getName()` action in a conditional statement to identify geometries, and respond differently to each, for example:

```
if (target.getName().equals("Red Cube")) {
    target.rotate(0, -intensity, 0); // rotate left
} else if (target.getName().equals("Blue Cube")) {
    target.rotate(0, intensity, 0); // rotate right
}
```

Build and run the sample. When you point with the center mark and click either the red or the blue cube, it rotates. You notice that the red cube rotates to the left and the blue cube to the right.

## What just happened?

Impressive: your application can now not only *feel* key presses and clicks coming from the user, but it can even *see* through the eyes of the user and know what he or she looked at in the scene! In our example, you can now tell the cubes apart, and respond with different actions accordingly: the red one rotates to the left because you used `-intensity` (negative), and the blue one to the right because you used `intensity` (positive) as rotation factors.

What does *seeing through the eyes of the user* mean? Mathematically, you aim an *invisible line* from the camera location forward, in its view direction. A line that has a fixed beginning and direction is called a **ray**. In the jMonkeyEngine, this corresponds to a `com.jme3.math.Ray` object. The ray starts at the 3D coordinates of the camera, which coincides with the center of the screen, the typical location of crosshairs. The ray travels in the view direction through the scene and intersects (**collides**) with scene objects. The `com.jme3.collision` package provides you with specialized methods that **detect collisions** between various mathematical objects, including between rays and the scene graph. This neat little trick for identifying click targets is called **ray casting**.

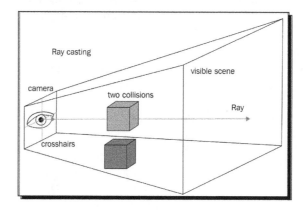

The code sample prints a bit of information so you can see what this picking algorithm is capable of. The `CollisionResults` object contains a list of all collisions between two scene elements, and accessors that let you pick the closest (or farthest) intersected object. In the jMonkeyEngine SDK, choose **Window | Output | Output** to open the console. When you run the application and click on the cubes, the output should look similar to the following:

```
Selection #0: Red Cube at (0.0, 1.1, 1.0), 9.048468 WU away.
Selection #1: Red Cube at (0.0, 1.4, -0.9), 11.090528 WU away.
Selection #0: Blue Cube at (0.1, -0.8, 1.0), 9.044685 WU away.
Selection #1: Blue Cube at (0.1, -1.0, -1.0), 11.054616 WU away.
```

Note that each cube is detected twice: the first impact point is on the front side, where the ray enters the geometry, and the second is the exit point on the backside of the geometry. In general, the clicked item is the closest geometry in the results list. Therefore, we use `results.getClosestCollision().getGeometry()` to identify the target.

In an actual game, you can use this crosshair-style picking method to implement an attack on an enemy; instead of simply rotating the picked geometry, you could play a gun sound and subtract health points from the identified target. If your conditional identifies the clicked geometry as a door, you could play a creaking sound, and trigger a closing or opening animation on the target, and so on. Your imagination is the limit!

## Time for action – pick a brick (using the mouse pointer)

Aiming fixed crosshairs is one way to pick objects in the scene. Another option is to make the mouse pointer visible, and allow free clicks.

1. Make a copy of the previous exercise, `TargetPickCenter.java`. You can keep the code that handles the mouse click actions and the key press actions for inspiration.

2. Rename the copy of the class to `TargetPickCursor.java`. Remember to also refactor the first line of the `main()` method to the following:

   ```
   TargetPickCursor app = new TargetPickCursor();
   ```

3. Keep the `myBox()` method, the constants, the `analogListener` object, and the two cubes. Remove the `attachCenterMark()` method, and the `AnalogListener` object implementation.

4. By default, the mouse pointer is hidden. To make it visible, add the following to the `simpleInitApp()` method:

   ```
   flyCam.setDragToRotate(true);
   inputManager.setCursorVisible(true);
   ```

Run `TargetPickCursor` to see the intermediate result.

## What just happened?

Again, you see the red cube above the blue cube. When you move the mouse, you notice that the pointer is a visible arrow now. But you also notice something else; earlier, the view rotated when you moved the mouse to the sides. This feature is part of the default camera behavior and is called **mouse look**, or **free look**. Mouse look does not get along with a visible mouse pointer. You can use the mouse either for navigating, or for pointing and clicking. Both at the same time is quite confusing for the player.

You deactivated mouse look when you set `flyCam.setDragToRotate(true);`. To rotate the camera and look around now, keep the left mouse button pressed while moving.

## Time for action – pick a brick (pointer with ray casting)

Now your player can click items, but how do you find out what he clicked? In principle, we can use the same ray casting algorithm as for the previous example with the crosshairs. Only instead of casting the ray from the camera forward, we now cast it forward from the 3D coordinates of the click location.

1. Implement the `AnalogListener` object on the `Analog()` method to test for our left-click action, `MAPPING_ROTATE`.

   ```
   private AnalogListener analogListener = new AnalogListener() {
       public void onAnalog(String name, float intensity, float tpf)
   {
           if (name.equals(MAPPING_ROTATE)) {
               // implement action here
           }
       }
   };
   ```

2. Replace the *implement action here* comment by the following code. To identify what was clicked, we use methods from the `com.jme3.collision` package. As before, we create an empty results list.

   ```
   CollisionResults results = new CollisionResults();
   ```

3. The next few steps are new. Since we are working with the mouse pointer, we get the 2D coordinates of the cursor position from the `inputManager` object:

   ```
   Vector2f click2d = inputManager.getCursorPosition();
   ```

4. We use the `cam.getWorldCoordinates()` method to convert these (x,y) coordinates into (x,y,z) coordinates with a depth (z) of zero.

   ```
   Vector3f click3d = cam.getWorldCoordinates(
       new Vector2f(click2d.getX(), click2d.getY()), 0f)
   ```

**5.** We want to cast the ray *forward* from this point. The following code calculates the direction vector of a temporary point that is 1 WU *deep into the screen* from the clicked location:

```
Vector3f dir = cam.getWorldCoordinates(
    new Vector2f(click2d.getX(), click2d.getY()), 1f).
      subtractLocal(click3d);
```

**6.** Instead of aiming the ray forward from the camera location in the camera direction, we now aim the ray starting from the click location into the calculated forward direction.

```
Ray ray = new Ray(click3d, dir);
```

**7.** Now that we have the ray, the rest of the code is the same as for the crosshairs example. We calculate intersections between this line-of-sight ray and all geometries attached to the `rootNode` object, and collect them in the results list.

```
rootNode.collideWith(ray, results);
```

**8.** If the user has clicked anything, the results list is not empty. In this case we identify the selected geometry—the closest item must be the target that the player picked! If the results list is empty, we just print some feedback to the console.

```
if (results.size() > 0) {
    Geometry target = results.getClosestCollision().getGeometry();
    if (target.getName().equals("Red Cube")) {
        target.rotate(0, -intensity, 0); // rotate left
    } else if (target.getName().equals("Blue Cube")) {
        target.rotate(0, intensity, 0); // rotate right
    }
} else {
    System.out.println("Selection: Nothing" );
}
```

Build and run the sample. When you point the mouse pointer at either the red or blue cube and click, the cube rotates as in the previous example. Congrats! Not even fancy-free mouse clicks can escape your notice now!

## *What just happened?*

Previously, when aiming with crosshairs, we assumed that the crosshairs were located in the center of the screen, where the camera is located—we simply aimed the ray forward from the (known) 3D camera location, in the (known) 3D camera direction. A mouse click with a pointer, however, can only identify (x,y) coordinates on a 2D screen.

```
Vector2f click2d = inputManager.getCursorPosition();
```

Similarly, we can no longer simply use the known camera direction as the direction of the ray. But to be able to cast a ray, we need a 3D start location and a 3D direction. How did we obtain them?

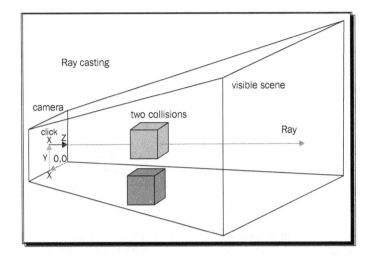

The `cam.getWorldCoordinates()` method can convert a 2D screen coordinate, plus a depth *z* from the camera forward, into 3D world coordinates. In our case, the depth *z* is zero—we assume that a click is *right on the lens* of the camera.

To specify the *forward* direction of the ray, we first calculate the coordinates of a temporary point `tmp`. This point has the same (x,y) coordinates as the mouse click, but is 1 WU deeper into the scene (1 WU is an arbitrarily chosen depth value). We use the `cam.getWorldCoordinates()` method once more with the click's 2D screen coordinate, but now we specify a depth of 1 WU:

```
Vector3f tmp = cam.getWorldCoordinates(
    new Vector2f(click2d.getX(), click2d.getY()), 1f);
```

We need to identify the direction from the 3D click location towards the temporary point 1 WU in front of it. Mathematically, you get this direction vector by subtracting the click's vector from `tmp` point's vector as in the following code:

```
Vector3f dir = tmp.subtractLocal(click3d);
```

Subtracting one vector from another is a common operation if you need to identify the direction from one point to another. You can do it in one step:

```
Vector3f dir = cam.getWorldCoordinates(
    new Vector2f(click2d.getX(), click2d.getY()), 1f).
        subtractLocal(click3d);
```

In these small examples, we collide the ray with the whole scene attached to the `rootNode` object. This ensures that all nodes are tested. On the other hand, too many tests may slow performance in large scenes. If you know that only mutually exclusive sets of nodes are candidates for a certain action, then restrict the collision test to this subset of nodes. For example, attach all spatials that respond to an *open/close* action to an `Openable` node. Attach all spatials that respond to a *take/drop* action to a `Takeable` node, and so on.

Experiment with either picking method, crosshairs or mouse pointer, and see which one suits your gameplay better.

## Pop quiz – input handling

Q1. In which order do you define and register the pairings for your input handler?

1. trigger-mapping, mapping-listener, listener-action
2. mapping-listener, listener-action, action-trigger
3. action-trigger, trigger-mapping, mapping-listener
4. listener-action, action-trigger, trigger-mapping

# How to steer spatials

Now your users can trigger game actions and select targets. But a video game also follows an internal rhythm and generates its own events—new enemies spawn and plot a path towards the player base, a timer ignites explosives, a dungeon door falls shut, and so on. How do you implement computer-controlled events that need to be updated in every frame of the game?

Look at the `Main.java` template of the `SimpleApplication` class again—there is a mysterious method that we have not yet used, the `simpleUpdate()` method. Let's find out what it does!

## Time for action – you are the CubeChaser

Let's do something more interactive than just look at rotating cubes. Can you write code that lets you *chase* one of the cubes? By chase we mean, if the camera moves closer than 10 WU to this cube, the cube should move away from the camera.

1. Make another copy of the `BasicGame` object's `Main.java` template.
2. Rename the copy to `CubeChaser.java`. Remember to also refactor the first line of the `main()` method to the following:

```
CubeChaser app = new CubeChaser();
```

**3.** Delete the blue cube and copy the `myBox()` convenience method from one of the previous target picking examples. Don't forget to copy the `mesh` class field.

**4.** Add a `makeCubes(40);` call to the `simpleInitApp()` method and fill the scene with 40 randomly positioned and randomly colored cubes. Use the built-in method `FastMath.nextRandomInt(min, max)` (from `com.jme3.math`) to generate random coordinates in the interval between `min` and `max`.

```
private void makeCubes(int number) {
  for (int i = 0; i < number; i++) {
    // randomize 3D coordinates
    Vector3f loc = new Vector3f(
      FastMath.nextRandomInt(-20, 20),
      FastMath.nextRandomInt(-20, 20),
      FastMath.nextRandomInt(-20, 20));
    rootNode.attachChild(
      myBox("Cube" + i, loc, ColorRGBA.randomColor()));
  }
}
```

**5.** Create a white cube geometry, `scaredCube`, as a class field, and position it in the origin.

```
private Geometry scaredCube;
...
public void simpleInitApp() {
  makeCubes(40);
  scaredCube = myBox("Scared Cube", Vector3f.ZERO, ColorRGBA.
White);
  rootNode.attachChild(scaredCube);
}
```

How would you write code that constantly monitors the distance between the camera location and the location of the `scaredCube` object? You write these kinds of tests in the `simpleUpdate(float tpf)` method.

**6.** Use the `vector1.distance(vector2)` method for the distance test. You get current object coordinates by calling the `cam.getLocation()` and `cube.getLocalTranslation()` methods.

```
public void simpleUpdate(float tpf) {
  System.out.println("Distance: "+
    cam.getLocation().distance(scaredCube.getLocalTranslation()));
}
```

**7.** Modify this code so that it tests whether the distance is less than 10 WU. If yes, then move the scared cube away from you, that is, in the direction that the camera is facing.

```
public void simpleUpdate(float tpf) {
  ...
  if (cam.getLocation().distance(scaredCube.getLocalTranslation())
< 10) {
    scaredCube.move(cam.getDirection());
  }
}
```

Run the class and use the *W, A, S,* and *D* keys and the mouse to navigate through the cube-filled scene. Keep an eye on the white cube!

> If you feel you are moving too slow, you can speed up the default camera. Add the following command somewhere in the `simpleInitApp()` method:
> ```
> flyCam.setMoveSpeed(100f);
> ```

## What just happened?

When you run this class you see that the `simpleUpdate()` method prints a lot of output to the console. The current camera location and the cube location are polled in every frame, and their distance is recalculated and printed. The `simpleUpdate()` method ensures that your test always returns the latest results, even while you and the scared cube are moving wildly through the scene.

If you back away and move around the cube—sneak up on it from behind, so to speak—you can chase it back into the cluster of cubes. Just like the camera location, the camera direction inside the `simpleUpdate()` method returns an updated value every frame. The vector points in the new direction while you navigate the camera around the cube, so that you can chase the cube back.

The `simpleUpdate()` method is one way to hook code directly into the main loop. Everything in this method is executed repeatedly, as fast as possible, as long as the game runs. (Hint: Be careful when creating new objects here!) Just like the `simpleInitApp()` method, you never call the `simpleUpdate()` method yourself. You only implement the method body, and jMonkeyEngine takes care of executing it.

## Time for action – chase all the cubes!

The other cubes are mightily impressed by your new-found cube chasing skills.
Can you change the code sample so that you can pick which cube you want to chase,
simply by looking at it? Use the ray casting method that you learned in the earlier
target picking examples!

1. Since you will detect cubes with the help of ray casting, create a class field for
   the ray object.

   ```
   private Ray ray = new Ray();
   ```

2. Completely remove the code pertaining to scaredCube—a real cube chaser
   doesn't need an extra class field to pick a cube.

3. Put the following code in the simpleUpdate() method loop to keep the ray
   up-to-date. Use the ray.setOrigin(cam.getLocation()) method and the
   ray.setDirection(cam.getDirection()) method to aim the ray in the
   direction of the camera. Identify collisions and pick the closest geometry as
   the target. Test the distance and change the target's location, just as before.

   ```
   public void simpleUpdate(float tpf) {
       CollisionResults results = new CollisionResults();
       ray.setOrigin(cam.getLocation());
       ray.setDirection(cam.getDirection());
       rootNode.collideWith(ray, results);
       if (results.size() > 0) {
           Geometry target = results.getClosestCollision().
                             getGeometry();
           if (cam.getLocation().
               distance(target.getLocalTranslation()) < 10) {
               target.move(cam.getDirection());
           }
       }
   }
   ```

Run the sample, navigate through the scene, and look around. Suddenly, none of the
cubes can withstand your awe-inspiring gaze!

## What just happened?

You cleverly combined two things that you have just learned. The ray casting algorithm is not
limited to input listeners—you can just as well use the simpleUpdate() method loop to
cast the ray, identify current collisions with the scene graph, and interact with the targets.

As your game grows more complex, you will find yourself putting more and more conditionals and actions in the simpleUpdate() method. But a long sequence of tests in one method of one class is not exactly an object-oriented solution—this will soon be a pain to maintain. Of course it's fine to experiment with new game mechanics in the simpleUpdate() method during development, just like we did with the ray casting algorithm. When a code block in the simpleUpdate() method does what it is supposed to do, consider encapsulating it as abstract, reusable behavior. Your game interactions will be much cleaner if you move behaviors into dedicated classes, so-called controls.

## Time for action – get these cubes under control

One type of dedicated jMonkeyEngine class that encapsulates a spatial's behavior is the Control class from the com.jme3.scene.control package. You can create a Control object based on the code mentioned earlier, and add it to an individual cube. This prompts the cube to automatically test its own distance to the camera, and move away when the player looks at it! Seeing is believing:

1.  Create a CubeChaserControl class. Make it extend the AbstractControl class from the com.jme3.scene.control package.

2.  Implement abstract methods of the CubeChaserControl class with the following template:

    ```
    @Override
    protected void controlUpdate(float tpf) { }
    protected void controlRender(RenderManager rm, ViewPort vp) {
    }
        public Control cloneForSpatial(Spatial spatial) {
            throw new UnsupportedOperationException(
                    "Not supported yet.");
        }
    ```

3.  Move the ray field from CubeChaser class to the CubeChaserControl class. Create additional class fields, a com.jme3.renderer.Camera field called cam, and a com.jme3.scene.Node field called rootNode.

    ```
    private Ray ray = new Ray();
    private final Camera cam;
    private final Node rootNode;
    ```

4.  Add a custom constructor that initializes cam and rootNode.

    ```
    public CubeChaserControl(Camera cam, Node rootNode) {
        this.cam = cam;
        this.rootNode = rootNode;
    }
    ```

5.  Move the ray casting block from the `simpleUpdate()` method of the `CubeChaser` class to the `controlUpdate()` method of the `CubeChaserControl` class.

    ```
    protected void controlUpdate(float tpf) {
        CollisionResults results = new CollisionResults();
        ray.setOrigin(cam.getLocation());
        ray.setDirection(cam.getDirection());
        rootNode.collideWith(ray, results);
        if (results.size() > 0) {
            Geometry target = results.getClosestCollision().
    getGeometry();
            // interact with target
        }
    }
    ```

6.  Test whether *I* (the controlled spatial, represented by the predefined `spatial` variable) *am a target* (one of the cubes that the player is looking at). If yes, test whether the player (represented by the camera) is close enough to chase me. Replace the *interact with target* comment with the following conditional statement:

    ```
    if (target.equals(spatial)) {
      if (cam.getLocation().distance(spatial.getLocalTranslation()) <
    10) {
        spatial.move(cam.getDirection());
      }
    }
    ```

7.  Back in the `CubeChaser` class, you want to add this control's behavior to some of the spatials. We create lots of spatials in the `makeCubes()` method; let's amend it so that every fourth cube receives this control while the rest remain unfazed. You can create instances of the control with the main camera and `rootNode` object as arguments. Replace the `rootNode.attachChild()` code line in the `makeCubes()` method with the following code:

    ```
    Geometry geom = myBox("Cube" + i, loc, ColorRGBA.randomColor());
    if (FastMath.nextRandomInt(1, 4) == 4) {
      geom.addControl(new CubeChaserControl(cam, rootNode));
    }
    rootNode.attachChild(geom);
    ```

Before you run this sample, make sure that you have indeed removed all code from the `simpleUpdate()` method of the `CubeChaser` class; it is no longer needed. By using controls, you can now chase specific group of cubes—defined by the subset that carries the `CubeChaserControl` class. Other cubes are unaffected and ignore you.

There are two equivalent ways to implement controls. In most cases, you will just extend the `AbstractControl` class from the `com.jme3.scene.control` package. Alternatively, you could also implement the control interface directly; you only implement the interface yourself in cases where your control class already extends another class, and therefore cannot extend `AbstractControl`.

If you get tired of finding out which cubes are chasable, go back to the `CubeChaserControl` class and add `spatial.rotate(tpf, tpf, tpf);` as the last line of the `controlUpdate()` method. Now the affected cubes spin and reveal themselves!

 Note that various built-in methods provide you with a float argument, tpf. This float is always set to the current **time per frame (tpf)**, equal to the number of seconds it took to update and render the last video frame. You can use this value in the method body to time actions, such as this rotation, depending on the speed of the user's hardware—the tpf is high on slow computers, and low on fast computers. This means, the cube rotates in few, wide steps on slow computers, and in many, tiny steps on fast computers.

## What just happened?

Every control has a `controlUpdate()` method that hooks code into the game's main loop, just as if it were in the `simpleUpdate()` method. You always add a control instance to a spatial; the control doesn't do anything by itself. Inside the control instance, you reach up to that spatial by referring to the predefined `spatial` variable. For example, if you add control instance `c17` to geometry instance `cube17`, then the `spatial` variable inside `c17` equals `cube17`. Every transformation that `c17` applies to `spatial`, is applied directly to `cube17`.

One *control class* (such as the `CubeChaserControl` class) can control the behavior of several spatials that have something in common—such as being chasable in this example. However, each spatial needs its own *control instance*.

One spatial can be affected by zero or more controls at the same time. You want to teach an old spatial new tricks? If you ever decide to change a game mechanic, you only have to modify one control; rebuild the application, and all controlled spatials immediately adhere to it. With only a few lines of code, you can add behavior to, or remove behavior from, an arbitrary number of spatials. Encapsulating behavior into controls is very powerful!

If you need various groups of nodes that share behavior, don't create subclasses of the `Spatial` class with added custom methods! You will get into hot water soon, because using inheritance, a spatial would be locked into the one role it inherited—for example, a shopkeeper NPC could never fight back to defend its shop, because its parent is not a fighter class. Controls on the other hand are modular and can add or remove roll-based behavior easily—every NPC with an `ArcheryControl` method can use crossbows and bows; every NPC with the `MerchantControl` method can buy and sell items, and so on.

The `spatial` object has a few interesting accessors, including a `getControl()` method that gives you access to other controls added to the same spatial. There is no need to pass objects as references if they are already accessible via a custom control's accessors. When you look at the custom constructor of the `CubeChaserControl` class, you see that we actually pass the camera and the `rootNode` object into it. It's untypical for a control to need that much information about the scene graph or the camera. The ideal control class is self-contained and gets all the information it needs directly from its spatial, using custom accessors that you define. Let's make it better!

## Time for action – get into the right AppState of mind

When you notice that a control class has ambitions to make decisions on the application level, this is a sign that this control class has evolved to something else—an **application state (AppState)**. We want the application to do the same thing as before—let us chase the random subset of cubes that carry the `CubeChaserControl` class.

1. Create an `AppState` class `CubeChaserState` that extends the `AbstractAppState` class from the `com.jme3.app.state` package. This class will contain our game logic.

2. Copy the following minimum template into the `CubeChaserState` class:

```
public class CubeChaserState extends AbstractAppState {
    @Override
    public void update(float tpf) {}
    @Override
    public void cleanup() {}
    @Override
    public void initialize(AppStateManager stateManager,
                           Application app) {}
}
```

3. Move the `makeCubes()` and `myBox()` methods from the `CubeChaserControl` class into the `CubeChaserState` class; we want to reuse them.

**4.** Move the class fields from the `CubeChaserControl` class into the `CubeChaserState` class. Add extra class fields for the `assetManager` object and the application `app`, because we are now operating on the application level.

```
private SimpleApplication app;
private final Camera cam;
private final Node rootNode;
private AssetManager assetManager;
private Ray ray = new Ray();
private static Box mesh = new Box(Vector3f.ZERO, 1, 1, 1);
```

**5.** Copy the implementation of the custom constructor of the `CubeChaserControl` class into the `initialize()` method of the `CubeChaserState` class. Similarly, initialize typical `SimpleApplication` variables such as `assetManager`, `rootNode`, and so on. You can also modify the scene graph here, as we do by calling our `makeCubes()` method.

```
@Override
  public void initialize(AppStateManager stateManager,
                                 Application app) {
      super.initialize(stateManager, app);
      this.app          = (SimpleApplication) app;
      this.cam          = this.app.getCamera();
      this.rootNode     = this.app.getRootNode();
      this.assetManager = this.app.getAssetManager();

      makeCubes(40);
  }
```

**6.** Move the ray casting code from the `controlUpdate()` method of the `CubeChaserControl` class into the `update()` method of the `CubeChaserState` class. Replace the `if (target.equals(spatial))` line that tests whether this is one certain spatial with a test that identifies all spatials of the `CubeChaserControl` class in the scene. We are operating on application level now, because we access the camera and the `rootNode` object.

```
public void update(float tpf) {
  CollisionResults results = new CollisionResults();
  ray.setOrigin(cam.getLocation());
  ray.setDirection(cam.getDirection());
  rootNode.collideWith(ray, results);
  if (results.size() > 0) {
    Geometry target = results.getClosestCollision().getGeometry();
    if (target.getControl(CubeChaserControl.class) != null) {
      if (cam.getLocation().
          distance(target.getLocalTranslation()) < 10) {
```

```
                    target.move(cam.getDirection());
            }
        }
    }
}
```

7.  Your `CubeChaserControl` class is now empty, save for the `rotate()` method that you added to make the controlled cubes reveal themselves.

    ```
    @Override
    protected void controlUpdate(float tpf) {
        spatial.rotate(tpf, tpf, tpf);
    }
    ```

8.  Your `CubeChaser` class is now almost empty, and its only remaining import statement is for the `SimpleApplication` class! In the `simpleInitApp()` method, create a new `CubeChaserState` object. To activate this `AppState`, you attach it to the `stateManager` object of the `SimpleApplication` class.

    ```
    @Override
    public void simpleInitApp() {
        flyCam.setMoveSpeed(100f);
        CubeChaserState state = new CubeChaserState();
        stateManager.attach(state);
    }
    ```

When you run the `CubeChaser` class now, you get the same chasing behavior, but your code is modular. Now you understand why it is best practice to move tests and action implementations from the `simpleUpdate()` method into control and the `AppState` classes.

## What just happened?

A control encapsulates a subset of accessors and update behaviors on the level of spatials, while an `AppState` class encapsulates a subset of the scene graph and of scene-wide behaviors. A control only has access to its `spatial`, while an `AppState` class has access to the whole application via `this.app`.

Certain kinds of behavior, such as animations, playing audio, or visual effects, or the `rotate()` call in this example, are independent of objects on the application level. This behavior only needs access to its spatial. Therefore, the `controlUpdate()` method of the `CubeChaserControl` class is the perfect place to encapsulate this spatial-level behavior. A spatial may need access to global game state data other than `SimpleApplication` fields, such as points or level—in this case, pass your central game state object in the control's constructor (and not the whole `SimpleApplication` instance).

The cube-chasing code snippet, however, needs access to `SimpleApplication` fields (here camera and `rootNode`) to perform its collision detection. Therefore, the `update()` method of the `CubeChaserState` class is the ideal class to encapsulate this type of application-level behavior. You see the different use cases?

Every `AppState` class calls the `initialize()` method when it is activated and the `cleanup()` method when it is deactivated. So if you want this `AppState` class to bring certain spatials, lights, sounds, inputs, and so on with it, you override the `initialize()` method. When you deactivate an `AppState` class, its `update()` method loop stops. If you want the detached `AppState` to take away the things it brought, you must similarly override the `cleanup()` method and detach those nodes, and so on.

You activate `AppState` classes by attaching them to the application state manager, and deactivate them by detaching them from it. Each `SimpleApplication` class inherits one application state manager—you access it via the `this.app.getStateManager()` method or the `stateManager` object. You can attach several `AppState` classes to your `stateManager` object, but the same state can only be attached once.

## Time for action – call me maybe?

In the `CubeChaser` class, the added `CubeChaserControl` classes mark individual cubes, and the `AppState` object identifies and transforms them when certain conditions are met. Combining both `AppState` objects and controls can be quite powerful! You often use `AppState` objects to work with certain subsets of spatials that all carry one specific control.

A control can add custom methods to its spatial, and the `AppState` object can call these methods to make individual spatials do the `AppState` object's bidding. As an example, let's make the scared cubes identify themselves by name, and count how often cubes get scared in total.

1.  Add the following custom method to the `CubeChaserControl` class:

    ```
    public String hello(){
            return "Hello, my name is "+spatial.getName();
    }
    ```

2.  In the `CubeChaserState` class, create a simple counter variable and a public accessor for it.

    ```
    private int counter=0;
    public int getCounter() { return counter; }
    ```

**3.** In the `CubeChaserState` class, call the `hello()` method on each `target` that you want to interact with. Place the following call after the `target.move(…)` line in the `update()` method:

```
System.out.println(
    target.getControl(CubeChaserControl.class).hello()
    + " and I am running away from " + cam.getLocation() );
counter++;
```

**4.** In the `simpleUpdate()` method of the `CubeChaser` class, add the following call to get some status information about the running `AppState` method:

```
System.out.println("Chase counter: "
        + stateManager.getState(CubeChaserState.class).
        getCounter());
```

When you run the `CubeChaser` class now and chase a cube, you see console output such as the **Hello, my name is Cube12 and I am running away from (-17, -13, 1)** message, together with a count of how often the `AppState` object has moved any cubes away.

## What just happened?

Just like a spatial has a `spatial.getControl()` method to let neighboring controls communicate with it, an `SimpleApplication` class has a `stateManager.getState()` method to access neighboring `AppState` objects in the same `appManager` class. For example, you can call the `AppStates.getCounter()` method of the `CubeChaserState` from every place where you have access to the central `stateManager`, as shown next:

```
int x = stateManager.getState(CubeChaserState.class).getCounter();
```

# Coordinating global game mechanics

Now you know three modular ways of running code as part of the main update loop: you can implement the `simpleUpdate()` method in the main class, you can add controls to spatials, and you can attach `AppState` objects.

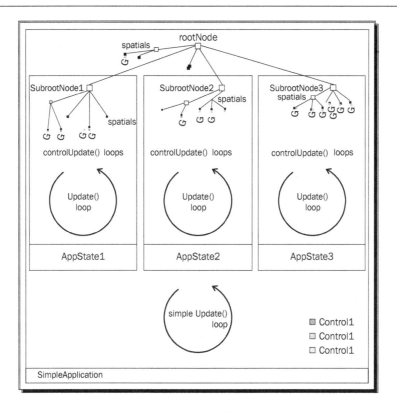

You can activate or deactivate an individual *chunk of behavior* by adding or removing a control, or by attaching and detaching an `AppState` object. You can move whole chunks of the scene graph out of the main `simpleInitApp()` method, and make them part of an `AppState` object. For example, a hypothetical `OutdoorsAppState` object's `initialize()` method attaches bright lights and a forest sound loop; its `cleanup()` method detaches what the `AppState` object brought, so you can switch to the `IndoorsAppState` object, which itself brings dim fluorescent lights and a factory sound loop. This modularization helps you keep your code reusable and maintainable.

Since your game behavior interacts, you have to be aware of the order in which its pieces execute during the update phase of the listen-update-render loop:

1. jMonkeyEngine calls the `update()` methods of all `AppState` objects in the order in which you attached them.

2. jMonkeyEngine calls the `controlUpdate()` methods of all controls in the order in which you added them.

3. jMonkeyEngine calls the `simpleUpdate()` method of the main `SimpleApplication` class.

You must call all *code that modifies the scene graph* from one of these three methods that hook into the update loop. This ensures that your changes are in sync with the main thread.

Outside the main loop, you can always use multi-threading and run other calculations *that do not* (directly or indirectly) modify the scene graph in threads of their own. Especially when you solve more complex tasks, be careful that one long-running algorithm (such as path finding) does not block the whole main thread. Start a new thread so that you don't slow down the whole application, and break up long-running tasks into self-contained, parallel-running *Callables* and use the returned results.

What happens if you modify the scene graph from an external thread? Well, your code will work as expected most of the time—but in seemingly random intervals, the engine will inexplicably complain that the scene graph is *out of date*. If you cannot avoid making modifications to the scene graph outside the main thread, you must enqueue these Callables in the main application using the app.enqueue() method to these calls in the main application! Find more about concurrency in jMonkeyEngine applications on our wiki at http://jmonkeyengine.org/wiki/doku.php/jme3:advanced:multithreading.

# The beauty of AppStates and controls

The ideal jMonkeyEngine application has an empty simpleUpdate() method in its main class—all entity behavior would be neatly modularized and encapsulated in controls and AppState objects.

The ideal jMonkeyEngine application's simpleInitApp() method would have only two lines of code: one that creates a custom StartScreenAppState instance, and a second line that attaches it to the stateManager object of the SimpleApplication class. Let's look at one simple example of how you can structure your application using several modular AppState objects:

1. The StartScreenAppState tab would display a main menu with buttons, such as **play**, **options**, and **quit**. It has a visible mouse pointer and its inputManager object responds to clicks on buttons.
2. When the user clicks on the **options** button, the StartScreenAppState method attaches an OptionsScreenAppState object and detaches itself.
3. The OptionsScreenAppState object displays user preferences and offers a user interface to customize options, such as keyboard layout, graphic quality, or difficulty.
4. When the user clicks on the **save** button, the OptionsScreenAppState object attaches the StartScreenAppState method again, and detaches itself.
5. When the user clicks on the **play** button, the StartScreenAppState method attaches the GameRunningAppState object, and detaches itself.

6. The `GameRunningAppState` object generates the new level content and runs the game logic. The `GameRunningAppState` object can attach several subordinate `AppState` objects—for example, a `WorldManagerState` object that attaches nodes to the `rootNode` object, a `PhysicsState` object that handles falling and colliding objects, and a `ScreenshotAppState` object that saves rendered scenes as image files to the user's desktop. The `inputManager` object of the `AppState` class hides the visible cursor and switches to in-game inputs, such as click-to-shoot and *WASD-keys* navigation.

7. When the user presses the *Esc* key, you save the game state, the `GameRunningAppState` object attaches the `StartScreenAppState` method, and detaches itself and its subordinate `AppState` objects.

8. When the user clicks on the **quit** button on the `StartScreenAppState` method, the game quits.

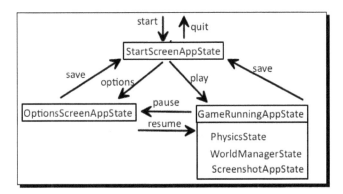

Many games also offer a key that pauses and resumes the game. The game loop freezes, but the game state remains in memory. In this chapter, you learned three ways of adding interaction to a game, namely the `InputListener` objects, the `simpleUpdate()` method, Controls, and `AppState` objects.

To implement pausing for your game, you need to write code that saves the current state and switches off all the in-game interactions again, one by one. This paused state is similar to the non-game `StartScreenAppState` method or the `OptionsScreensAppState` state. This is why many games simply switch to the `OptionsScreensAppState` state while paused. You can also use a conditional to toggle an `isRunning boolean` variable that temporarily disables all update loops.

A paused game typically also temporarily switches to a different set of the input manager settings to stop responding to user input—but make sure to keep responding to your resume key!

## Pop quiz – how to control game mechanics

Q1. Combine the following sentence fragments to form six true statements:

The simpleUpdate() method...    b) An AppState object...    c) A Control...

1.   ... lets you add accessors and class fields to a spatial.
2.   ... lets you hook actions into the main update loop.
3.   ... can be empty.
4.   ... can initialize a subset of the scene graph.
5.   ... defines a subset of application-wide game logic.
6.   ... defines a subset of game logic for one type of spatial.

## Have a go hero – shoot down the creeps!

Return to the Tower Defense game that you created in the previous chapter—let's add some interaction to this static scene of creeps, towers, and the player base. You want the player to click to select a tower, and press a key to charge the tower as long as the budget allows. You want the creeps to spawn and walk continuously along the z axis and approach the base. Each creep that reaches the base decreases the player's health until the player loses. You want the towers to shoot at all creeps in range as long as they are charged with ammunition. Killing creeps increases the player's budget, and when the last creep is destroyed, the player wins. Use what you learned in this chapter!

1.   Create a `GamePlayAppState` class that extends the `AbstractAppState` class. Move the code that initializes the scene nodes from the `simpleInitApp ()` method into the `GamePlayAppState` object's `initialize()` method. In the `cleanup()` method, write the code that detaches these nodes along the same lines. Add an instance of this state to the `stateManager` object of the Main class.

2.   To have a game state to interact with, you first need to define user data. In the `GamePlayAppState` class, define `integer` class fields for the player's `level`, `score`, `health`, and `budget`, and a Boolean variable `lastGameWon`, including accessors. In your code that creates towers, use the `setUserData()` method to give each tower index and `chargesNum` fields. Where you create creeps, use the `setUserData()` method to give each creep index and health fields.

3.   Create a `Charges` class. The charges that the towers shoot are instances of a plain old Java object that stores a damage value and the number of remaining *bullets*. (You can extend this class and add accessors that support different types of attacks, such as freeze or blast damage, or different forces.)

4. Create a `CreepControl` class that extends the `AbstractControl` class and lets creep spatials communicate with the game. The constructor takes the `GamePlayAppState` object instance as an argument—because the creep needs access to player budget and player health. Write accessors for the creep's user data (index and health). In the code block where you create creeps, use the `addControl(new CreepControl(this))` method on each creep.

5. Implement the `controlUpdate()` method of the `CreepControl` class to define the behavior of your creep spatials: creeps storm the base. As long as the creep's health is larger than zero, it moves one step closer to the player base (at the origin). It then tests whether its z coordinate is zero or lower. If yes, it has stormed the player base: the creep subtracts *one life* from the player's health and it detaches itself. If the creep's health is below zero, the towers have killed the creep: the creep adds a bonus to the player budget, and detaches itself.

6. Create a `TowerControl` class that extends the `AbstractControl` class and lets tower spatials communicate with the game. The constructor takes the `GamePlayAppState` object instance as an argument because the towers need access to the list of creeps and the beam_node object. Write accessors for the tower's user data (index, height, and ChargesNum). In the code block where you create towers, use the `addControl(new TowerControl(this))` method on each tower.

7. Implement the `controlUpdate()` method of the `TowerControl` class to define the behavior of your tower spatials: towers shoot at creeps. Each tower maintains an array of charges. If the tower has one or more charges, it loops over the ArrayList of creep objects that it gets from the `GamePlayAppState` object, and uses the `creep_geo.getControl(CreepControl.class)` method to get access to the `CreepControl` object. The tower determines whether the distance between itself and each creep is lower than a certain value. If yes, it collects the `CreepControl` object into a `reachable` ArrayList. If this list has one or more elements, creeps are in range, and the tower shoots one bullet of the top charge at each reachable creep until the charge is empty. For now, we use the `com.jme3.scene.shape.Line` class to visualize the shots as plain lines that are drawn from the top of the tower towards the location of the creep. Attach all lines to the beam `Node` object in the scene graph. Each hit applies the charge's damage value to the creep, and decreases the number of bullets in the charge. If a charge's bullet counter is zero, you remove it from the tower's `Charge` array and stop shooting.

8. In the `Main.java` `simpleInitApp()` method, create an input mapping that lets the player select a tower with a left-click, and one that charges the selected tower by pressing a key. Implement an `ActionListener` object that responds to these two mappings. When the player clicks to select, use ray casting with a visible mouse pointer to identify the clicked tower, and store the tower's index in a class field `selected` (otherwise `selected` should be -1). If the player presses the charge key, and the budget is not zero, use, for example, the `rootNode.getChild("tower-" + selected).getControl(TowerControl.class)` method to get the `TowerControl` instance. Add a new `Charge` object to the tower control, and subtract the charge's price from the budget.

9. In the `GamePlayAppState` object's `update()` method, you maintain timed events using two float class fields, `timer_budget`, and `timer_beam`. The `timerBudget` variable adds the tpf (time per frame in seconds) to itself until it is larger than 10 (such seconds), then it resets itself to zero and increases the player budget. The `Timer_beam` field does the same, but it only waits for one second before it clears all accumulated beam geometries from the `beam Node` node.

10. In the `GamePlayAppState` object's `update()` method, you also check whether the player has won or lost. Test whether health is lower than or equal to zero. If yes, you set the `lastGameWon` variable to false and detach this `GamePlayAppState` object (which ends the game). If the player is still healthy and no creeps are alive, then the player has won. Set the `lastGameWon` object to true and detach this `GamePlayAppState` object (which ends the game). Else, the player is healthy but the creeps are still attacking. The `TowerControl` class and the `CreepControl` class handle this case.

# Summary

Congratulations! By completing this chapter, you have made a big leap ahead in your game developer career.

You now know how to respond to user inputs, such as mouse clicks and motions, touch events, joysticks clicks and motions, and key presses. You have learned two different ways to identify the target spatial that the user has clicked. You know how to use the `simpleUpdate()` method to poll and update the game state, how to use controls to implement game logic in spatials, and how to use `AppState` objects to implement global game logic.

Since pushing cubes around gets old after a while, let's continue to the next chapter, where you will learn how to load scenes and character models!

# 4

# Adding Character to Your Game

*There comes a time when you leave the basic shapes behind and make
something fancier. Whether the 3D game of your dreams is set on a terrain,
in a city, or in a space station; whether the characters roaming your maps are
unicorns, warriors, or race cars: unless you generate procedural graphics on the
fly, you need 3D models to populate your world.*

In the previous chapters, you acquired the two essential skills that a 3D game developer
needs: you can initialize a scene, and you can make it interactive using the update loop and
input listeners. With what you know, you could already write your own Blockout! Granted,
falling cubes are not very exciting. Where are the ninjas, space ships, and cities?

In this chapter you will learn:

- ◆ How to build anything from triangles
- ◆ How to create 3D models and scenes
- ◆ How to store and load 3D models
- ◆ How to animate 3D models
- ◆ How to load 2D icons and text

Let's add some character to our game!

## Making a Mesh

A 3D engine needs geometric information about scene objects before it can render
anything. How would you describe a box? You need to tell the engine where the eight
corners are, and which corners connect to form the box's faces. For a cuboid shape this
is pretty straightforward. Let's look at a box through the eyes of the rendering engine.

## Time for action – meshing around with cubes

The following code sample is again based on the familiar BasicGame template that creates a blue cube.

**1.** Make a copy of `Main.java` and name the class `WireframeShapes.java`. Remember to also refactor the first line of the `main()` method to: `WireframeShapes app = new WireframeShapes();`

**2.** In the `simpleInitApp()` method, after the creation of the material `mat`, change the following material property: `mat.getAdditionalRenderState().setWireframe(true);`

The WireframeShapes code sample now looks like the following code:

```
public class WireframeShapes extends SimpleApplication {

  @Override
  public void simpleInitApp() {
    Box mesh = new Box(Vector3f.ZERO, 1, 1, 1); // create box mesh
    Geometry geom = new Geometry("Box", mesh);

    Material mat = new Material(assetManager,
        "Common/MatDefs/Misc/Unshaded.j3md");
    mat.setColor("Color", ColorRGBA.Blue);
    mat.getAdditionalRenderState().setWireframe(true);
    geom.setMaterial(mat);
    rootNode.attachChild(geom);
  }

  public static void main(String[] args) {
    WireframeShapes app = new WireframeShapes();
    app.start();
  }

}
```

**3.** Run the class. Move around using the *W*, *A*, *S*, and *D* keys and the mouse, and inspect the polygons that outline the shape of the cube.

## What just happened?

You see that each of the six cube faces are broken down into two triangular parts. What looks like a cube to you is actually a polygon mesh made up of 12 triangles.

Typically, you apply materials to geometries to cover up the polygon mesh. But now, for learning purposes, you made the internals below the material visible. When you use `mat.getAdditionalRenderState().setWireframe(true);` on a material, the engine renders a wireframe view of the **mesh** shape for all geometries using this material.

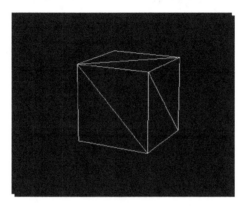

Being able to see the wireframe can be useful when debugging transformation issues of more complex objects in larger scenes. Let's look at some shapes more complex than cubes next.

## Time for action – meshing around with spheres

What about round surfaces, such as spheres are they triangle meshes too?

1.  Go back to the `WireframeShapes` class you just created.

2.  Comment out the line that creates the `Box()` mesh.

3.  Replace the box mesh with code that creates a sphere mesh instead. Use the Sphere class from the `com.jme3.scene.shape` package: `Sphere mesh = new Sphere(16, 16, 1.0f);`

4.  This line of code creates a sphere mesh with a radius of 1.0f. The other arguments of the constructor specify the smoothness of the sphere.

5.  Run the class. Move around using the *W*, *A*, *S*, and *D* keys and the mouse, and inspect the polygon mesh that outlines the shape of the sphere.

## What just happened?

When you run the sample application, you realize that even a sphere is quite a triangular business, from the point of view of a 3D engine!

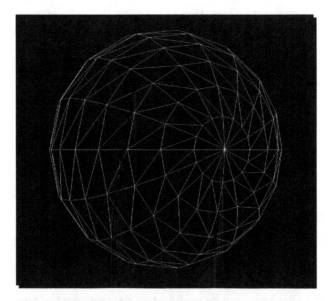

The quality of a sphere is determined by its radial samples; that is, the number of triangles along the equator and meridian of the sphere. This is why the sphere constructor takes two integer arguments. In our example Sphere (16, 16, 1.0f), both values are 16.

For a small sphere, 16 triangles for each sampling dimension results in very good quality. For bigger spheres, you can go up to 32 triangles for both dimensions. There is no hard limit though, and the values do not have to be powers of two either. Just remember not to be wasteful: the more triangles in the scene, the slower the framerate. Your players cannot even see the difference between spheres with 32 or 64 radial samples—but they will notice a sluggish framerate immediately.

You see now that a polygon mesh is a simple triangle grid that is sculpted to outline a more complex shape. Whether they are round or angular, bugbears or buildings, terrains or teapots—all 3D models and shapes are made up of polygon meshes. The teapot in the following screenshot, for example, is a polygon mesh made up of hundreds of triangles:

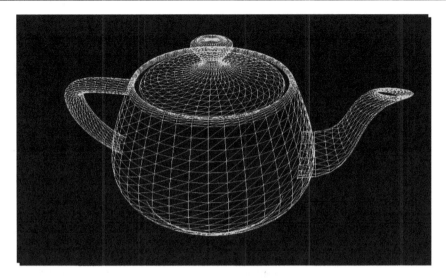

The advantage of meshes is that they are mathematically simple enough to render in real time, while being detailed enough to be recognizable. This is a typical example of the kind of smart compromises that 3D game developers have to make to strike the balance between speed and visual quality.

The polygons' corners—the crossing points of the wireframe—are called **vertices**. Every **vertex** is positioned at a 3D coordinate. Sculpting the vertices of a mesh is a lot of work, which is why you typically create meshes using special **3D modeling software**. This chapter demonstrates how you create and export your artwork, and load it into a jMonkeyEngine scene graph.

# From mesh to geometry

From previous chapters you remember that a scene is made up of spatials. A spatial can either be an invisible node, or a visible geometry. Have another look at the following two lines from our `WireframeShapes.java` example:

```
Box mesh = new Box(Vector3f.ZERO, 1, 1, 1);
Geometry geom = new Geometry("Box", mesh);
```

You notice that the magic ingredient that makes a geometry visible is a polygon mesh: first you create a mesh shape (here the box), then you wrap the geometry object around it. The advantage is that you can reuse the same mesh in several geometries.

The mesh data type is just a shape—pure, unaltered vertex data. The com.jme3.scene.Geometry data type combines the inner mesh, the surface material, and transformations into one object. When a mesh is used in a geometry, the geometry's transformations (position, scale, rotation) and material (for example its color) are applied to the mesh. This combination makes it a visible element of the 3D scene.

The jMonkeyEngine class that is used to hold mesh data is com.jme3.scene.Mesh. The mesh inside a geometry gives us a lot of modeling flexibility, because it can be one of the following three things:

- **A shape**: The simplest type of meshes are the jMonkeyEngine's default shapes, such as boxes, spheres, and cylinders from the com.jme3.scene.shape package. You can attach several simple shapes to one node to build a more complex geometry. Shapes are built-in and can be created without loading 3D models and without using the assetManager object.

- **A 3D model**: 3D models are meshes that are more complex than a shape. Sets of models are called scenes, and are even more complex. You create models as well as scenes in external 3D modeling tools. You use the assetManager object to load models into the application.

- **A custom mesh**: Advanced users can create meshes programmatically. This option is used by 3D artists who generate procedural or fractal worlds on the fly. You can find custom mesh documentation on the jMonkeyEngine.org wiki.

 Curious about the inner workings of a mesh? In the jMonkeyEngine SDK's source editor, you can control-click classes, inherited fields, and overridden methods to jump to the source. For example, control-click a Box() constructor and see firsthand how this custom mesh was implemented. The jMonkeyEngine is open source, after all!

Now you know what meshes are, and where they are used. But where do you get them from?

# Beg, steal, or borrow

A video game typically needs 3D models, animations, materials, icons, background music, sound effects, and maybe even voices and a cinematic clip for cut scenes. Unless you are Leonardo da Vinci, you won't produce all of this artwork yourself. Luckily, there are many game resource repositories where you can find **game assets** for download, and game developer communities with freelancing 3D artists.

You can either download free assets or buy pre-made multimedia collections. Each option has its pros and cons. Free models may not be available in the right formats. Commercial art packages may be expensive and in either case, you may not get precisely what you want. If you require maximum control over certain assets, your development team needs designated multimedia artists—and good multimedia software.

# The right wrench to pound in the screw

The jMonkeyEngine SDK bundles many tools, but a mesh editor is not among them. This is because there are countless flavors of 3D modeling tools: Blender, Maya, 3DS Max, Trimble SketchUp, MilkShape3D, ArtOfIllusion, and many others. The choice depends on your operating system, your work style, your level of expertise, and finally, your wallet.

The jMonkeyEngine does not restrict you to use one particular mesh editor. You can keep using the tools you are familiar with. The only requirement is: *your 3D modeling software must be able to export files in a format that jMonkeyEngine can load*. At the time of writing, the jMonkeyEngine supports Wavefront, Ogre XML/Ogre DotScene, and Blender binary formats.

| Model format | File suffix | Usage |
|---|---|---|
| Ogre3D Mesh | `.mesh.xml` or `.meshxml`, `.material` | A 3D model plus material. You can download the plugin for all major editors. Use the Ogre Mesh format for skeleton animations or static models. |
| Ogre3D DotScene | `.scene` | A set of Ogre Mesh models. |
| Wavefront | `.obj`, `.mtl` | A 3D model plus material. Nearly all editors export to Wavefront out of the box. Use this format for static models. |
| Blender | `.blend` | 3D models in Blender's binary format. |

In the jMonkeyEngine SDK, open **Tools | Plugins** from the menu, and look at the available plugins and installed tabs. Note, among others, Wavefront OBJ Support, OgreXML Support, OgreXML Tools, Blender Support, and the Model Importer Tool—these plugins need to be installed and active for model import features to work.

Whichever 3D modeling tool you choose, familiarize yourself with the user interface: practice how to create meshes, navigate the 3D scene, select meshes, transform them, give them materials and so-called **UV textures**, animate them, and export the result.

For the course of this book, we will use Blender. You can download the software from `http://blender.org` for free.

If you haven't done so yet, install Blender 2.63 or higher now. Give it a shot for the sake of demonstration—you can always switch to another modeling tool later.

# Time for action – installing the Blender-to-Ogre3D plugin

Look into the export menu of your Blender installation. If it does not export to Ogre Mesh/ Ogre DotScene yet, it's time to install a free plugin from `ogre3d.org`. There you also find plugins for other 3D modeling tools.

The jMonkeyEngine SDK assists you in installing the Ogre XML plugin into Blender 2.63+, so you can follow the examples in this book:

1.  In the top-right search box of the jMonkeyEngine SDK, type "**Install Blender Ogre XML**".

2.  A list of the actions and help resources appears. Select the "**Install Blender Ogre XML**" action and press *Enter*. A dialog box opens.

3.  Click on **change** to set the path. Browse to your Blender script directory and click on **OK**. The default paths in various operating systems are as follows:

    ```
    Windows 7 - C:\Users\%username%\AppData\Roaming\
                Blender Foundation\Blender\2.63\scripts\
    Windows XP - C:\Documents and Settings\%username%\
                 Application Data\Blender Foundation\Blender\2.63\
                 scripts\
    Mac OS X - /Applications/Blender 2.63/blender.app/
               Contents/MacOS/2.63/scripts
    Linux - /home/$user/.blender/2.63/scripts/
    ```

4.  Click on **Install Exporter Script** and the exporter plugin is installed.

5.  Re-open Blender and look into the **Export** menu to confirm the installation was successful.

## What just happened?

Your Blender installation can now export to Ogre3D format, additionally to Wavefront, which Blender supports by default. Blender is a professional, full-featured modeling tool that is available for all three major operating systems. The jMonkeyEngine team also likes Blender because it is open source software, and supported by an enthusiastic community, just like jMonkeyEngine is.

Model editors such as Blender can import and export a variety of common model file formats. This means that you can use your editor to convert between formats, to a certain degree. For example, you can import a model in .3ds (3dsMax) format into Blender, and then save it either as a `.blend` file, or export it as Ogre `mesh.xml`.

# Time for action – sculpting the mesh

Let's create a 3D model. This book cannot replace a complete Blender 2.63+ tutorial, so you will have to go through additional tutorials on `blender.org`. There are also great free video tutorials on `cgcookie.com/blender/` and the iTunes University!

Start Blender. The 3D view pane contains a simple mesh, a cube. Let's work with the untitled cube for now. Remember to drag the middle mouse button to look at the mesh from different angles; use the mouse wheel to zoom in and out on the mesh.

1.  In your file explorer, create the `BasicGame/assets/Textures/MyModel/` and `BasicGame/assets/Models/MyModel/` directories. Here you will store your assets.

2.  In Blender, choose **File | Save As** and save the untitled Blender file as `mymodel.blend` into the `BasicGame/assets/Textures/`. (Note, *not* `assets/Models/`!)

3.  Switch from **Object Mode** to **Edit Mode**. In the **Mesh Tools** panel, click on **Subdivide** two or three times. The cube mesh is subdivided into more polygons.

4.  Switch from **Edit Mode** to **Sculpt Mode**. The mouse pointer changes to a brush circle.

5.  Left-click and drag the mouse over the mesh and sculpt it! In the **Brush** panel, click on **Add** or **Substract** to pull or push the mesh; change **AutoSmooth**, **Radius**, and **Strength** to change the pressure and impact on the mesh.

6.  Play with the tools a bit and sculpt whatever you fancy; for example, a head. When you are done, choose **File | Save** to save your work.

## What just happened?

Blender lets you edit polygon meshes like modeling clay, which is a very user-friendly approach for organic shapes. Don't subdivide the mesh too much though: high-polygon meshes may look prettier in the 3D model editor, but for a fast-paced video game, the rendering speed of low-polygon models trumps static smoothness!

Instead of a cube, you can use the **Add | Mesh | ...** menu to start out with other base meshes to sculpt, including a **Monkey** mesh that you can use as a test model. This chimpanzee head model is called Suzanne—nice to meet a fellow monkey out there!

Blender offers many sculpting brushes. Follow one of the Blender tutorials to familiarize yourself with the effects you can achieve. Sculpting is just one of the many mesh editing modes that Blender supports. Other common modeling methods you should look into are vertex/edge/face editing and extrusion.

# Time for action – coloring the mesh

When you are done sculpting the mesh, switch back from **Sculpt Mode** to **Edit Mode**. Now you create the mesh's surface—its material and texture. For this we use a professional technique called **UV mapping**.

1.  Verify that the model is selected in **Edit Mode** (it has an orange outline). If it isn't, right click to select it.

2.  In the Outliner panel, find the model entry (marked with an orange triangle). Open the node and rename the mesh to `mymodel`. Delete the camera and the light, if there are any.

3.  In the **Properties** panel (the one with the long row of small icons) click on the **Material** button (a reddish chequered circle). If your model doesn't have a material yet, click on the plus sign to add one. Rename the material to `mymodel`—just like the filename, so the two can be associated with each other more easily.

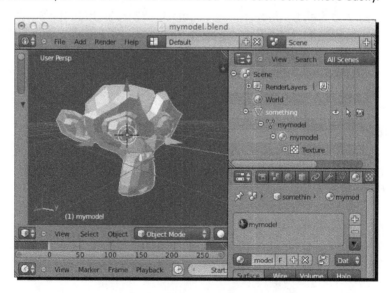

Now let's add the actual texture to the model.

1. Verify the model is still selected and in **Edit Mode**. In the **Mesh Tools** panel on the left-hand side, scroll down to **UV Mapping**. Click on the **Unwrap | Smart UV Project**, accept the defaults, and click on **OK**.

2. To see the **UV Mapping**, switch the main pane from **3D View** editor (a white 3D cube icon) to **UV/Image Editor** (a reddish landscape-with-sunset icon). You should see your 3D mesh broken down into flat 2D pieces.

3. Click on **New** to create a texture image. Name the untitled image `mymodel` again—just like the file—accept the defaults, and click on **OK**. You see a black texture.

4. Switch back from the **UV/Image Editor** option to the **3D View** editor. Switch from **Edit Mode** to **Texture Paint** mode. You now see your model with the black texture.

5. Use the **Brush** tool from the left-hand side pane to select colors, and paint the model. It's not important to get it perfect, just highlight areas in different colors so you can recognize them—you will make the texture look perfect later in the chapter.

6. Switch from **3D View** editor to **UV/Image Editor**. You now see that the colors that you painted on the 3D mesh are represented on the corresponding pieces of the 2D texture. If the UV mapping looks messy, consult a Blender tutorial for how to define optimal UV seams.

7. Choose **Image\* | Save as Image**. Save the texture as `mymodel.png` under `BasicGame/assets/Textures/MyModel/`.

8. Switch from **UV/Image Editor** to **3D View** editor. Switch from **Texture Paint** mode back to **Edit Mode**. In the **Properties** pane, choose the **Textures** section (reddish chequered square) next to the **Material** section (reddish chequered circle).

9. Click on **New** to add texture data to the model. Where it says **Type: Clouds**, choose **Type: Image or Movie**. Click on **Open**, and browse to the `mymodel.png` that you just saved, and click on **Open Image**. The image you selected should appear in the preview.

10. Choose **File | Save** to save your work to the `mymodel.blend` file.

## What just happened?

A color is the most basic material a model can have. For video games, you typically define the color of a model using texture files. The type of texture that we use for game models is called **UV-mapped texture**. The term **UV Mapping** stems from the fact that a 3D mesh has three coordinates (X, Y, and Z), while a 2D image has two coordinates (U and V); the model editor maps the image's UV coordinates onto your mesh's XYZ coordinates when creating the texture.

The finished UV texture looks a lot like a sewing pattern! The model editor unwraps the mesh, lets you paint right on it, and saves the texture as a compact image—pretty cool feature. It's worth going through your model editor's tutorials to learn its best practices for creating UV textures, such as marking optimal seams manually. After creating the UV texture, you open `mymodel.png` in an image editor of your choice, and paint the final model texture over the color-coded areas of the "sewing pattern". The jMonkeyEngine supports UV textures and can piece them together again when you load the model.

You will learn how to make the most of materials and textures in the next chapter.

## Time for action – a model for to go, please

Since every model editor has its own native format, you typically export the model to an exchange format. In the case of jMonkeyEngine, these formats are Ogre Mesh or Wavefront.

Keep using the `mymodel.blend` file that you just saved to `BasicGame/assets/Textures/MyModel/`. Let's start by practicing an Ogre Mesh conversion in Blender:

1. Press *A* and verify that the model is selected (orange outline).
2. Choose **File | Export | Ogre 3d (Scene and Mesh)** from the menu. The exporter window opens.
3. In the path field, make sure that the path ends in .../`BasicGame/assets/Textures/MyModel/`. Name the target file as `mymodel.mesh.xml`.
4. Under **Export Ogre**, keep the defaults, but uncheck **Force Camera**, **Force Lamps**, and **Export Scene**; choose **Swap Axis: xyz**.
5. Click on **Export Ogre**.

Return to the model. As an exercise, we export it a second time, now in Wavefront format.

1. Press *A* and verify that the model is selected (orange outline).
2. Choose **File | Export | Wavefront (.obj)** from the menu. The exporter window opens.
3. In the path field, make sure that the path ends in .../`BasicGame /assets/Textures/MyModel/`. Name the target file as `mymodel.obj`.
4. Under **Export OBJ**, keep the defaults, and check **Triangulate Faces** and **Include Normals**.
5. Click on **Export Wavefront Obj**.

You have now exported your model from the model editor in two different formats.

## *What just happened?*

Some Blender models have a camera and light source included. Since you already inherit camera and light from the **SimpleApplication**, delete them from the model. The **Swap Axis: xyz** setting ensures that your model is exported the right way up: 3D engines and model editors can use different coordinate systems.

Look into the `BasicGame/assets/Textures/myModel/` directory. Additional to the original Blender file (`.blend`), the directory now contains your model in two formats:

```
BasicGame/assets/Textures/MyModel/
mymodel.blend
mymodel.mtl
mymodel.obj
mymodel.material
mymodel.mesh.xml
mymodel.png
```

The `.mtl` and `.obj` files are the Wavefront model. The `mesh.xml` and `.material` files are the Ogre3D models. Note that the `mymodel.png` UV texture is used by both! In a real-life scenario, you export each model to only one format: for example, export all static models as Wavefront, and all animated models as Ogre3D files.

## Time for action – loading a model (just testing)

The 3D model is ready for its journey into the 3D game world. Switch over to your BasicGame project in the jMonkeyEngine SDK again.

1. Make a copy of `Main.java` and name the class `LoadModel.java`. Remember to also refactor the first line of the `main()` method to:

   ```
   LoadModel app = new LoadModel ();
   ```

2. Replace the `simpleInitApp()` method with the following code snippet:

   ```
   public void simpleInitApp() {
     Spatial mymodel = assetManager.loadModel(
         "Textures/MyModel/mymodel.mesh.xml");
     rootNode.attachChild(mymodel);
     DirectionalLight sun = new DirectionalLight();
     sun.setDirection((new Vector3f(-0.5f, -0.5f, -0.5f)));
     sun.setColor(ColorRGBA.White);
     rootNode.addLight(sun);
   }
   ```

Since the `load()` method returns both nodes and geometries, you load models as generic Spatials. Run the application and have a look at your loaded model.

The same loading method also works with the Wavefront `.obj` file. Replace the path, and try it yourself:

```
Spatial mymodel = assetManager.loadModel(
    "Textures/MyModel/mymodel.obj");
```

When you load the two copies of the model, both formats should end up looking the same in the jMonkeyEngine. Your test was successful!

## What just happened?

You use the `assetManager` object inherited from `SimpleApplication` to load the models. The `assetManager` object automatically looks for files in the assets directory of your project. This means you reference the file `BasicGame/assets/Textures/MyModel/mymodel.obj` as `Textures/MyModel/mymodel.obj` when loading it.

Note that we do not use the `Unshaded.j3md` default material that we used when we loaded plain boxes. `Unshaded.j3md` is a very plain, colored material that works without a light source—hence the name, "unshaded". Models typically have more than one color, which is why you use more professional-looking UV textures that you tailor directly in the 3D model editor. You export the model together with its materials and UV textures, and save the texture under the same name as its model into the same textures subdirectory, just as you did with `mymodel.png`. This way the `load()` method can automatically identify the right material and texture files, no manual assignment needed.

Did you notice that we added a directional light to the `rootNode` object? If you do not use `Unshaded.j3md`, a light is required to make a model's material visible! Always ensure that at least one of the model's parent nodes (typically, the `rootNode` object) has a light source added to it. If you forget the light, your models will be black and featureless.

**Troubleshooting models**

You only see the model in the scene if both the mesh and its material load correctly. If you encounter problems, try replacing the material with a temporary material based on the built-in `ShowNormals.j3md`:

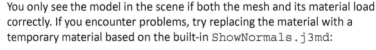

```
Material mat = new Material(assetManager,
    "Common/MatDefs/Misc/ShowNormals.j3md");
mymodel.setMaterial(mat);
```

This displays the model in contrasting colors, without textures or shading. This workaround allows you to at least load the model and continue working while the graphic designer fixes the material.

# Time for action – loading a model (for real)

Loading the meshes straight from the Ogre Mesh or Wavefront file is something that you only do for testing purposes. When you load a model from a .mesh.xml or .obj file, jMonkeyEngine converts it internally into an optimized binary format called .j3o.

If you have made up your mind to use a certain model in your game, you convert it to .j3o, and only load the .j3o file:

1. In the jMonkeyEngine SDK's Project window, browse to the assets/Textures/MyModel/ directory.

2. Right-click on mymodel.mesh.xml and choose **Convert to j3o Binary** from the context menu. The SDK creates mymodel.j3o.

3. Move mymodel.j3o into the BasicGame/assets/Models/MyModel/ directory.

4. Open LoadModel.java again. Keep the light source in simpleInitApp().

5. Replace the load() path in simpleInitApp() with the following code:

```
Spatial mymodel = assetManager.loadModel(
    "Models/MyModel/mymodel.j3o");
rootNode.attachChild(mymodel);
```

6. Run the LoadModel sample. The j3o version of the model should load and look the same as before.

## What just happened?

You recall that we saved the original Blender, Ogre3D, and Wavefront models in the assets/Textures directory. Did you wonder whether it would not make more sense to store them under assets/Models? It wouldn't: from a jMonkeyEngine developer's point of view, Ogre3D and Wavefront are just intermediate formats. For the final release, you convert all models to the more powerful .j3o format. Only the .j3o files go into the assets/Models directory, which remains nicely clutter-free.

j3o is the internal binary format for all jMonkeyEngine spatials and scenes. Other formats only store meshes, materials, and animations; the .j3o format can additionally store game-relevant information, such as user data (health and so on), shadow settings, and instances of attached audio nodes, light nodes, particle emitters, and controls. j3o files are optimized for gaming, which means they load faster than converting external formats on the fly.

> When you build the game in the SDK using the provided build script (which is what we recommend), only .j3o models and scenes from inside your assets directory are bundled into your application! Original Blender, Ogre3D, and Wavefront models are excluded, as is everything outside the assets directory. If your loadModel() code does not point to the .j3o copy of the file, you will get an AssetNotFoundException message at runtime when trying to load any external model formats.

# Managing assets – best practices

A modern 3D Java game is made up of more than just Java files; it runs on more than one operating system; it may be deployed to several platforms. Developers want a flexible way to load assets that works the same in every situation: this is why the jMonkeyEngine team introduced the AssetManager class.

The AssetManager API is independent of the operating system (Windows, Mac OS, Linux), the data format (straight files, JAR files, ZIP files, APK packages), or the platform (desktop, web, mobile). Using the assetManager object, you no longer need to change the code or structure of the project to make it work on another platform.

## Time for action – sorting your stuff out

When you start coding, you may want to load sample models to test a scene or interaction. Since your own artwork is most likely not ready yet, you typically use free models or mock-ups. Now it's time to decide on a directory structure for your assets:

1. Create subdirectories under assets/Textures/. Keep original models, their textures, and materials together!

2. Create parallel subdirectories for .j3o models under assets/Models/.

For example, in a racing game, you would prepare the following for your car models:

◆ assets/Textures/Vehicles/Cars/ for ferrari.obj and porsche.obj— including material and textures

◆ assets/Models/Vehicles/Cars/ for ferrari.j3o and porsche.j3o

Or in a shooter, you would prepare the following directories for your monster NPCs:

◆ assets/Textures/NPCs/Monsters/ for gremlin.mesh.xml/ and orc.mesh. xml—including material and textures

◆ assets/Models/NPCs/Monsters/ for gremlin.j3o and orc.j3o

Create some mock-ups, convert them, and try to load them from different paths.
By default, the `SimpleApplication` method's `assetManager` looks for files in the `assets/` `directory`. You only need to specify the rest of the path in the `load()` method. For example:

```
assetManager.loadModel("Models/NPCs/Monsters/gremlin.j3o")
```

```
assetManager.loadModel("Models/Vehicles/Cars/ferrari.j3o")
```

 Did you notice that your `CubeChaser` code used the `assetManager` method to load a material definition from `Common/MatDefs/Misc/` `Unshaded.j3md`? Why does this work, although your project does not have a directory named `assets/Common/MatDefs/Misc/`? jMonkeyEngine finds this built-in file in the jMonkeyEngine JAR. This JAR is on the classpath of every jMonkeyEngine game—and the classpath is also registered as a default root directory for asset loading.

## What just happened?

You create subdirectories in the `assets` directory because you want to keep the same file structure from beginning to end of the project. This advice applies to models, as well as sounds and textures, and so on. If you ever change the assets (sub)directory structure, you must manually update all affected asset paths in your code.

 The `.j3o` file under `assets/Models/` uses the same absolute path to locate textures in the `Textures` directory as the original Blender, Ogre3D, or Wavefront file did. You can still modify and update a model's textures during the development phase; but do not move, rename, or delete the textures after creating the j3o file. If you change subdirectories of `assets/Models` or `assets/Textures`, or rename textures or models, remember that you also must re-export all affected original models from the model editor, and regenerate all affected .j3o files!

To give you a picture of what this means, open the BasicGame project in a file explorer. The following overview outlines the default assets subdirectories, and explains which file types go into which directory:

| BasicGame/ assets/... | Content | Usage |
| --- | --- | --- |
| Interface/ | .fnt | A bitmap font in the `AngelCode` font format. A typical use case for text is displaying the score or the game rules in your user interface, which is one of the things you will learn next. |
| Interface/ | .jpg, .png, .xml | Image formats used for icons and background images in the user interface. Also optional XML files used for user interfaces created with jMonkeyEngine's **Nifty GUI** integration. |

| BasicGame/ assets/... | Content | Usage |
|---|---|---|
| `MatDefs/` `Shaders/` | `.j3md` `.vert,` `.frag` | Special file formats used by jMonkeyEngine's shaders: advanced users can create custom material definitions and shaders. Unless you know what that means, you can simply ignore the `assets/MatDefs` and `assets/Shaders` directories. |
| | | Common material definitions (such as `Unshaded.j3md`) and shaders for most use cases are built into the engine and ready for use. |
| `Materials/` | `.j3m` | jMonkeyEngine's format for materials. |
| `Models/` | `.j3o` | jMonkeyEngine's binary format for 3D models. |
| `Scenes/` | `.j3o` | jMonkeyEngine's binary format for 3D scenes. |
| `Sounds/` | `.ogg` `.wav` | Audio formats used to store sounds, ranging from noises and voices to background music. |
| `Textures/` | `.jpg` `.png` `.tga` | Image formats for storing textures that belong to models. Keep textures and the original models together. |
| `Textures/` | `.mesh.xml,` `.material,` `.scene` `.obj+.mtl` `.blend` | Original 3D models in Ogre3D XML, Wavefront Object, or Blender format, respectively. Keep textures and the original models together. |

The directory structure that you see here is a best practice that the jMonkeyEngine team came up with. The subdirectory names (`Models`, `Scenes`, and so on) are examples only. When you start a new project, you are free to delete, create, or rename directories inside the assets directory as you see fit—and stick with it.

Also keep the name of the `assets` directory: this ensures that the build script packages your assets automatically!

## Time for action – saving and loading .j3o files

Right-clicking a model in the SDK is not the only way to create j3o files. Another common situation is that you want to save the current scene when the player quits, and restore the game when the player restarts the application.

You can use `com.jme3.export.binary.BinaryExporter` to create `j3o` files, and the `com.jme3.asset.plugins.FileLocator` to register custom directories as `AssetManager` root directories. Switch over to your BasicGame project in the jMonkeyEngine SDK again.

1. Make a copy of `LoadModel.java` and name the class `SaveModel.java`. Remember to also refactor the first line of the `main()` method to:

```
SaveModel app = new SaveModel();
```

2. Keep the light source. Replace the model loading code in the `simpleInitApp()` method with the following code snippet. It loads your j3o file from the `assets/Models` directory and moves the model to a random position:

```
Spatial mymodel = assetManager.loadModel(
    "Models/MyModel/mymodel.j3o");
mymodel.move(
    FastMath.nextRandomFloat()*10-5,
    FastMath.nextRandomFloat()*10-5,
    FastMath.nextRandomFloat()*10-5);
rootNode.attachChild(mymodel);
```

3. Run the code. You should see your model.

4. Add a new method that overrides this `SimpleApplication` class `stop()` method. When the game ends, you want to save the current scene to a file:

```
@Override
public void stop() {
    String userHome = System.getProperty("user.home");
    File file = new File(
        userHome + "/SavedGames/" + "savedgame.j3o");
    BinaryExporter exporter = BinaryExporter.getInstance();
    try {
        exporter.save(rootNode, file);
    } catch (IOException ex) {
        Logger.getLogger(SaveModel.class.getName()).log(
        Level.SEVERE, "Error: Failed to save game!", ex);
    }
    super.stop(); // continue quitting the game
}
```

**5.** In the beginning of `simpleInitApp()`, add code that loads the previously saved game again.

```
String userHome = System.getProperty("user.home");
assetManager.registerLocator(userHome, FileLocator.class);
try {
    Node loadedNode = (Node) assetManager.loadModel(
                              "/SavedGames/savedgame.j3o");
    rootNode.attachChild(loadedNode);
} catch (com.jme3.asset.AssetNotFoundException e) {}
```

**6.** Run your sample. Press *Esc* key to quit, and run and quit it again. Every time you run this sample and quit it, another model is added to the scene.

## What just happened?

You can now save any spatial—even the whole rootNode object—as a j3o file, and then restore it again.

1. The `simpleInitApp()` method first loads the previously saved scene from `savedgame.j3o`. You register the `user.home` directory to the `assetManager`, so you can load `/SavedGames/savedgame.j3o` just like any asset. If the file does not exist, you catch an `AssetNotFoundException` message.

   ```
   assetMaanager.registerLocator(userHome, FileLocator.class);
   ```

2. The `simpleInitApp()` method then loads and attaches a new copy of your model to the scene.

3. When you press the *Esc* key, the `SimpleApplication` method executes its `stop()` method. You override the `stop()` method to save the scene as `savedgame.j3o` before quitting.

   ```
   File file = new File( userHome + "/SavedGames/" + break line from
   here "savedgame.j3o");
   BinaryExporter exporter = BinaryExporter.getInstance();
   exporter.save(rootNode, file);
   ```

When you look into your home directory, you see a new folder called `SavedGames` containing the `savedgame.j3o` file.

 If you do not use the jMonkeyEngine SDK for whatever reason, you can write a custom Java class for your project using the described process. Use it to load all models and convert them to j3o files before the release.

## Pop quiz

Q1. Your teammate asks you why you save the original models into assets/Textures and move the .j3o models into `assets/Models`. What is the best reply?

1. Oops, sorry, I keep swapping the two!

2. Let's not create any j3o's and load all models in their original format.

3. The .j3o stores the full project-level texture paths, so don't move them.

4. Not so important, we can always rename the directories later.

# Animating a model

Up until now, you have only dealt with static 3D objects. Maybe you have a daring piece of update loop code that transforms models so they move around like chess pieces on a board. But if the moving objects are characters, you would like to see their legs and arms move while they walk. It's time to animate your 3D models.

In 3D games, a method called **skeletal animation** is used to animate characters. But in principle, the skeleton approach can be extended to any 3D mesh – even an opening crate's hinge can be considered a simple joint.

 Your wizard fidgets, your ninja moonwalks, and your brawny warrior skips along like a balloon animal? Unless you are animating toons, the realism of an animated character's motion is generally a problem. Professional game designers invest a lot of effort to make characters animate in a natural way, including the use of motion capturing.

## Time for action – rig, skin, and animate

The jMonkeyEngine only loads and plays recorded animations. You must use a model editor to add animations to an existing model. This process is very different depending on the model editor and we cannot cover it here—please consult your editor's documentation for details.

In general, you have to complete three steps: you rig, skin, and animate the model in your model editor.

1.  Rig your model using a bone armature. Parent all bones to one root bone. Locate the root bone at the origin (typically, on the floor between the feet of the character).

2.  Skin your model using vertex groups and weight painting.

3.  Animate the model by specifying keyframes. If your model contains several animations, turn the keyframes into action strips, and layer them in Blender's NLA editor. For example, create an idle and a walk animation.

4.  Give each animation a name, for example "Idle" and "Walk". Export the animated model as Ogre3D mesh with skeleton.

5.  In the end you should have the files `mymodel.mesh.xml`, `mymodel.skeleton.xml`, `mymodel.png`, and `mymodel.material`.

> For more details on how to rig, skin, and animate with Blender, search the free tutorials on `cgmasters.net` for Blender Armatures and Animation in Blender, search `wiki.blender.org` for Non-Linear Animation Editor, and search `youtube.com` for video tutorials such as Animations in Blender 2.6 and JME3.

Go through some tutorials, and animate `mymodel.blend`—or you can use an included sample: you find a free animated model under `BookSamples/ assets/Textures/Jaime/`.

## What just happened?

To animate a 3D model, you rig the internal skeleton (the **bones** or **armature**), you link the bones to the external mesh (the **skin**), and specify animation data (the **keyframes**).

1.  **Rigging** is the construction of a character's **skeleton**. You add bones to the model, and connect them in a parent-child hierarchy to a root bone. Moving one bone pulls other bones with it (for example, moving the arm also moves the hand). Create as few bones as possible to decrease complexity. After exporting, the bones will be invisible to the player.

2.  **Skinning** means associating individual bones with corresponding skin sections. For characters, the skin includes clothing. Animating the invisible bone pulls the visible skin with it (for example, the thighbone moves the upper leg skin), distorting it if necessary. One part of the skin can be affected by more than one bone (think of knees and elbows). The connection between bones and skin is gradual: you assign **weights** how much each skin polygon is affected by each bone's motion. For example, when the thighbone moves, the leg is fully affected, the hip joints less so, and the head not at all.

3.  **Keyframes** finally define the overall animation. A keyframe is one pose on a timeline. A series of keyframes makes up one animation. Each model can have several animation sequences (for example: walking, idling, attacking, jumping). Each animation sequence has a unique name.

In your game code, you load the model as before. If it's an animated model, you load an animation into a channel, and you tell the engine when to play the channel.

## Time for action – loading an animated model

Animated Ogre models come as a set of files: when you look at the included Jaime model, the model is in `Jaime.mesh.xml`, and the animation details are in `Jaime.skeleton.xml`.

Copy the content of the Jaime directory to a new BasicGame's `assets/Models/Jaime/` directory. Open the directory in the SDK and use the context menu to convert the `mesh.xml` file to `.j3o`. Move the `Jaime.j3o` file to a new corresponding `assets/Models/Jaime` directory.

Your goal is to add the model to the scene, and then animate it when the user presses the Space bar. To trigger the animation, you want to use the familiar input handling that you learned when you were interacting with the user previously.

1.  Make a copy of `LoadModel.java` and name the class `AnimateModel.java`. Remember to also refactor the first line of the `main()` method to:

    ```
    AnimateModel app = new AnimateModel ();
    ```

2.  Create a class field that represents the model. Let's call it `player`. Initialize the `player` in the `simpleInitApp()` method by loading the `Jaime.j3o` model. If necessary, rotate it so it faces the camera.

    ```
    private Node player;
    ...
    @Override
    public void simpleInitApp() {
        ...
        player = (Node) assetManager.loadModel(
            "Models/monkeyExport/Jaime.j3o");
        player.rotate(0, FastMath.DEG_TO_RAD * 180, 0);
        rootNode.attachChild(player);
        ...
    }
    ```

3. If your model uses materials, add a light source to make the material visible. You will learn more about lights and materials in the next chapter.

```
DirectionalLight sun = new DirectionalLight();
sun.setDirection(new Vector3f(-0.5f, -0.5f, -0.5f ));
sun.setColor(ColorRGBA.White);
rootNode.addLight(sun);
```

4. Create one class-level `AnimControl` field for each animated model, and initialize the `object` in the `simpleInitApp()` method. Internally, jMonkeyEngine automatically generates a `com.jme3.animation.AnimControl` instance for each animated model.

```
private AnimControl control;
...
@Override
    public void simpleInitApp() {
        ...
        control = player.getControl(AnimControl.class);
        ...
}
```

5. If you created this model, you already know which animations you defined for it. If you use `Jaime.j3o`, use the following code snippet to print the list of animations that are exposed by this control:

```
for (String anim : control.getAnimationNames())
    { System.out.println(anim); }
```

6. Run the application and note down the animation names, then remove the line again. Create string constants for the animations you want to use.

```
private static final String ANI_IDLE = "Idle";
private static final String ANI_WALK = "Walk";
```

7. Create at least one class-level animation channel for this control. In the `simpleInitApp()` method, initialize the channel, and specify a default animation. In our example, we want the model to be `Idle` by default.

```
private AnimChannel channel;
...
@Override
public void simpleInitApp() {
    ...
  channel = control.createChannel();
  channel.setAnim(ANI_IDLE);
      ...
}
```

You have loaded an animated model, created at least one channel, and you have access to its animation control methods.

# What just happened?

You remember that we use controls to call methods (accessors) on a spatial. You know that the getControl(MyControl.class) method gives us access to a spatial's control of type MyControl. One spatial can carry many controls.

When you load a spatial and jMonkeyEngine identifies it as an animated model, the engine automatically generates **animation control** (com.jme3.animation.AnimControl) and **bone control** (com.jme3.animation.SkeletonControl) instances for it.

The animation control is an instance of com.jme3.animation.AnimControl. It exposes special animation accessors for this spatial. You use the model's AnimControl to create **animation channels**, instances of com.jme3.animation.AnimChannel. Each channel plays one animation sequence at a time. In our example, you create one channel and set it to ANI_IDLE to play the idle animation.

You can create several AnimChannels in one AnimControl, then set different animations in each AnimChannel, and play them in parallel. For example, for a charging wizard, you can play a walking animation on a character's lowerBodyChannel, while playing a spell casting animation on its upperBodyChannel.

The optional SkeletonControl instance gives you access to bones and their **attachment nodes**—geometries attached to these nodes move along with the animation; for example, a weapon moves with the hand bone. You can play animations without using the SkeletonControl.

## Time for action – playing an animated model

Everything is set up, but if you run the application now, the model is stuck in its idle pose. Use what you learned in the previous chapter about the AnalogListener and ActionListener, and configure the Space bar to make the character walk toward you gradually, while playing the walk animation!

1. Write an ActionListener that waits for the MAPPING_WALK trigger, and then tests whether the key is pressed or up. If the key is pressed, test if ANI_WALK is still playing on the animation channel; if it isn't, play ANI_WALK again. If the key is not pressed, play ANI_IDLE again.

```
private ActionListener actionListener = new ActionListener() {
  public void onAction(String name, boolean isPressed, float tpf)
  {
      if (name.equals(MAPPING_WALK) && isPressed) {
        if (!channel.getAnimationName().equals(ANI_WALK)) {
          channel.setAnim(ANI_WALK);
        }
```

```
        }
        if (name.equals(MAPPING_WALK) && !isPressed) {
          channel.setAnim(ANI_IDLE);
        }
      }
    };
```

2. Write an `AnalogListener` that also waits for the `MAPPING_WALK` trigger, and moves the player along the z axis towards the camera.

```
private AnalogListener analogListener = new AnalogListener() {
  public void onAnalog(String name, float intensity, float tpf) {
    if (name.equals(MAPPING_WALK) ) {
      player.move(0, 0, tpf);
    }
  }
};
```

3. In `SimpleInitApp()`, add the new input mapping that triggers the walk forward action when the Space bar is pressed. Register the mapping to the `AnalogListener` and `ActionListener`.

```
private static final String MAPPING_WALK = "walk forward";
@Override
public void simpleInitApp() {

    ...
    inputManager.addMapping(MAPPING_WALK,
                    new KeyTrigger(KeyInput.KEY_SPACE));
    inputManager.addListener(analogListener, MAPPING_WALK);
    inputManager.addListener(actionListener, MAPPING_WALK);
}
```

4. Run the application. Jaime should stand around idly. Press the Space bar. Jaime walks toward you.

## What just happened?

Animations are often triggered by user interaction, such as navigational key input. When the player triggers `MAPPING_WALK`, you call `channel.setAnim(ANI_WALK)`, and you also use the `move()` function to move the model. Note the use of the familiar tpf (time per frame) factor to make the character `move()` with the same speed on slow and fast hardware.

Additional to `channel.setAnim()`, you can set the following properties:

♦ Use the `channel.setSpeed()` method to set the speed of this animation: a speed of 1.0f is default, a value smaller than 1 plays it slower, a value larger than 1 plays it faster.

♦ Use the `channel.setTime()` method to fast-forward or rewind an animation to a certain second on the timeline. The value is clamped to the interval between zero and `channel.getAnimMaxTime()`.

In contrast to user-triggered animations, your game may also contain animations such as grazing animal NPCs or swaying trees. Such animations are controlled by the main loop.

Use `channel.setLoopMode(LoopMode.Loop)` to specify whether an animation should repeat itself. The `LoopMode` can be:

♦ `LoopMode.Loop`: The animation plays repeatedly. When reaching the end, the animation starts from the beginning. This is the default behavior.

♦ `LoopMode.Cycle`: The animation cycles back and forth repeatedly. When reaching the end, the animation plays backward until it reaches the first frame, then it plays forward again, and so on.

♦ `LoopMode.DontLoop`: The animation plays once, and stops at the last frame. You typically trigger the next animation at this point using the `AnimEventListener` method's `onAnimCycleDone()` interface.

## Time for action – responding to animation events

What if you want to play the sound loop of footsteps while walking, or reset the model to a neutral pose after crouching, or before jumping? To detect the start and end of animation events, your `SimpleApplication` must implement the `com.jme3.animation.AnimEventListener` interface.

```
public class AnimateModel extends SimpleApplication
        implements AnimEventListener {…}
```

*1.* Register the `AnimEventListener` (this) to each `AnimControl` instance:

```
control.addListener(this);
```

*2.* Now you can implement the `onAnimChange()` method. It is called every time a new animation starts.

```
public void onAnimChange(AnimControl control,
                    AnimChannel channel, String animName) {
    if (animName.equals(ANI_WALK)) {
```

```
        System.out.println(control.getSpatial().getName()
        + " started walking.");
      } else if (animName.equals(ANI_IDLE)) {
        System.out.println(control.getSpatial().getName()
        + " started being idle.");
      }
    }
```

3. You can also implement the `onAnimCycleDone()` method of the interface. It is called every time when an animation ends.

```
public void onAnimCycleDone(AnimControl control,
                    AnimChannel channel, String animName)
{
  if (animName.equals(ANI_WALK)) {
    System.out.println(control.getSpatial().getName()
    + " completed one walk loop.");
  } else if (animName.equals(ANI_IDLE)) {
    System.out.println(control.getSpatial().getName()
      + " completed one idle loop.");
  }
}
```

4. Run the sample, press the Space bar, and watch the output.

## What just happened?

Now you know how to hook in other game events so they happen in sync with the animation. The `AnimEventListener` interface notifies you every time when an animation ends (`onAnimCycleDone()`), or when a new animation starts (`onAnimChange()`). The method arguments give you information about which control, which channel, and which animation was involved in the event. You can now test for various combinations of states and react to them.

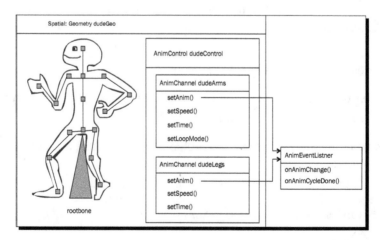

## Pop quiz

Q1. Which of the following statements about animations are true?

1. Each animated model has a) none; b) one; c) one or several `AnimControl` instances.

2. `AnimControls` have a) none; b) one; c) one or several `AnimChannels`.

3. An `AnimChannel` controls a) rigging, skinning, keyframes; b) time, speed, looping; c) saving, loading, converting.

4. Code in the `AnimEventListener` object's `onAnimChange()` method is always executed a) after `onAnimCycleDone()`; b) after `createChannel()`; c) after `setAnim()`.

# Loading a simple user interface

3D models are not the only assets that you load using the `assetManager`. Elements of the graphical user interface (GUI) are also loaded from files. A typical use case for a GUI would be to display the score, framerate, or status icons on the screen.

## Time for action – displaying text

From `SimpleApplication` you inherit a special guiNode for displaying 2D elements such as text, the guiNode. Let's re-use the blue cube sample as a base.

1. Make a copy of `Main.java` and name the class `SimpleUserInterface.java`. Remember to also refactor the first line of the main() method to:

   ```
   SimpleUserInterfaceapp = new SimpleUserInterface();
   ```

2. Before you create a custom GUI in `simpleInitApp()`, remove the default GUI from the application:

   ```
   public void simpleInitApp() {
       setDisplayStatView(false);
       setDisplayFps(false);
       . . .
   }
   ```

3. Create an integer class field tracking a value; say, a distance. You want to display the value as text on the screen, so you also create a `com.jme3.font.BitmapText` class field for it:

   ```
   private int distance=0;
   private BitmapText distanceText;
   ```

4. In the `simpleInitApp()` method, you load a font, initialize the BitmapText object, and attach it to the guiNode.

```
public void simpleInitApp() {
   ...
   guiFont = assetManager.loadFont("Interface/Fonts/Default.fnt");
   distanceText = new BitmapText(guiFont);
   distanceText.setSize(guiFont.getCharSet().getRenderedSize());
   distanceText.move(
      settings.getWidth()/2,           // X
      distanceText.getLineHeight(),    // Y
      0);                              // Z (depth layer)
   guiNode.attachChild(distanceText);
}
```

5. In this example, let's simply track the distance of the camera to the origin. To keep the distance value up-to-date, and display it, add the following lines to your `simpleUpdate()` method:

```
public void simpleUpdate(float tpf) {
   distance = Vector3f.ZERO.distance(cam.getLocation());
   distanceText.setText("Distance: "+distance);
}
```

When you build and run the sample, you see the distance display at the bottom center of the screen. Move around the scene and watch the number update.

## What just happened?

The guiNode that you inherit from `SimpleApplication` is a root node for flat ("orthogonal") elements. Orthogonal means these visual elements don't change their perspective when the camera moves. guiNode elements are always superimposed over the 3D scene, just like the framerate display in the bottom-left corner.

Use the default font size `guiFont.getCharSet().getRenderedSize()`, because bitmap fonts don't scale too well. You could also set a default text using `distanceText.setText("")`, or change the font color to yellow using `distanceText.setColor(ColorRGBA.Yellow)`. For this demo, just leave the defaults.

Next, you want to move the text to a nice position on the screen, relative to the current size of the display. Keep in mind that the origin (the 0,0 coordinate) of the 2D screen is in the bottom left-hand side. The location of the text is relative to the top-left corner of the text block.

Here are a few tips for positioning text:

- ◆ Use `settings.getWidth()` and `settings.getHeight()` to get the screen size. If you want to position a 2D element in the middle of the screen, start out with `getWidth()/2`, and subtract half the width of the element to center it. This value is the x coordinate of the 2D element.

- ◆ Use `distanceText.getLineHeight()`, `getLineWidth()`, and `getLineCount()` to get the size of the text object. If you want to shift a text block up, so one full line is visible at the bottom of the screen, use `distanceText.getLineHeight()` as the y coordinate of the 2D element.

- ◆ Use `distanceText.move(x,y,z)` to position the text object. The extra z coordinate of a flat GUI element is used for depth layering. A GUI element with a higher z value is drawn over GUI elements with lower z values. Leave the depth at 0 for now.

In this example, we just display a simple distance value. In an actual game, you would have variables in the update loop that contain interesting metrics about the game state: the score, the player's lives, amount of ammunition, secrets unlocked, and so on.

## Time for action – loading AngelCode fonts

In your own game project, you will want to use a font that emphasizes your game's atmosphere. The Font Creator plugin makes it easy to create bitmap fonts from system fonts.

1. Install a cool font into your system; for example, a free font from `http://www.theleagueofmoveabletype.com/`.

2. Go to **Tools | Plugins**, and then go to the **Available Plugins** tab. Choose the **Font Creator** plugin and click on **Install**. Restart the SDK.

3. Choose **File | New File | GUI | Font** from the main menu. The font creator wizard opens.

4. Select the free font and click on **Next**.

5. Specify font style and size, and click on **Finish**. The font is saved into your project's `assets/Interface/Fonts` directory.

6. Load `yourCustomFont.fnt` from your project directory with the same command as you used before to load the default font:

```
BitmapFont customFont = assetManager.loadFont(
    "Interface/Fonts/yourCustomFont.fnt");
fancyText = new BitmapText(customFont);
```

## What just happened?

The jMonkeyEngine supports bitmap fonts in the popular format provided by `angelcode.com`. The **Font Creator** plugin generates the bitmap font as a `.png` plus a `.fnt` file in your `assets/Interface/Fonts` folder.

Two free `AngelCode` fonts are included: `Interface/Fonts/Default.fnt` and `Interface/Fonts/Console.fnt`. Note that you can load these default fonts from `Interface/Fonts/`, although they are not in your project's `assets/Interface/Fonts/` directory. This is another example of loading a common asset that is included in the jMonkeyEngine JAR. The two default fonts are always available, which means you can use them for testing, as fallback, or to display debug information.

## Time for action – loading icons into the GUI

Additionally to 2D text, a GUI can contain pictures—as decorations, icons, or status indicators. For example, a flight simulator is framed by an image of a cockpit with windows, gauges, and dials. Another use case is an inventory browser. These are just two examples—depending on your game type and genre, you encounter many different uses for icons in the GUI.

1. Save images for the user interface in your project's `Interface` directory.

2. The following code sample loads a GUI element named `frame.png` and attaches it to the `rootNode`:

```
Picture frame = new Picture("User interface frame");
frame.setImage(assetManager, "Interface/frame.png", false);
frame.move(settings.getWidth()/2-265, 0, -2);
frame.setWidth(530);
frame.setHeight(10);
guiNode.attachChild(frame);
```

**3.** The next code sample loads an icon with transparency and attaches it to the rootNode.

```
Picture logo = new Picture("logo");
logo.setImage(assetManager, "Interface/Monkey.png", true);
logo.move(settings.getWidth()/2-47, 2, -1);
logo.setWidth(95);
logo.setHeight(75);
guiNode.attachChild(logo);
```

**4.** Run the application to see the results. You should see a frame at the bottom center of the page, and also a monkey face icon.

If you kept the code from the previous `SimpleUserInterface` example where you loaded the distance text, the text is printed over the frame and logo. If you want to keep both GUI elements, add an x and y offset to the text's `move()` method and move it away from the frame; for example:

```
distanceText.move(settings.getWidth()/2+50, distanceText.
getLineHeight()+20,0);
```

## What just happened?

The `frame.png` image has no transparency, which is why you set the boolean in the `setImage()` method to false. The `monkey.png` icon uses an alpha channel, which is why you set the boolean in the `setImage()` method to true.

You position the bottom-left corner of both images so they are centered at the bottom of the screen. You move the `monkey.png` to depth layer -1, so it is drawn above the `frame.png` in layer -2.

You can resize the image using `setWidth()` and `setHeight()` as shown here, but be aware that you achieve more professional-looking results by resizing images in a graphic editor, and loading them in full-size. Finally, you attach both images to the guiNode.

## Time for action – display interactive status icons

You use the `SimpleUpdate()` method to calculate `Vector3f.ZERO.distance(cam. getLocation())`. Depending on whether the distance is more or less than 10f, let's toggle the monkey icon between two different states: smiling and sad:

```
public void simpleUpdate(float tpf) {
    distance = Vector3f.ZERO.distance(cam.getLocation());
    distanceText.setText("Distance: " + distance);
```

```
    if (distance < 10f) {
      logo.setImage(assetManager,
        "Interface/chimpanzee-smile.gif", true);
    } else {
      logo.setImage(assetManager,
        "Interface/chimpanzee-sad.gif", true);
    }
  }
}
```

## What just happened?

You often use graphics not only as decorations but also to display game state. As shown, you can use conditional setters in the `simpleUpdate()` method to keep your icons up-to-date. You create a series of icons representing game states—in this example, the states are "happy monkey" and "sad monkey". The monkey is happy when the camera is close to the origin, and sad when it is farther away.

How would you implement a clickable icon, a button, so to speak? Use what you learned previously about ray casting, and determine ray collisions with the guiNode—this is the trivial solution. For advanced GUIs, jMonkeyEngine integrates the Nifty GUI library that supports various controls, such as buttons, text input fields, and sliders, as well as effects and sounds. You can find more info on our wiki and on `nifty-gui.lessvoid.com`.

## Time for action – 3D objects in the 2D GUI?

Up to now, all assets you attached to the guiNode were two-dimensional, such as fonts and icons. What happens if you attach a 3D object, such as the blue cube geom, the blue cube, to the guiNode instead of the rootNode? Why not try and see yourself.

Modify a fresh BasicGame and add the following change:

```
geom.setLocalTranslation(
    settings.getWidth()/2,
    settings.getHeight()/2,
    0);                        // center the box
geom.scale(10f);              // scale the box
guiNode.attachChild(geom);
```

When you run the sample code, it seems the jMonkeyEngine renders the box as before. But when you move the mouse, the box does not turn along as objects attached to the rootNode would.

## What just happened?

A 3D object on the GUI node is treated as a flat 2D image, which is pinned to a coordinate on the 2D screen. If that's the effect you want, go ahead and do it: many games use "orthogonal" 3D objects to display the active weapon on the bottom edge of the screen.

Some GUI caveats:

1. Assets attached to the guiNode are not measured in world units, but in pixels. Our blue box is 2 wu wide and will therefore appear as a tiny 2x2 pixel cubelet when you attach it to the guiNode! This is why the code sample scales the box by a factor of ten.

2. As a general tip, rotate orthogonal 3D objects a bit. That gives them a more interesting, dynamic angle in the GUI.

3. If the 3D model uses a material based on anything other than `Unshaded.j3md` or `ShowNormals.j3md`, you must add a light source to a parent node to make the material visible. In this case, the parent node is the guiNode!

You learn more about materials and lights in the next chapter.

# The art pipeline

Additionally to code, a game needs 3D models, textures, icons, music, sounds, fonts, and much more. Considerable time of the game development process is spent managing these assets. The procedure of creating, converting, and loading multimedia files is called the **art pipeline**.

Since artwork may go through several iterations, your team will be looking for ways to make the art pipeline and hand-off process as painless as possible—for designers as well as developers.

1. The team decides on a directory structure and creates asset subdirectories.

2. Developers start writing code in the SDK. They create the overall frame of the game, including start and options screens, and the main game screen. Developers clean and build the application, and make test runs straight from the SDK.

3. Graphic artists create textures and low-polygon models in the native format of their editors. They save their work in a supported format (Blender, Ogre3D, or Wavefront; PNG, or TGA) into `assets/Textures` subdirectories.

4. Graphic artists create fonts, icons, background images, and splash screens in the native format of their editors. They save their work in a supported format (PNG, TGA, FNT) into `assets/Interfaces` subdirectories.

5. Audio artists record music, voices, and sounds in the native format of their editors. They save their work in a supported intermediate format (ogg or wav) into `assets/Sounds` subdirectories.

6. Developers convert all original models in `assets/Textures` to `.j3o` format. They move the `.j3o` files to the corresponding `assets/Models` subdirectories. They verify that all `loadModel()` paths point to j3o files.

7. Developers clean and rebuild the application. All team members test the executable in the project's dist directory.

 A popular best practice in development teams is file version control. Versioning lets you track, merge, and revert project changes to code or assets. Using a shared project repository for code and assets integrates your artists fully into the development process, and lowers the risk of losing team members' submissions "in the mail". You find built-in version control tools in the SDK's **Team** menu.

## Have a go hero – furnishing the tower defense game

Let's return to our little tower defense game. Currently, it's all boxes and spheres. That's fine considering the stage of development we are at. Getting the game mechanics to work comes first: the creeps storm in and the towers shoot. But they're still all cubes.

 **Boxes have their place**

We don't want to disrespect cubes: if all you want to do is, say, test your mouse-picking implementation, you don't need to load a 3D model. In the development phase it's actually a good practice to start out with boxes or spheres: they are built-in and never throw null pointer exceptions. If a method works with a box, but not with a model, you know the model is the problem. If a method does not even work with a box, then the method is the problem.

Make sure that your TowerDefense game is the active main project. You need towers, a home base, and some creeps.

Let's furnish the place a bit.

1. In the SDK, open **Window | AssetPackBrowser**. From the **AssetPackBrowser** window, install the three **AssetPacks**—they contain cool free models that you can use.

2. Browse through the list and note Armoury, Donjon, Bailey, Temple; Spider, Bear, and others; various pieces of walls and palisades. Double-click to preview them. (Remember to click the light bulb and zoom in or out if necessary.)

3.  Right-click the ones that you like and right-click them and choose **Add to Project**.

4.  Use what you learned to load tower models instead of the oblong cubes.

5.  Use what you learned to load a wild animal model instead of the creep cubes.

6.  Use what you learned to load text that displays how many lives the player has left, and show a (permanent) text hint which key to press to recharge the tower.

Of course you also use models that you created yourself, or from other free sources, such as http://opengameart.org/. Apart from the flat floor and the boring sky, your game should look much cozier already!

# Summary

A good video game is more than just the code: in this chapter, we learned a lot about how to create and integrate external artwork into our games. This includes static and animated models, as well as icons, textures, and fonts.

Specifically, we covered meshes and looked at one way of sculpting them. You learned how to export models from a model editor such as Blender, and how to import them into a jMonkeyEngine application. You know the advantages of converting models to the j3o format, of structuring your directories well. You learned how to save and load the rootNode including all game data. You learned the basic concepts of model animation, and you know how to load animated models and control them using triggers, the update loop, or listeners. You understand how to display text, images, and even 3D objects in the user interface. You also heard of several resources where you can get free models and fonts.

You see that the jMonkeyEngine SDK was not designed for hardcore Java hackers only. The SDK helps you integrate developers and non-techie team members, such as audio and graphic artists, more closely.

Now that you've heard a lot about models and their special "skins", let's have a closer look at materials, and the effects you can achieve with them.

# 5
# Creating Materials

*You know how to create complex shapes from polygon meshes and animate them. Up to now, the materials that you applied to your geometries were all very plain looking. Where are the glows, the shininess, and all the other small details that make a material look great? It's time to pull out all the stops and make use of the awesome shader features of jMonkeyEngine.*

You can now populate your game with characters, vehicles, and buildings, and you can load text and icons for the graphical user interface. In this chapter you will learn:

- ◆ Why light sources are important
- ◆ How to texture objects
- ◆ How to make objects transparent
- ◆ How to make objects appear more detailed than they are
- ◆ How to make surfaces appear rough or smooth
- ◆ How to make an object glow

Cool screenshots and some nifty tricks are waiting for you, so let's go!

## What is a material?

What we colloquially call color is actually visible light reflecting off an object. The human brain is pretty smart in inferring an object's material, simply from the reflective properties of its surface. You never think about it, but the reflected light is what makes the difference between milk and chalk, skin and rubber, water and plastic, and so on! To understand the difference between various illumination properties, let's start with the default case: unshaded materials.

# Time for action – unshaded materials

In the previous chapters, you used a plain, unshaded material to create a simple blue cube. Look at the blue cube's code again. The cube's material is based on the `Unshaded.j3md` material definition, and it has a `Color` property that is set to `ColorRGBA.Blue`.

```
Material mat = new Material(assetManager,
  "Common/MatDefs/Misc/Unshaded.j3md");
mat.setColor("Color", ColorRGBA.Blue);
```

Let's see what else this material can do:

1. Make a copy of `Main.java` and name the class `MaterialsUnshaded.java`. Remember to also refactor the first line of the `main()` method to `MaterialsUnshaded app = new MaterialsUnshaded();`.

2. Copy the provided image `assets/Interface/Monkey.png` into your project's `assets/Interface/` directory.

3. Replace the blue cube code in `simpleInitApp()` with the following code:

```
Sphere sphereMesh = new Sphere(16, 16, 1);
Geometry sphereGeo = new Geometry("Unshaded textured sphere",
  sphereMesh);
sphereGeo.move(-2f, 0f, 0f);
sphereGeo.rotate(FastMath.DEG_TO_RAD * -90,
  FastMath.DEG_TO_RAD * 120, 0f);
Material sphereMat = new Material(assetManager,
  "Common/MatDefs/Misc/Unshaded.j3md");
sphereMat.setTexture("ColorMap",
  assetManager.loadTexture("Interface/Monkey.png"));
sphereGeo.setMaterial(sphereMat);
rootNode.attachChild(sphereGeo);
```

Run the code sample. You should see a sphere with a monkey texture. The sphere is rotated and moved aside a bit, simply so you can see the texture better.

## What just happened?

For the blue cube, you used the `setColor()` setter to set the material's `Color` property to the value `ColorRGBA.Blue`. In addition to colors, materials that are based on `Unshaded.j3md` also support textures.

The previous example uses the `loadTexture()` method of `assetManager` to load a monkey logo from the `assets/Interface` directory into the material. The material layer that contains the texture of an unshaded material is called `ColorMap`. You use the material's `setTexture()` method to set its `ColorMap` layer:

```
spereMat.setTexture("ColorMap",
    assetManager.loadTexture("Interface/Monkey.png"));
```

When you run the code and navigate around the sphere, you notice that the sphere has no brighter or darker side. Even if you add a light source, an unshaded box always looks as if it were evenly lit from all sides.

If you need to increase the contrast of a material that is based on `Unshaded.j3md`, you can add a pre-computed texture layer containing static brightness values. This texture layer is called `LightMap`. For a game of Blockout, for example, an unshaded LightMap'ped material is sufficient. To see the difference, copy the included `assets/Interface/Monkey_light.png` image into your `assets/Interface` directory, and add the following code below the first `setTexture()` call. `Monkey_light.png` adds a static gradient to the sphere.

```
spereMat.setTexture("LightMap",
    assetManager.loadTexture("Interface/Monkey_light.png"));
```

The advantage of materials based on `Unshaded.j3md` is that they are rendered fast. You can use unshaded materials in situations where rendering speed is more important than dynamically lit-and-shaded surfaces—for example, when visualizing molecules in a scientific application. If your game is going for a "classic 80s' 8-bit" style, a fast, unshaded LightMap'ped material also does the trick for you.

| Common/MatDefs/Misc/Unshaded.j3md properties | |
| --- | --- |
| **Parameter** | **Data type** |
| Color | ColorRGBA |
| ColorMap | Texture |
| LightMap | Texture |

# Material definitions and shaders

For comparison with the unshaded material you just saw, what does a material look like that takes dynamic lighting into consideration?

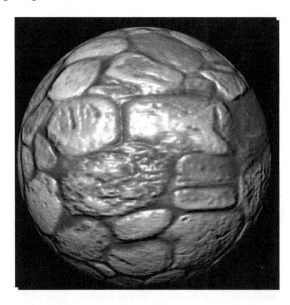

Now, this material has a definite "smooth rock" vibe to it! You can almost touch the bumps where individual pebbles jut out! Be aware that this sphere mesh is completely featureless! The whole trick is that the material makes use of **Phong illumination** and **Blinn bump mapping**. These shader techniques are named after their inventors, Bui Tuong Phong and Jim Blinn.

Internally, 3D engines use shaders when rendering your 3D graphics. Shaders are special instructions that are executed on your system's **graphic processing unit (GPU)**, taking advantage of the GPU's hardware acceleration. OpenGL-based jMonkeyEngine supports vertex and fragment shaders written in **OpenGL Shading Language (GLSL)**:

- **Vertex shaders** can modify existing shapes in your scene without requiring a computationally more expensive mesh—jMonkeyEngine uses them to animate water, cloth, or flags.

- **Fragment shaders** (also known as **pixel shaders**) produce color effects on existing materials without requiring computationally more expensive textures —jMonkeyEngine uses them for glows, reflections, or lens flares.

These are just a few examples of what shaders do for you "backstage". Don't worry about the details; shaders do their thing automatically as part of the rendering pipeline:

1. The main application sends mesh data to the vertex shader.

2. The vertex shader computes new vertex positions, if necessary.

3. The vertex shader passes the vertices' new screen coordinates to the fragment shader.

4. The fragment shader computes each pixel's new color, if necessary.

5. The result is displayed on screen.

jMonkeyEngine exposes shader features to you through user-friendly material definitions, such as Unshaded.j3md. As you have seen in previous examples, these material definitions are a simple interface that let you set parameters on materials, such as setTexture(). Internally, jMonkeyEngine then uses these parameters to configure how the shader should handle the material. Let's have a closer look at the material definition that makes illumination and bump mapping possible: Lighting.j3md.

# Good-bye unshaded, hello lighting!

Lighting.j3md is a Phong-illuminated material definition that makes the most of your materials. It's probably the material definition that you will use most often.

All examples in this category show illuminated materials; this means you must add a light source to the scene to be able to see them! Here is a code snippet that creates two useful light sources from the com.jme3.light package, and attaches them to your rootNode. More details about lights later.

```
DirectionalLight sun = new DirectionalLight();
sun.setDirection(new Vector3f(1, 0, -2));
sun.setColor(ColorRGBA.White);
rootNode.addLight(sun);

AmbientLight ambient = new AmbientLight();
ambient.setColor(ColorRGBA.White);
rootNode.addLight(ambient);
```

Let's look at the simplest case first: A material with plain material colors, without textures, but with shading.

## Time for action – no frills, just color

First we create an illuminated sphere with a blue material, using a normal geometry with a material based on the Lighting.j3md material definition:

1. Make a copy of Main.java and name the class MaterialColor.java. Remember to also refactor the first line of the main() method to MaterialColor app = new MaterialColor ();.

2. Replace the blue cube code in the simpleInitApp() method with the following:

```
Sphere sphereMesh = new Sphere(32,32, 1f);
Geometry sphereGeo = new Geometry("Colored lit sphere",
    sphereMesh);
Material sphereMat = new Material(assetManager,
    "Common/MatDefs/Light/Lighting.j3md");
sphereMat.setBoolean("UseMaterialColors", true);
sphereMat.setColor("Diffuse", ColorRGBA.Blue );
sphereMat.setColor("Ambient", ColorRGBA.Gray );
sphereGeo.setMaterial(sphereMat);
rootNode.attachChild(sphereGeo);
```

Remember to add light sources to make the illuminated material visible!

Run the sample. As opposed to our plain blue cube, this blue, illuminated sphere clearly has a darker and a lighter side. You see that applying lit materials to geometries makes them immediately look more three-dimensional to our eyes.

### What just happened?

To colorize an illuminated geometry, you set three material color properties. First you enable the Boolean parameter UseMaterialColors. Then you set the two material color properties, the Diffuse and the Ambient color. Note that you use a setBoolean() setter for the Boolean parameter, and a setColor() setter for the colors.

**Common/MatDefs/Light/Lighting.j3md**

| Parameter | Data type |
| --- | --- |
| UseMaterialColors | Boolean |
| Diffuse | ColorRGBA |
| Ambient | ColorRGBA |

The uniform base color of a geometry is called its **diffuse color**. The diffuse color (together with UseMaterialColors) is the minimum property that an illuminated material needs to be visible.

The ambient color property is optional. If you don't set it, the ambient color is a neutral gray by default, which works well with all kinds of scenes. In scenes where one color clearly prevails, you can set Ambient to the main color of the scene to support the overall atmosphere—white for Antarctica, green for a jungle, red for a demon lair... You get the idea.

# Time for action – oooh, shiny!

Shininess is an illumination property that gives onlookers a better idea whether the surface is smooth or rough. The Lighting.j3md material definition not only supports plain material colors but can also render specular highlights (what we colloquially call shininess) on top of the material colors.

Let's make a smooth geometry:

1. Make a copy of Main.java and name the class MaterialColorShiny. java. Remember to also refactor the first line of the main() method to MaterialColorShiny app = new MaterialColorShiny();.

2. Replace the blue cube code in the simpleInitApp() method with the following:

```
Sphere sphereMesh = new Sphere(32,32, 1f);
Geometry sphere1Geo = new Geometry("rough sphere", sphereMesh);
Material sphere1Mat = new Material(assetManager,
   "Common/MatDefs/Light/Lighting.j3md");
sphere1Mat.setBoolean("UseMaterialColors",true);
sphere1Mat.setColor("Ambient", ColorRGBA.Gray );
sphere1Mat.setColor("Diffuse", ColorRGBA.Cyan );
sphere1Mat.setColor("Specular", ColorRGBA.White );
sphere1Mat.setFloat("Shininess", 8f); // [1,128]
sphere1Geo.setMaterial(sphere1Mat);
sphere1Geo.move(-2.5f, 0, 0);
rootNode.attachChild(sphere1Geo);
```

3. Remember to add light sources.

In the line where you set the shininess property, try different values between 1 and 128. Rerun the code sample and note the different specular lights on the surface.

The following screenshot shows difference in shininess from left to right: a rough surface (no shininess), a plain surface (shininess 8f, specular color white), and a smooth surface (shininess `128f`, specular color white).

## *What just happened?*

Shininess is a value between 1 and 128 that specifies how smooth or rough a surface is. Here are some examples:

- Glass, water, and silver have very smooth surfaces; they have tiny, clearly outlined specular highlights. Their shininess is high (>`16f`).

- Metal, plastic, stone, and polished materials are somewhere in the middle; they have wide, blurry specular highlights. Their shininess is low (<`16f`).

- Cloth, paper, wood, and snow have soft or uneven surfaces; they have no specular highlights. These objects are not shiny.

**Specular color** is a material color property that you only specify for materials with a shininess greater than zero. Specular color defines the color of the reflected highlights—it's generally the same as the emissive color of the main light source; for example, white in a sunlit scene.

Soft, non-shiny objects don't use the specular color property; reset it to `ColorRGBA.Black` to deactivate shininess.

| Common/MatDefs/Light/Lighting.j3md | |
| --- | --- |
| **Parameter** | **Data type** |
| UseMaterialColors | Boolean |
| Ambient | ColorRGBA |
| Diffuse | ColorRGBA |
| Specular | ColorRGBA |
| Shininess | Float |

Note that you use a `setFloat()` setter to specify the shininess, and a `setColor()` setter for the `Specular ColorRGBA` property.

Are you getting the hang of how to use setters to change material properties? Good, then let's move on to the next level and add a texture to the equation: a geometry's texture can be opaque, translucent, or transparent. With the right textures, you can produce a variety of interesting effects. We'll look at some code samples.

## Time for action – illuminated opaque textures

In the simplest case, a material loads one image file and slaps it onto the geometry's surface. Let's see what that looks like.

1.  Make a copy of `Main.java` and name the class `TexturesOpaqueTransparent.java`. Remember to also refactor the first line of the `main()` method to `TexturesOpaqueTransparent app = new TexturesOpaqueTransparent();`.

2.  Copy the provided `assets/Interface/Monkey.png` image to your project's `assets/Interface` directory. This will be our texture.

3.  Replace the blue cube code in the `simpleInitApp()` method with the following:
    ```
    Sphere sphereMesh = new Sphere(16, 16, 1);
    Geometry sphereGeo = new Geometry("lit textured sphere",
      sphereMesh);
    Material sphereMat = new Material(assetManager,
      "Common/MatDefs/Light/Lighting.j3md");
    sphereMat.setTexture("DiffuseMap",
      assetManager.loadTexture("Interface/Monkey.png"));
    sphereGeo.setMaterial(sphereMat);
    sphereGeo.move(-2f, 0f, 0f);
    sphereGeo.rotate(FastMath.DEG_TO_RAD * -90,
      FastMath.DEG_TO_RAD * 120, 0f);
    rootNode.attachChild(sphereGeo);
    ```

4.  Again, remember to add the two light sources.

When you run the code, you see a sphere with an opaque monkey texture. It has a lit and a shaded side.

 If you want to move around the scene faster, you can speed up the camera by adding `flyCam.setMoveSpeed(50)` in the `simpleInitApp()` method. If you want to increase the contrast, change the background color of the scene using `viewPort.setBackgroundColor(ColorRGBA.LightGray)` in the `simpleInitApp()` method.

## *What just happened?*

The material property that handles the main texture layer for illuminated materials is called `DiffuseMap`. The `DiffuseMap` property in `Lighting.j3md` works just like the `ColorMap` property that you already know from `Unshaded.j3md`. `DiffuseMap` is the minimum texture needed to create an illuminated textured material.

**Common/MatDefs/Light/Lighting.j3md**

| Parameter | Data type |
| --- | --- |
| UseMaterialColors | Boolean |
| Diffuse | ColorRGBA |
| Ambient | ColorRGBA |
| DiffuseMap | Texture |

You can use material colors together with a texture in the same material—this will result in an evenly tinged texture. For example, by using three different `Diffuse` colors, you can use one generic grayscale wood texture for three types of wood.

## Time for action – semitransparent texture

The previous material was opaque, but materials can also be semitransparent. Applying a semitransparent material makes the geometry partially see-through and blends the geometry's color with what is visible behind it. For this, you need an image file with an alpha channel that has grayscale in it.

Let's try to create a fancy window:

**1.** Copy the `assets/Textures/mucha-window.png` image to your project's `assets/Textures/` directory.

**2.** Back in `TexturesOpaqueTransparent.java`, add the following code in the `simpleInitApp()` method:

```
Box windowMesh = new Box(new Vector3f(0f, 0f, 0f),
    1f, 1.4f, 0.01f);
Geometry windowGeo = new Geometry(
    "stained glass window", windowMesh);
Material windowMat = new Material(assetManager,
    "Common/MatDefs/Light/Lighting.j3md");
windowMat.setTexture("DiffuseMap",
    assetManager.loadTexture("Textures/mucha-window.png"));
windowMat.getAdditionalRenderState().
    setBlendMode(BlendMode.Alpha);
windowGeo.setMaterial(windowMat);
windowGeo.setQueueBucket(Bucket.Transparent);
windowGeo.setMaterial(windowMat);
windowGeo.move(1f,0f,0f);
rootNode.attachChild(windowGeo);
```

**3.** Keep the light sources and the other geometry.

When you run the sample and move around, you see a stained glass window next to the opaque textured sphere. The frame of the glass window is opaque, while the stained glass is transparent.

## *What just happened?*

The `mucha-window.png` image has an alpha channel that influences its opacity. You create images with alpha channels in an external graphic editor, such as Gimp. Create your transparent texture with 32-bit RGBA color, and save the file in PNG format.

Transparent textures contain RGB channels (containing the color of the picture) and one alpha channel (containing the opacity of the picture). Every white pixel in the alpha channel makes the corresponding RGB pixels opaque (100 percent opacity). Every black pixel makes the corresponding RGB pixel transparent (0 percent opacity). Darker or lighter grayscales in the alpha channel make the corresponding RGB pixels more or less semitransparent.

To activate transparency in a jMonkeyEngine material, you add a `RenderState` to it. A `RenderState` specifies material rendering properties that are not controlled by shaders; this includes blending, which is used for transparency.

```
windowMat.getAdditionalRenderState().
  setBlendMode(BlendMode.Alpha);
```

There are various `BlendMode` options, but `BlendMode.Alpha` is the one that you typically use.

When rendering a 3D scene with transparent geometries, the rendering order is essential. The background color or sky must be rendered behind everything. Opaque geometries must be drawn first, and they must occlude each other depending on their depth. Transparent geometries must be rendered on top of opaque geometries, and they must blend with what is behind them. Finally, the GUI must be rendered on top of everything.

jMonkeyEngine uses a `RenderQueue` that categorizes all geometries into "buckets", sorts each bucket by depth, and renders everything in the right order. The default queue is `Bucket.Opaque`. You place all transparent geometries into `Bucket.Transparent` using the following call:

```
windowGeo.setQueueBucket(Bucket.Transparent);
```

When a transparent geometry overlaps other geometries, this bucket ensures that you can see them through the transparent parts of the transparent geometry.

What's the difference between `Bucket.Transparent` and `Bucket.Translucent`? Objects in `Bucket.Translucent` (such as a fire particle effect) are not affected by visual effects (such as drop shadows). Objects in `Bucket.Transparent` (such as window geometries, foliage textures) are affected by other rendering effects (such as shadows). You will learn more about visual effects in later chapters.

## Time for action – transparent textures

How transparent can we go? Let's try to make a part of the monkey sphere disappear:

1.  Back in `TexturesOpaqueTransparent.java`, add the following lines before `sphereGeo.setMaterial()`:

    ```
    sphereMat.getAdditionalRenderState().setAlphaTest(true);
    sphereMat.getAdditionalRenderState().setAlphaFallOff(0.5f);
    sphereGeo.setQueueBucket(Bucket.Transparent);
    ```

2.  Run the code. The monkey sphere is partially gone!

# What just happened?

A semitransparent material (such as the stained-glass window) lets you see through, but the geometry is still there—its color simply blends with what is behind it. For a stained-glass window, a slab of ice, or a bottle, this is just what you want.

Fully transparent materials, however, make part of their geometry disappear. Fully transparent textures are commonly used for foliage, flowers, or hair textures.

The background of `Monkey.png` has an alpha channel of zero; this is why the background disappeared when you used it as `DiffuseMap` and activated the alpha test `RenderState`. The float value controls how much of the geometry disappears. Start with `.5f` and work your way up or down until you get the outcome you were aiming for.

You can also use your alpha texture as `AlphaMap` to "punch holes" into a geometry. Black areas in the `AlphaMap` outline the areas that will disappear from the geometry; white areas remain solid. Which shades of gray remain visible depends on the `AlphaFallOff` value that you specified.

**Common/MatDefs/Light/Lighting.j3md**

| Parameter | Data type |
| --- | --- |
| DiffuseMap | Texture |
| AlphaMap | Texture |
| geo.setQueueBucket() | Bucket.Sky, Bucket.Opaque, Bucket.Transparent, Bucket.Gui, Bucket.Translucent |

| Material RenderState | Data type |
| --- | --- |
| getAdditionalRenderState().setAlphaTest(); | Boolean |
| getAdditionalRenderState().setAlphaFallOff(); | Float [0f, 1f] |
| getAdditionalRenderState().setBlendMode(); | BlendMode.Alpha |

## Pop quiz – transparent versus opaque

Q1. You assign geometries to render buckets. In what order does jMonkeyEngine render the buckets so that they get drawn on top of one another correctly?

1. Bucket.Sky—Bucket.Opaque—Bucket.Transparent—Bucket.Gui

2. Bucket.Gui—Bucket.Opaque—Bucket.Transparent—Bucket.Sky

3. Bucket.Sky—Bucket.Transparent—Bucket.Opaque—Bucket.Gui

4. Bucket.Gui—Bucket.Transparent—Bucket.Opaque—Bucket.Sky

# Multimapping

Okay, the material colors, shininess, and textures are nice, but these materials still don't look like the shiny pebbles that you saw in the beginning of the chapter. How do you make your materials more life-like? Time to learn about multimapping!

The more layers of information the 3D artists provide additionally to the basic texture, the higher the degree of detail and realism they can achieve in a rendered geometry. Note, however, that the more layers you use, the slower the model renders. So, use this feature wisely.

In our previous examples, we used only a `DiffuseMap` texture, and a few other properties. Modern 3D graphics can use several layers of information for one material. Each layer contains one image file. This layering method is referred to as multimapping.

**Common/MatDefs/Light/Lighting.j3md**

| Parameter | Data type |
| --- | --- |
| DiffuseMap | Texture |
| NormalMap | Texture |
| ParallaxMap | Texture |
| SpecularMap | Texture |
| Shininess | Float |
| UseMaterialColors | Boolean |
| Diffuse | ColorRGBA |
| Ambient | ColorRGBA |
| Specular | ColorRGBA |

You already know shininess, and that the DiffuseMap layer adds a texture to illuminated materials. Additionally, Lighting.j3md supports SpecularMaps for light reflection effects, and several kinds of bump maps (including ParallaxMap and NormalMap) to add extra detail to a surface. We'll look at each effect.

# Time for action – meet the hover tank

The provided assets directory contains the Models/HoverTank/Tank.j3o model.

1. Copy Tank.j3o and its four textures into a new assets/Models/HoverTank/ directory in your project.

2. Make a copy of Main.java and name the class HoverTank.java. Remember to also refactor the first line of the main() method to HoverTank app = new HoverTank();.

3. Replace the blue cube code in the simpleInitApp() method with the following:

```
Node tank = (Node) assetManager.loadModel(
    "Models/HoverTank/Tank.j3o");
Material mat = new Material(
    assetManager, "Common/MatDefs/Light/Lighting.j3md");
TextureKey tankDiffuse = new TextureKey(
    "Models/HoverTank/tank_diffuse.jpg", false);
mat.setTexture("DiffuseMap",
    assetManager.loadTexture(tankDiffuse));
tank.setMaterial(mat);
rootNode.attachChild(tank);
```

Run the code. You should see a textured sci-fi vehicle with a monkey logo.

## What just happened?

Creating a texture for a cube is easy, but what about this nifty sci-fi vehicle? As explained in the previous chapter, the textures for more complex objects are designed just like sewing patterns: one UV texture contains the outline of the front, back, and side of the object, all pieces next to one another.

The following screenshot shows the hover tank model and its `DiffuseMap` texture (model by Rémy Bouquet):

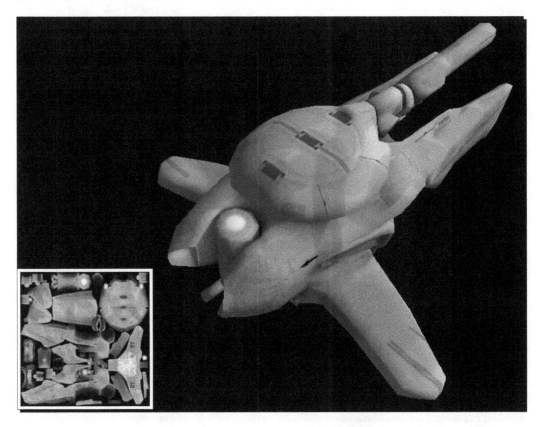

The UV textures for this model were exported from the model editor, as described in the previous chapter. You load the UV texture into the `DiffuseMap` layer like any other texture, using `mat.setTexture(DiffuseMap, assetManager.loadTexture(tankDiffuse));`

One thing that is new here is that you created a `com.jme3.asset.TextureKey` object for the texture:

```
TextureKey tankDiffuse = new TextureKey(
    "Models/HoverTank/tank_diffuse.jpg", false);
```

Having access to the texture objects lets you flip the texture by setting a Boolean parameter in the `TextureKey` constructor to `false`. This is sometimes necessary because editors export files with different orientations.

## Time for action – let the hover tank be groovy

Currently, the surface of the hover tank looks a bit like a cheap toy: the grooves in the material look painted on, and the material looks more like plastic than metal. One thing you want to avoid is adding extra polygons to the mesh just to make the grooves three-dimensional.

Let's try a more professional solution and add a so-called normal map:

1. Make sure you have the `Models/HoverTank/tank_normals.png` texture in your `assets` directory.

2. This line generates the tangent data that describes your model's surface. Add it before the `setMaterial()` line in your `HoverTank.java`'s `simpleInit()` method:

   ```
   TangentBinormalGenerator.generate(tank);
   ```

3. Load the normal map into the material. Again, add these lines before the `setMaterial()` line:

   ```
   TextureKey tankNormal = new TextureKey(
      "Models/HoverTank/tank_normals.png", false);
   mat.setTexture("NormalMap",
      assetManager.loadTexture(tankNormal));
   ```

4. Run the code sample.

Your hover tank is looking better and better. In addition to its texture, the grooves now appear to be carved into the surface, while others seem to jut out into the third dimension. And all that without having to change the mesh!

The following screenshot shows the hover tank with added grooves and embossed surface details; the `NormalMap` visualizes the degree of displacement as colors (model by Rémy Bouquet):

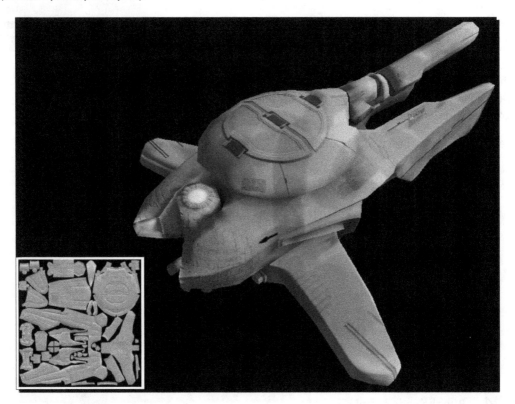

## What just happened?

Bump maps are used to add depth and surface details that would be too hard (or simply too inefficient) to sculpt in a mesh editor. The category of bump map texture includes height maps, normal maps, and parallax maps.

You use **normal maps** to simulate fine cracks in walls, a chipped rusty surface, natural skin texture, or a soft canvas weave—without actually changing the mesh. A typical normal map looks like a bluish false-color version of the `DiffuseMap`. Each color value encodes a surface normal vector of the desired slope at this point, hence the name normal map. The shifted surface normals are passed on to the shader, which renders the surface as if it were really as bumpy as the fake slope data pretends. It's hard to draw normal maps by hand. Professional 3D artists calculate them off high-polygon versions of 3D models, and some mesh editors may offer to compute fake normal maps from a diffuse or height map.

If you added a normal map and see no effect, your model is missing tangent data that describes its shape mathematically. You pre-calculate tangent data by calling `TangentBinormalGenerator.generate(model)` on your geometry.

In contrast, **height maps** are used to describe height differences, such as hills and valleys of a terrain. The grayscales in the height-map image look similar to a topographic map, and you can draw them by hand in a graphic editor. You will learn more about height maps in *Chapter 8, Creating Landscapes*.

The **parallax map** technique (also called virtual displacement) is an enhancement of the bump mapping technique. You use a model editor to generate parallax maps of height maps. Parallax maps look best when used for medium-scale displacements, such as deep cracks or gaps in walls or floors.

# Time for action – give your hover tank a shine

Next, let's make the surface look more metallic and less plastic. Similar to the Specular color for plainly colored shiny materials, multimapped materials have a SpecularMap layer that defines varying degrees of shininess of the surface.

Using a graphic editor, you can create a specular map from an existing diffuse texture as follows:

1. Copy the DiffuseMap tank_diffuse.jpg image as a template and save it as tank_specular.jpg.

2. Desaturate the image (decrease contrast and brightness) so the whole map is evenly medium gray.

3. Paint white and light gray over areas of the hover tank that you want to be smooth and shiny.

4. Paint black and dark gray over dull, rough, worn-out areas of the hover tank.

The resulting SpecularMap typically looks similar to a grayscale version of the color map. A working example is included as assets/Models/HoverTank/tank_specular.jpg.

Let's apply what you learned about texture mapping in HoverTank.java. Add the following lines to the existing code sample:

```
TextureKey tankSpecular = new TextureKey(
  "Models/HoverTank/tank_specular.jpg", false);
mat.setTexture("SpecularMap",
  assetManager.loadTexture(tankSpecular));
```

```
mat.setBoolean("UseMaterialColors", true);
mat.setColor("Ambient", ColorRGBA.Gray);
mat.setColor("Diffuse", ColorRGBA.White);
mat.setColor("Specular", ColorRGBA.White);
mat.setFloat("Shininess", 100f);
```

Run the sample. Now your hover tank is not only textured and bumpy but also smooth and shiny on top, and rough around the edges at the bottom.

The following screenshot shows a shiny hover tank and its specular map that defines smoother and rougher areas (model by Rémy Bouquet):

## *What just happened?*

Previously, you learned how to use the specular material color together with the shininess property to make a colored surface shiny. Using only material colors, the surface is either all smooth, or all rough. In reality, however, an object can have rough and smooth spots. The specular map further improves this kind of realism for an object's surface because it lets you add extra information about where exactly a lit material is smooth or rough.

## Time for action – make your hover tank glow

Let's add one last cool effect. We want the jet engines and the energy grid on the bottom of the tank to shine with an electric glow:

1. Make sure you have the `Models/HoverTank/tank_glow_map.jpg` texture in `Models/HoverTank/` in your `assets` directory.

2. Import the `com.jme3.post` package and add the following code snippet to your `simpleInitApp()` method:

```
FilterPostProcessor fpp = new FilterPostProcessor(assetManager);
viewPort.addProcessor(fpp);
BloomFilter bloom =
    new BloomFilter(BloomFilter.GlowMode.SceneAndObjects);
fpp.addFilter(bloom);
```

3. The following lines load the glow map, and specify the glow color for the model. Add them before the `setMaterial()` line:

```
TextureKey tankGlow = new TextureKey(
    "Models/HoverTank/tank_glow_map.jpg", false);
mat.setTexture("GlowMap",
    assetManager.loadTexture(tankGlow));
mat.setColor("GlowColor", ColorRGBA.White);
```

4. Run the sample.

You are now a proud owner of the ultimate textured, shiny, bumpy, glowing hover tank. What else could one wish for?

The following screenshot shows the hover tank's `GlowMap` that contains white and light gray pixels for all areas that should glow (model by Rémy Bouquet):

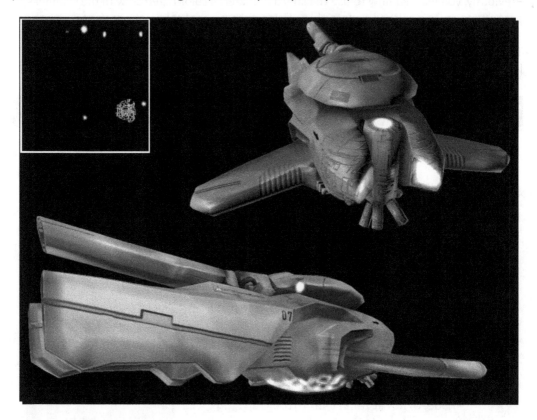

## What just happened?

You can add visual effects, such as glows, to the scene after it is rendered. jMonkeyEngine handles post-processing glow effects using the `FilterPostProcessor` and `BloomFilter` classes. You will learn more about post-processing in *Chapter 7, Adding Spark to Your Game*. For now, all you need to know is that your `SimpleApplication` class provides you with a `viewPort` object that manages additional effects. To specify which effect you want to activate, you create a `BloomFilter` object and add it to the `FilterPostProcessor` object:

```
FilterPostProcessor fpp = new FilterPostProcessor(assetManager);
viewPort.addProcessor(fpp);
BloomFilter bloom = new BloomFilter(BloomFilter.GlowMode.Objects);
fpp.addFilter(bloom);
```

The glow color (also called emissive color) is the color of light emitted by a fluorescent object. Only glowing materials (lamps, lights, the moon, blinking controls, cat eyes, and so on) have a glow color. Normal objects (trees, houses, persons) typically do not use this property. You can create a GlowMap texture layer that specifies which areas of your object should glow, as we did with the hover tank:

```
TextureKey tankGlow = new TextureKey(
  "Models/HoverTank/tank_glow_map.jpg", false);
mat.setTexture("GlowMap",
  assetManager.loadTexture(tankGlow));
mat.setColor("GlowColor", ColorRGBA.White);
```

The following screenshot shows (from left to right) a non-glowing sphere, a sphere with a checkered GlowMap, and a sphere with a random noise GlowMap:

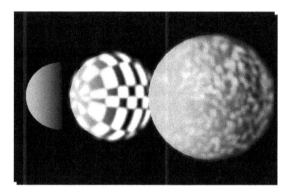

You can easily create a GlowMap from a copy of the object's DiffuseMap. Paint everything black that should not glow. Then you set white, gray, or colored highlights that define the glowing areas. The glow color is often white, but you can create special glow effects by using colors.

| Common/MatDefs/Light/Lighting.j3md | |
| --- | --- |
| Parameter | Data type |
| GlowMap | Texture |
| GlowColor | ColorRGBA |

# Time for action – deep-freeze your materials

When you are working with multimapped materials, you base them, for example, on the `Lighting.j3md` material definition. Material definitions come bundled with the jMonkeyEngine library. The above examples taught you how to use a series of setters to specify material properties in Java. This is typically how you start when you create a new, one-off material.

Look at your hover tank code again. It takes 10 lines of Java code to configure this material, plus four lines for `TextureKeys`! If you ever need the same material with the same settings for other models, it would be handy to create and configure your custom materials once, and then load them simply with one `setMaterial(mat)` line from a file.

Return to the SDK; now, let's learn how to store material settings in a material file:

**1.** Right-click on the **assets/Material** directory and choose **New...Other**. Then go to **Materials | Empty Material File**. Click on **Next**.

**2.** Name the new file `tank.j3m` and save it to your project's `assets/Materials/` folder.

**3.** The file opens in the Material Editor. Choose **Lighting.j3md** as a material definition. Recreate your material settings by assigning textures (**DiffuseMap**, **NormalMap**, **SpecularMap**, **GlowMap**) and colors (**Specular**, **Diffuse**, **Ambient**, **Glow**) as before. Enable the **UseMaterialColors** checkbox and enter the **Shininess** value. Press the **Return** key in the last input field to save the file.

**4.** Loading the material from `tank.j3m` now only takes one line that replaces over a dozen lines of material creation, material setters, and `TextureKeys`:

```
Material mat = assetManager.loadMaterial
    ("Materials/tank.j3m");
```

Run the code sample and confirm that the outcome is the same.

## What just happened?

Return to the SDK and look at `tank.j3m` in the Material Editor again. Click on **Source**. You see that `tank.j3m` has the following content:

```
Material my hovertank material : Common/MatDefs/Light/Lighting.j3md {
  MaterialParameters {
    SpecularMap : Models/HoverTank/tank_specular.jpg
    NormalMap   : Models/HoverTank/tank_normals.png
    DiffuseMap  : Models/HoverTank/tank_diffuse.jpg
```

```
GlowMap        : Models/HoverTank/tank_glow_map.jpg
UseMaterialColors : true
Ambient   : 0.5 0.5 0.5 1.0
Diffuse   : 1.0 1.0 1.0 1.0
Specular  : 1.0 1.0 1.0 1.0
GlowColor: 1.0 1.0 1.0 1.0
Shininess : 100
    }
}
```

Note that the first word, `Material`, is a keyword and has to stay as it is. The words `my hovertank material` are a description that you can choose freely. Go through the lines and note how they map to the settings—the Java code and the file encode the same information.

The SDK's Material Editor makes it easy to create and preview a material file. On the other hand, the syntax is human-readable and you are free to write a `.j3m` file by hand in any text editor.

After you load the material from a file, you can still change individual properties by overriding them with Java setters. For example, to temporarily deactivate shininess, change the following lines:

```
Material mat = assetManager.loadMaterial("Materials/tank.j3m");
mat.setColor("Specular",ColorRGBA.Black);
tank.setMaterial(mat);
```

Loading a custom material in a `.j3m` file is not only faster but also gives you full control over all supported features of multi-textured materials, independent of your model editor.

## Pop quiz – multimapping

Q1. Combine the first part and the last part of the sentences to form true statements about multimapping.

a) `DiffuseMap`..., b) `NormalMap`..., c) `SpecularMap`..., d) `GlowMap`..., e) `AlphaMap`...

1.   ... requires a `BloomFilter` post-processor and a color.

2.   ... uses a texture channel to make parts of the geometry transparent.

3.   ... is the minimum texture and can be used on its own.

4.   ... makes your model look bumpy without adding polygons to the mesh.

5.   ... lets you give your models a smooth shine.

# Different types of textures

jMonkeyEngine supports various kinds of textures:

- **UV Mapped textures** are professionally created textures that look like sewing patterns. Take your time to learn how to create them in your model editor; you will most likely use them in your games.

- **MIPmaps** (MIP stands for "multum in parvo," meaning "many in one") provide several different levels of detail (LODs) for one texture in one file. Depending on how close (or far) the camera is, the engine automatically renders a more (or less) detailed texture for the object; this improves performance. jMonkeyEngine generates MIPmaps internally for all textures when a texture is sent to the GPU. This optimization happens "behind the scenes"—you don't have to do anything.

- **Seamless Tiled textures** are very simple and are commonly used for simple objects such as walls and floors. When texturing a wide area such as a wall, you don't load one huge picture of a wall. It's more efficient to repeat one small picture of some bricks and fill the area. You have to design the image to be seamlessly tileable: the right edge must match the left edge, and the top edge must match the bottom edge. Tiling easily creates the illusion of a huge texture (unfortunately, the cheap trick becomes painfully obvious as soon as the surface is viewed from a distance). In jMonkeyEngine you activate tiling in a particular texture layer as follows:

```
floorMat.getTextureParam("DiffuseMap").
  getTextureValue().setWrap(WrapMode.Repeat);
```

  You can get different `WrapMode` options from the `com.jme3.texture` package that let you repeat, mirror, or clamp your tiled texture to achieve different tilings.

- **Procedural textures** are generated by repeating one small image with added pseudo-random gradient variations called **Perlin noise**. Procedural textures look significantly more natural than seamless tiled textures; they appear less distorted on spheres, and on wide meshes their repetitiveness is much less noticeable. Procedural textures are ideal for "natural" textures such as meadows, mountains, rusty warehouses, zombie brains, and irregular piles of stones.

  The jMonkeyEngine SDK supports the optional NeoTextureEditor plugin for creating and loading procedural textures. You can find more details and code samples on the jMonkeyEngine wiki.

- **Texture Splatting** is a technique that makes it possible to use several multimapped textures in one texture. A typical usage example is one terrain texture that includes grass, rock, and road textures "painted" on it. You use the `AlphaMap` layers as a mask to tell the engine which of the textures should be visible where on the terrain. You will learn all about this technique in Chapter 8, *Creating Landscapes*.

# Time for action – scaling and tiling textures

Since it's used quite often, let's create a material with a seamless tiled texture, and use it as the floor under the hover tank:

**1.** Go back to `HoverTank.java`.

**2.** Copy the provided `assets/Textures/BrickWall/` directory to your `assets/Textures` directory.

**3.** Add the following code to the `simpleInitApp()` method:

```
Box floorMesh = new Box(new Vector3f(-20,-2,-20),
                        new Vector3f(20,-3,20));
floorMesh.scaleTextureCoordinates(new Vector2f(8,8));
Geometry floorGeo = new Geometry("floor", floorMesh);
Material floorMat = new Material(assetManager,
"Common/MatDefs/Light/Lighting.j3md");
floorMat.setTexture("DiffuseMap", assetManager.loadTexture(
    "Textures/BrickWall/BrickWall_diffuse.jpg"));
floorMat.setTexture("NormalMap", assetManager.loadTexture(
    "Textures/BrickWall/BrickWall_normal.jpg"));
floorMat.getTextureParam("NormalMap").getTextureValue().
    setWrap(WrapMode.Repeat);
floorMat.getTextureParam("DiffuseMap").getTextureValue().
    setWrap(WrapMode.Repeat);
floorGeo.setMaterial(floorMat);
rootNode.attachChild(floorGeo);
```

Run the code sample. You should see a repeatedly tiled floor under the hover tank.

## What just happened?

The correct tiling of a seamless texture depends on the image you choose. If your pebbles are as huge as rocks, and your blades of grass as long as branches, then your texture scale is too small. If your impressive hangar has a cute checkered pattern, or your stacked logs are textured like a pile of pencils, your texture scale is too big. Note that texture coordinates are not an issue in your texture, but in your mesh!

```
floorMesh.scaleTextureCoordinates(new Vector2f(8,8));
```

If you just set the texture, and scale its texture coordinates, the outcome is usually quite ugly: the texture is rendered once in one corner of the geometry, and the rest of the geometry is filled with blurry, distorted pixels. If you see this happen, you forgot to set the `WrapMode` for the tiled texture, for each texture layer individually.

```
floorMat.getTextureParam("NormalMap").getTextureValue().
    setWrap(WrapMode.Repeat);
```

```
floorMat.getTextureParam("DiffuseMap").getTextureValue().
  setWrap(WrapMode.Repeat);
```

Keep `HoverTank.java` with its new floor open—it's a good code sample to test different light sources in.

# Time for action – lights on!

You can use any combination of light sources from the `com.jme3.light` package: ambient lights, directional lights, point lights, and spot lights. Remove the lights from `HoverTank.java` file's `simpleInit()` method, and add them back one by one to see the difference.

1. Add an ambient light. Try multiplying the color by different scalars, larger or smaller than 1.0f, to increase or decrease its brightness. Note how it illuminates the whole scene evenly. Try setting the color to something other than `White`.

   ```
   AmbientLight ambient = new AmbientLight();
   ambient.setColor(ColorRGBA.White.mult(5f));
   rootNode.addLight(ambient);
   ```

2. Remove the ambient light and add a point light. Move it to different locations to see the difference. Try different colors and multiply them by a scalar to see the difference in brightness.

   ```
   PointLight lamp = new PointLight();
   lamp.setPosition(Vector3f.ZERO);
   lamp.setColor(ColorRGBA.Yellow);
   rootNode.addLight(lamp);
   ```

3. Remove the point light and add a directional light. Try different directions, colors, and brightness.

   ```
   DirectionalLight sun = new DirectionalLight();
   sun.setDirection(new Vector3f(1,0,-2));
   sun.setColor(ColorRGBA.White);
   rootNode.addLight(sun);
   ```

4. Remove the directional light. Add a `SpotLight` as a private field and initialize it in `simpleInitApp()`. Add two update loop calls that keep the `SpotLight` pointed from the camera location toward the camera direction. Look around in the scene and note the cone of light.

   ```
   private SpotLight spot;
   public void simpleInitApp() {
     ...
     spot = new SpotLight();
     spot.setSpotRange(100);
   ```

```
        spot.setSpotOuterAngle(20 * FastMath.DEG_TO_RAD);
        spot.setSpotInnerAngle(15 * FastMath.DEG_TO_RAD);
        rootNode.addLight(spot);
    }
    public void simpleUpdate(float tpf) {
        spot.setDirection(cam.getDirection());
        spot.setPosition(cam.getLocation());
    }
```

You see that the four light types illuminate the scene in very different ways.

**Have a light?**

In the jMonkeyEngine SDK, you can easily add a light using the `Palette` from the Windows menu. Drag-and-drop the code snippet from the palette right into your Java code. When you see a light bulb icon in the SDK's editor, click on it to make the SDK add the correct import statements and you're done. If you are editing a `.j3o` scene in the `Scene Composer`, click on the scene node in the `Scene Explorer` window to add a light source.

## What just happened?

As you have seen in this chapter, all lit materials require a light source to be visible. A light is added to a parent node from where it illuminates all children. In the simplest case, you add a light source directly to the `rootNode`. But you can also create nice effects by adding extra lights to individual nodes only. Be aware that using too many light sources has an impact on performance.

The following lights are at your disposal:

- An **ambient light** is the simplest light source that makes materials visible. The only property this light has is its color. This light evenly illuminates the whole scene and does not cause any shading. Typically, we add an ambient light to the `rootNode` to influence the scene's "temperature" (color) and overall brightness.

- A **point light** is one of the most commonly used individual light sources in a scene. In addition to color, it has a location from which it radiates in all directions, before it fades out. We typically attach it to candles, lamps, camp fires, and so on.

- A **directional light** lets you specify a color and a direction. Use it to simulate outdoor sunlight. You can add code to the update loop that modifies the color (brightness and temperature) and incidence angle to simulate different times of the day. Of course, astronomically speaking, the Sun is a gigantic point light. But the few beams that reach Earth are practically parallel, and reach us from one direction only, so a directional light is the best fit for sunlight in a video game.

◆ A **spot light** is the most complex light source. From its location, it casts a light cone in a given direction. You also specify the range and width of the light cone. You can use it for car headlights, helmet-mounted or hand-held flashlights, or to highlight a scene element, such as an altar, a treasure, or an entrance.

All lights have a color. When you give the light a cooler (say, `ColorRGBA.Cyan`) or warmer (say, `ColorRGBA.Orange`) color, this influences the atmosphere of its surroundings. The default light color is white (`ColorRGBA.White`). If a model looked good in the mesh editor, but appears dreary or discolored when loaded into your game, shine a white light source on it to see the model's true colors:

```
light.setColor(ColorRGBA.White);
```

 You can also control the brightness of a light source by setting its color: dark colors result in a gloomy light; 100 percent colors (such as `ColorRGBA.White`, and other constants) result in a bright, well-lit scene. If you ever need to simulate blindingly bright lights, multiply the color constant by a scalar, using the method `ColorRGBA.White.mult(5)`.

Against human intuition and experience, light and shadow are two separate effects in 3D graphics. You will learn how to add shadows in Chapter 7, *Adding Spark to Your Game*.

## Have a go hero

Return to the Tower Defense game that you started building. In the previous chapter, you added `.j3o` objects from `AssetPackBrowser` to your project; you loaded these models from your `assets/Models` directory into your Tower Defense game's scene. Let's have a closer look at these models:

1. Open your Tower Defense game in the SDK's **Projects** window. Open the `Project Assets` node.

2. Note that using the `AssetPackBrowser` window has added a new directory, `assets/3d_objects`. It contains the UV textures for the `.j3o` models that you added from the `AssetPackBrowser` window.

   Do not rename or move this directory, or its contents; these paths are hardcoded into the imported `.j3o` models!

3. Browse the textures. Note that each texture directory contains three PNG files: `D.png` is the `DiffuseMap`, `N.png` is the `NormalMap`, and `S.png` is the `SpecularMap`.

4. Open those images in a graphic editor and "improve" them: for example, add "your" coat of arms to the models (in the `DiffuseMaps`) and change the emblem's smoothness (in the `SpecularMaps`). Paint the `NormalMap` under the emblem in a neutral blue to flatten it (editing `NormalMaps` by hand is untypical; we just do it for the exercise's sake).

5. Do a web search for free seamless textures, and give the floor geometry an interesting repeating material.

Add some interesting light effects to your scene by performing the following steps:

1. Add an `AmbientLight` that emphasizes the gloomy atmosphere of your game.

2. Add a low `DirectionalLight` to increase contrast. Place it, for example, behind the camera, shining toward the player base.

3. Add some `PointLights` inside buildings and towers so they shine through the windows.

4. Add a searchlight on top of the player base (at the origin) that shines along the Z-axis; write update loop code that makes the `SpotLight` swivel back and forth automatically.

5. Add a `BloomFilter` and specify a spooky `GlowColor` for the creeps. Make a copy of the creeps' `DiffuseMap` and name it `G.png`. Use `getMaterial().setTexture()` on these geometries (cast `Spatial` to `Geometry`, if necessary) to add `G.png` as `GlowMap`. Open `G.png` in a graphic editor, darken and desaturate it, and paint on it with a bright color to make your creeps glow in the dark ominously.

Those are just examples; have fun and experiment!

# Summary

In this chapter, you have learned how to create custom materials, and use them to make geometries look more spiffy. You're on your way to become a 3D graphics expert! Now that you know essential concepts such as shaders and multimapping, it will be easier for you to use a search engine to find good textures, or to ask the right questions on forums.

Specifically, we covered how to work with opaque and transparent materials, how to make parts of geometries invisible, how to use multimapped textures to make materials reflect light in a more natural way, and how to "deep-freeze" materials that you use repeatedly.

With the 3D graphic skills that you have learned by now, your scenes will look pretty awesome already! Your walls are made up of the bumpiest bricks, you can render differently tinged wood types, and your rubber duckies have just the right amount of specularity. But do they also act their part? Read on to make the brick wall solid, to push around your wooden boxes, and to teach your rubber ducky how to bounce like a boss.

# 6
# Having Fun with Physics

*Thanks to built-in game physics, jMonkeyEngine can treat geometries as solid matter and simulate the effects of gravity and other physical forces. In the simplest case, you use game physics to make walls and floors solid—this is called **collision detection**. Game physics also simulate friction, impulse, bouncing, skidding, and many more fun and exciting physical interactions.*

In bowling, marble run, or billiard games, little balls roll, spin, and bounce off solid obstacles; in physics puzzles, the player interacts with pendulums, wheels, chains, or rope bridges. In car racing games, vehicles with suspensions and tire friction speed over uneven terrain and jump over ramps; in space racing games, you accelerate space vessels in a zero-gravity, zero-friction environment. In ragdoll games, you push dummies down the stairs; in destruction games, you crash cars and blow stuff up. These are all examples of physics simulation.

In this chapter we will:

- ◆ Walk through a solid town
- ◆ Shoot cannon balls at a brick wall
- ◆ Ride an elevator
- ◆ Learn some tricks from professional game developers

You already know how to position geometries using `setLocalTranslation()`. You may have noticed that you can place geometries in mid-air, they can overlap, or move through floors and walls. In this chapter, you will learn how to make scenes more physically realistic.

Internally, the jMonkeyEngine uses jBullet, a Java port of the open source Bullet Physics Engine. This is why you find the physics classes in a package named `com.jme3.bullet`.

# Solid floors and walls

Many genres of video game use the first-person perspective. The camera shows the scene from the player's point of view running through the level, avoiding physical obstacles, chasing enemies, jumping from platform to platform, and so on. You already know how to load static models into the scene—now, let's make a first-person player walk among solid walls and floors.

## Time for action – fortify the town

We start with a simple game that loads a model of a town:

1. Make a copy of `Main.java` and name the class `PhysicsTown.java`. Remember to also refactor the first line of the `main()` method to the following:

   ```
   PhysicsTown app = new PhysicsTown();
   ```

2. Download a sample town model in the Ogre DotScene format from `http://jmonkeyengine.googlecode.com/svn/trunk/engine/town.zip`. Save it directly into your project directory (not into `assets/`).

3. Register a `com.jme3.asset.plugins.ZipLocator` for `town.zip` to the `assetManager`. Now you can use the `assetManager` to load the model's `main.scene` into the `sceneNode` class field. Since the model is quite small, scale it a bit bigger. As always, you attach the loaded model to the `rootNode`. Remember to add light sources to the scene.

   ```
   private Node sceneNode;
   public void simpleInitApp() {
       assetManager.registerLocator("town.zip", ZipLocator.class);
       sceneNode = (Node)assetManager.loadModel("main.scene");
       sceneNode.scale(1.5f);
       rootNode.attachChild(sceneNode);

       AmbientLight ambient = new AmbientLight();
       rootNode.addLight(ambient);
       DirectionalLight sun = new DirectionalLight();
       sun.setDirection(new Vector3f(1.4f, -1.4f, -1.4f));
       rootNode.addLight(sun);
   }
   ```

**4.** Optionally, make the sky blue by adding the following line to the `simpleInitApp()` method:

```
viewPort.setBackgroundColor(ColorRGBA.Cyan);
```

When you run the `SimpleApplication` now, you should see the model of a town. You can move around using the WASD keys as usual—currently, you can still fly through obstacles.

> To load a zipped asset right from the project directory, we registered a `com.jme3.asset.plugins.ZipLocator` to the `assetManager` as follows:
>
> ```
> assetManager.registerLocator("town.zip", ZipLocator.class);
> ```
>
> A `registerLocator()` path always starts inside your project directory. Remember, however, that the default build script does not bundle any files in external formats into the final executable. Your users will get an `AssetNotFoundException` for any Ogre3D model that you did not convert to j3o. If you want to offer users a way to load zipped levels in external formats from the project directory, you must customize `build.xml` yourself to copy these external assets to the `dist/` directory after the JAR was built.

After loading the scene, you want to make the walls and floors solid. After that, you want to be able to walk through the town from a first-person perspective.

**1.** Start by activating the physics simulation. This is always the same: create a `com.jme3.bullet.BulletAppState` object in the beginning of `simpleInitApp()` and attach it to the `AppStateManager`.

```
private BulletAppState bulletAppState;
public void simpleInitApp() {
    bulletAppState = new BulletAppState();
    stateManager.attach(bulletAppState);
    ...
}
```

**2.** After attaching the `sceneNode`, you add a so-called `RigidBodyControl` to it. Because you want `sceneNode` to be static (not moving), you specify a mass of `0f` as an argument of the `RigidBodyControl` constructor.

```
private RigidBodyControl scenePhy;
...
public void simpleInitApp() {
    ...
    scenePhy = new RigidBodyControl(0f);
    sceneNode.addControl(scenePhy);
}
```

**3.** Add the `scenePhy` control to your model `sceneNode`. Register the `sceneNode` to the physics `AppState` to activate it.

```
sceneNode.addControl(scenePhy);
bulletAppState.getPhysicsSpace().add(sceneNode);
```

The physical scene is ready; you're halfway there! Let's look at how we made this scene a solid object.

## What just happened?

jMonkeyEngine provides the built-in `BulletAppState` as part of its jBullet physics integration. Do you remember how you learned to implement game behavior in *Chapter 2, Creating Your First 3D Scene*? You used application states and custom controls to specify how objects should respond.

```
private BulletAppState bulletAppState;
public void simpleInitApp() {
    bulletAppState = new BulletAppState();
    stateManager.attach(bulletAppState);
}
```

The physics simulation is a typical example where application states and controls interact to define complex global behavior. The `BulletAppState` manages the *physics space* of your game. You know that a geometry defines the visible properties of an object and is managed by the `rootNode`. Think of the physics space as a root node that additionally manages physical object properties.

```
RigidBodyControl thingPhy = new RigidBodyControl(0f);
bulletAppState.getPhysicsSpace().add(thingPhy);
thingGeo.addControl(thingPhy);
rootNode.attachChild(thingGeo);
```

The following code snippet shows how you detach physical objects, including their geometries, from the scene:

```
bulletAppState.getPhysicsSpace().remove(thingPhy);
thingGeo.removeFromParent();
```

In the physics space, you also specify global parameters, such as default gravity and simulation accuracy. You can override the global default by setting those properties directly on individual physical objects after adding them. Specify the defaults before adding physical objects to the physics space—changing the defaults later has no effect on physical objects that are already in the physics space!

Gravity is typically a vector pointing into the downward direction, along the negative y axis. For zero-gravity environments, set this to `new Vector3f(0,0,0)`. For an Earth-like gravity, set this property to `-9.81` meters per second squared.

```
bulletAppState.getPhysicsSpace().
                setGravity(new Vector3f(0, -9.81f, 0));
```

The standard simulation accuracy is *1.0f/60f= 60 fps = 0.016f*. You can decrease the simulation accuracy if your game type can afford to trade lower accuracy for higher performance; or increase accuracy if you have enough processing power.

```
bulletAppState.getPhysicsSpace().setAccuracy(0.016f); // default
bulletAppState.getPhysicsSpace().setAccuracy(0.005f); // low accuracy
```

If you have situations such as a space ship passing close to a black hole in Zero-G, you can also set different gravity vectors for individual objects. The physical properties of a spatial are stored in its physics control. The `com.jme3.bullet.control` package offers you various specialized `com.jme3.bullet.control.PhysicsControls`. Here are the most common physics controls:

| Physics control | Usage | Examples |
|---|---|---|
| RigidBodyControl | Use this for solid objects in the scene. Apply it to objects that are freely affected by physical forces, be it by static collision or tipping over and falling down. This is the most commonly used physics control. It is used with dynamic as well as static objects. | Floors, walls, fences, immobile furniture, obstacles, and so on (all static).<br><br>Rolling and pushable objects such as crates, bricks, balls, flying projectiles, and so on (all dynamic). |
| BetterCharacter Control | Use this for characters that walk on a solid surface and bump into solid obstacles. This supports special `jump()` and `setWalkDirection()` methods, and jump and gravity properties. | Walking player avatars, animals, NPCs, and so on. |
| GhostControl | Use this physics control to detect and respond to overlap with physical objects. Attach this non-solid collision shape to a RigidBodyControl or BetterCharacter Control spatial and use its getOverlapping Objects() method. | Motion sensors, aggro radius, sonar, and so on. |

# Time for action – first-person navigation

One of the reasons why you extend `SimpleApplication` is that basic camera navigation (WASD keys and MouseLook) is already preconfigured. But when you run the `PhysicsTown` sample, you notice that the first-person camera keeps running straight through walls. Have we not just added a `RigidBodyControl` to the model to make the town solid?

We have, but the camera is not a solid object yet. The default navigation of `SimpleApplication` uses the non-physical `setLocalTranslation()` method to move the camera. To make this sample work, we first need to define a so-called collision shape for the invisible player, since the camera object has no mesh. We also update the keyboard navigation to use physics-aware methods.

Return to `PhysicsTown.java` and perform the following steps:

1.  In the `simpleInitApp()` method, create a `playerNode`. In this demo, our player is an invisible first-person character, but you could also attach a model to this node.

    ```
    private Node playerNode;
    public void simpleInitApp() {
        ...
        playerNode = new Node("the player");
        playerNode.setLocalTranslation(new Vector3f(0, 6, 0));
            rootNode.attachChild(playerNode);
    ```

2.  Create a `playerControl`. The `BetterCharacterControl` constructor expects three floats: the character's collision shape (radius, here `1.5f`, and height, here `4f`), and weight (here `30f`). You also specify the character's jump force and gravity.

    ```
    private BetterCharacterControl playerControl;
    public void simpleInitApp() {
        ...
        playerControl = new BetterCharacterControl(1.5f, 4, 30f);
        playerControl.setJumpForce(new Vector3f(0, 300, 0));
        playerControl.setGravity(new Vector3f(0, -10, 0));
    ```

3.  Add the `playerControl` to the `playerNode`, and register the `playerControl` to the `PhysicsSpace`.

    ```
        playerNode.addControl(playerControl);
        bulletAppState.getPhysicsSpace().add(playerControl);
    ```

Your physical player is ready, but if you run the code now, your player would still just sit there. The next step is to hook the `playerControl` into the navigation, and tie the first-person camera to `playerControl`.

1. In the `simpleUpdate()` method, disable the default `flyCam`, and make the camera follow the `playerNode`. This way, users see the scene from the player's point of view.

```
private CameraNode camNode;
public void simpleUpdate(float tpf) {
    ...
    camNode = new CameraNode("CamNode", cam);
    camNode.setControlDir(CameraControl.
                            ControlDirection.SpatialToCamera);
    camNode.setLocalTranslation(new Vector3f(0, 4, -6));
    Quaternion quat = new Quaternion();
    quat.lookAt(Vector3f.UNIT_Z, Vector3f.UNIT_Y);
    camNode.setLocalRotation(quat);
    playerNode.attachChild(camNode);
    camNode.setEnabled(true);
    flyCam.setEnabled(false);
}
```

2. Since we deactivated the `flyCam`, we want the WASD keys to steer the `playerControl`. Start by implementing the `ActionListener` interface, as you learned in a previous chapter.

```
public class PhysicsTown extends SimpleApplication implements
ActionListener { ... }
```

3. In the `simpleInitApp()` method, we overwrite the default WASD key mappings, because we want to customize them. Additionally, you map the Space bar to a custom `Jump` action.

```
inputManager.addMapping("Forward",
  new KeyTrigger(KeyInput.KEY_W));
inputManager.addMapping("Back",
  new KeyTrigger(KeyInput.KEY_S));
inputManager.addMapping("Rotate Left",
  new KeyTrigger(KeyInput.KEY_A));
inputManager.addMapping("Rotate Right",
  new KeyTrigger(KeyInput.KEY_D));
inputManager.addMapping("Jump",
  new KeyTrigger(KeyInput.KEY_SPACE));
inputManager.addListener(this, "Rotate Left",
  "Rotate Right");
inputManager.addListener(this, "Forward", "Back", "Jump");
```

4. We customize walking and jumping actions to use physics-aware methods. Physics-aware navigation does not directly set the character's new location; instead it moves the character into a `walkDirection` until it hits an obstacle. Create a few new class fields to track the player's motion.

```
private Vector3f walkDirection = new Vector3f(0,0,0);
private Vector3f viewDirection = new Vector3f(0,0,1);
private boolean rotateLeft = false, rotateRight = false,
                forward = false,   backward = false;
private float speed=8;
```

5. Implement the `onAction()` method of the `ActionListener` to track the keys that the user presses. If a certain `isPressed` Boolean is `true`, we know that the user wants to move in that direction. If the "jump" key is pressed, the `jump()` method of the `playerControl` is called directly. Note that no walking happens here yet!

```
public void onAction(String binding, boolean isPressed, float tpf)
{
    if (binding.equals("Rotate Left"))
    { rotateLeft  = isPressed; }
    else if (binding.equals("Rotate Right"))
    { rotateRight = isPressed; }
    else if (binding.equals("Forward"))
    { forward      = isPressed; }
    else if (binding.equals("Back"))
    { backward     = isPressed; }
    else if (binding.equals("Jump"))
    { playerControl.jump(); }
}
```

6. The actual walking is handled in the update loop. Here you poll the player's rotation and calculate the `walkDirection` and `viewDirection` vectors from it. Then, you use the `setWalkDirection()` and `setViewDirection()` methods to move the physics-aware player.

```
public void simpleUpdate(float tpf) {
    // Get current forward and left vectors of the playerNode:
    Vector3f modelForwardDir =
    playerNode.getWorldRotation().mult(Vector3f.UNIT_Z);
    Vector3f modelLeftDir    =
    playerNode.getWorldRotation().mult(Vector3f.UNIT_X);
    // Determine the change in direction
    walkDirection.set(0, 0, 0);
    if (forward) {
```

```
      walkDirection.addLocal(modelForwardDir.mult(speed));
    } else if (backward) {
      walkDirection.addLocal(modelForwardDir.mult(speed).
      negate());
    }
    playerControl.setWalkDirection(walkDirection); // walk!
    // Determine the change in rotation
    if (rotateLeft) {
      Quaternion rotateL = new Quaternion().
      fromAngleAxis(FastMath.PI * tpf, Vector3f.UNIT_Y);
      rotateL.multLocal(viewDirection);
    } else if (rotateRight) {
      Quaternion rotateR = new Quaternion().
      fromAngleAxis(-FastMath.PI * tpf, Vector3f.UNIT_Y);
      rotateR.multLocal(viewDirection);
    }
  playerControl.setViewDirection(viewDirection); // turn!
  }
```

Run the sample, and press the W, A, S, D keys to walk around. You should now bounce off walls and obstacles when you run into them. Approach the statue, press the Space bar, and try to jump on it. Congrats to this piece of solid workmanship! Just be careful not to fall off the edge of the world.

## What just happened?

As opposed to the standard setLocalTranslation() method, the setWalkDirection() method of the BetterCharacterControl takes the physical environment into account. When the user navigates the player close to a RigidBodyControl obstacle (such as the town model), the method tests for collisions with the obstacle's collision shape first, and stops moving the player in this direction.

The actual walking is handled in the simpleUpdate() loop.

1. The walkDirection vector expresses in which direction the first-person player is going: forward or backward, left or right, or a combination thereof. Before you can calculate the directional vector walkDirection, you get the current world rotation vectors of the playerNode (modelForwardDir and modelLeftDir).

2. Before each step, you reset the walkDirection vector to (0,0,0). Poll the input Booleans to determine whether the user wants to go forward or backward, left or right, or a combination thereof. If a Boolean is true, add the corresponding directional vector to walkDirection. Then, use setWalkDirection(walkDirection) to move the physics-aware player in this combined direction.

3. Turning left or right similarly multiplies the player's current `viewDirection` with a small value that depends on the `update` loop's time per frame (tpf). Then, you use `setViewDirection(viewDirection)` to rotate the player.

Using the demonstrated method, a physical player walks, for example, forward and to the right when the user presses *W* and *D* together.

 The `BetterCharacterControl` is a simple implementation of a walking character. In your game, you may want to control first- and third-person players, animated characters, collisions between players, and other special interactions. Use the default `BetterCharacterControl` as a template to learn from, if you need to write custom controls that implement more complex behavior.

`BetterCharacterControl` gives you access to the following methods:

| Method | Character motion |
| --- | --- |
| `setWalkDirection(new Vector3f(0f,0f,0.1f))` | This moves a physical character. Characters are locked upright to prevent falling over. Use `setWalkDirection(Vector3f.ZERO)` to stop a directional motion. |
| `setViewDirection(new Vector3f(1f,0f,0f))` | This rotates a physical character. Characters are locked upright to prevent falling over. |
| `jump()` | This makes a physical character jump "up", against the direction of gravity. |
| `setDuckedFactor(.5f)` `setDucked(true)` | This toggles whether the character ducks or not, and specifies how small a ducked character becomes. |

Similar to the `RigidBodyControl`, a `BetterCharacterControl` generates a collision shape (from the `com.jme3.bullet.collision.shapes` package). Collision shapes were invented as an optimization, because calculating collisions for every triangle of every mesh is not feasible in a fast-paced video game. Since the collision shape is invisible to the user, you can choose the simplest (and therefore fastest) collision shape that makes sense for an object. A fast collision shape can be as primitive as a sphere, box, or cylinder, or compounds thereof.

For example, a good default collision shape for a walking character is a `CapsuleCollisionShape`—an upright cylinder capped with a semi-sphere on each end. The capsule's roundedness helps the character to walk around corners and to move smoothly on uneven ground.

If you have a very complex physical scene with many default collision shapes, some manual optimization may be in order. Create primitive collision shapes manually (BoxCollisionShape, SphereCollisionShape, CapsuleCollisionShape, and so on from com.jme3.bullet.collision.shapes) for objects that would otherwise receive a complex default collision shape (HullCollisionShape, MeshCollisionShape, CompoundCollisionShape, and so on). You force the usage of a custom collision shape by passing the new shape as first argument into the physics control's constructor.

If you don't specify a collision shape as an argument, the RigidBodyControl() constructor generates a best-guess collision shape internally. For a complex scene, the RigidBodyControl() constructor generates a static mesh-accurate collision shape. The following screenshot shows the town scene with its otherwise invisible CompoundCollisionShape highlighted:

# Fun with rigid bodies

Let's try something more entertaining than a static scene now—what about a bit of destruction physics?

# Time for action – falling bricks

With what you have learned, you can create a scene with a floor, build a wall out of brick geometries, and shoot some cannon balls at it.

1. Make a copy of `Main.java` and name the class `PhysicsFallingBricks.java`. Remember to also refactor the first line of the `main()` method to:

   ```
   PhysicsFallingBricks app = new PhysicsFallingBricks();
   ```

2. Make this a physical game by attaching a `BulletAppState` instance.

   ```
   private BulletAppState bulletAppState;
   @Override
   public void simpleInitApp() {
     bulletAppState = new BulletAppState();
     stateManager.attach(bulletAppState);
   }
   ```

3. Prepare some class fields for the objects in your scene. The scene uses boxes for the bricks, spheres for the cannon balls, and another box for the floor. You also prepare fields for three materials and three `RigidBodyControls`.

   ```
   /** Materials for bricks, cannon balls, floor. */
   Material brickMat, stoneMat, woodMat;
   /** Meshes for bricks, cannon balls, floor. */
   private static final Sphere ballMesh;
   private static final Box    brickMesh;
   private static final Box    floorMesh;
   private static       Node   wallNode;
   /** PhysicsControls for bricks, cannon balls, floor. */
   private RigidBodyControl brickPhy;
   private RigidBodyControl ballPhy;
   private RigidBodyControl floorPhy;
   ```

4. To keep the code more readable and extendable, let's declare a few constants for the size of the bricks and the brick wall.

   ```
   private static final float BRICK_LENGTH = 0.4f;
   private static final float BRICK_WIDTH  = 0.3f;
   private static final float BRICK_HEIGHT = 0.25f;
   private static final float WALL_WIDTH   = 12;
   private static final float WALL_HEIGHT  = 6;
   ```

**5.** All bricks and all cannon balls use the same box and sphere shape, respectively, so go ahead and initialize the meshes in a static block.

```
static {
    floorMesh  = new Box(Vector3f.ZERO, 10f, 0.5f, 5f);
    brickMesh  = new Box(Vector3f.ZERO,
                    BRICK_LENGTH, BRICK_HEIGHT, BRICK_WIDTH);
    ballMesh   = new Sphere( 32, 32, 0.25f, true, false);
    ballMesh.setTextureMode(TextureMode.Projected);
        floorMesh.scaleTextureCoordinates( new Vector2f(4f,4f) );
}
```

We use these objects to initialize the scene with a wall made of brick geometries standing on a floor.

**1.** In the `simpleInitApp()` method, you initialize objects, and set up the scene. Create three `.j3m` files as you learned in the previous chapter (or use the sample materials provided with this book).

```
@Override
public void simpleInitApp() {
    ...
    brickMat  =
    assetManager.loadMaterial("Materials/brick.j3m");
    stoneMat  =
    assetManager.loadMaterial("Materials/pebbles.j3m");
    woodMat   =
    assetManager.loadMaterial("Materials/bark.j3m");
```

**2.** Create a floor, a simple box geometry with a wood material and a `RigidBodyControl`. Since the floor is static, set its mass to zero. Move the floor a bit down to ensure it's below the lowest brick.

```
Geometry floorGeo = new Geometry("Floor", floorMesh);
floorGeo.setMaterial(woodMat);
floorGeo.move( 0f, - BRICK_HEIGHT *2f, 0f );
rootNode.attachChild(floorGeo);
// PhysicsControl with zero mass,
// and default BoxCollisionShape:
floorPhy = new RigidBodyControl(0.0f);
floorGeo.addControl(floorPhy);
bulletAppState.getPhysicsSpace().add(floorPhy);
```

3. Create a `wall` node that groups together several rows of brick geometries. The following loop calculates the offsets, and calls a `makeBrick()` method that returns brick geometries. In the end, you attach the wall node to the `rootNode`.

```
wallNode=new Node("wall");
float offsetH = BRICK_LENGTH / 3;
float offsetV = 0;
for (int j = 0; j < WALL_HEIGHT; j++) {
  for (int i = 0; i < WALL_WIDTH; i++) {
    Vector3f brickPos = new Vector3f(
        offsetH + BRICK_LENGTH * 2.1f * i
        - (BRICK_LENGTH*WALL_WIDTH),
        offsetV + BRICK_HEIGHT,
        0f );
    wallNode.attachChild(makeBrick(brickPos));
  }
  offsetH = -offsetH;
  offsetV += 2 * BRICK_HEIGHT;
}
rootNode.attachChild(wallNode);
```

4. Implement the `makeBrick()` method to create the actual physical bricks, using the `brickMesh` shape and `brickMat` material. Position the brick geometry at its start position `loc`. Create a `RigidBodyControl` and specify a mass (here 5 kg), so the bricks become dynamic physical objects.

```
public Geometry makeBrick(Vector3f loc) {
  Geometry brickGeo = new Geometry("brick", brickMesh);
  brickGeo.setMaterial(brickMat);
  wallNode.attachChild(brickGeo);
  brickGeo.move(loc);
  // PhysicsControl with 5f mass, default BoxCollisionShape:
  brickPhy = new RigidBodyControl(5f);
  brickGeo.addControl(brickPhy);
  bulletAppState.getPhysicsSpace().add(brickPhy);
}
```

5. As always, add an `AmbientLight` and a `DirectionalLight` in the `simpleInitApp()` method.

When you run the code now, you see a physical brick wall on a physical wooden floor. All that is missing now is some cannon balls to "interact" with it.

Frames per second: 411

## What just happened?

You created a wall out of several rows of identical brick geometries. You run two loops over the height and width of the wall, from bottom to top. The first loop lays a row of bricks. After completing a row, the second loop moves the horizontal offset back to the start, and moves the vertical offset one row up.

The core of the loop calculates the next brick position, and attaches individual bricks to the wallNode. The makeBrick() method returns the physical brick geometries. Re-using static meshes for objects of the same shape (here bricks) is a neat trick that saves memory, especially in more complex scenes.

The `RigidBodyControl` constructor internally generates a default `CollisionShape`, in this case a `BoxCollisionShape` for a `Box` mesh. You only need to specify the mass.

```
brickPhy = new RigidBodyControl(5f);
```

Physical objects with a mass (such as falling bricks, rolling boulders, and pushable crates) are "dynamic"; this means they are affected by gravity and forces. The mass of dynamic physical objects is a float value in kilograms larger than zero. Contrast this to static physical objects (such as floors, walls, and whole levels), which always get a mass of zero.

```
floorPhy = new RigidBodyControl(0.0f);
```

Typically, it's fine to use the default collision shape that `RigidBodyControl()` generates.

# Time for action – flying cannon balls

Let's keep the default navigational inputs in our `PhysicsFallingBricks.java`, and simply add a shoot action. Every time the user clicks, you want to shoot a cannon ball from the camera position forward.

1. Write a `shootCannonBall()` method that creates a new physical geometry `ballGeo` from our `ballMesh` shape and `stoneMat` material. The `setLinearVelocity()` line defines the initial speed and direction of the object. In this case, we accelerate the cannon ball forward.

```
public void shootCannonBall() {
    Geometry ballGeo = new Geometry("cannon ball", ballMesh);
    ballGeo.setMaterial(stoneMat);
    ballGeo.setLocalTranslation(cam.getLocation());
    rootNode.attachChild(ballGeo);
    ballPhy = new RigidBodyControl(5f);
    ballPhy.setCcdSweptSphereRadius(.1f);
    ballPhy.setCcdMotionThreshold(0.001f);
    ballPhy.setLinearVelocity(cam.getDirection().mult(50));
    ballGeo.addControl(ballPhy);
    bulletAppState.getPhysicsSpace().add(ballPhy);
}
```

2. Create an `actionListener` and a `SHOOT` string constant. Test whether a `SHOOT` action was triggered. The `SHOOT` action calls the `shootCannonBall()` method.

```
private static final String SHOOT = "shoot";
private ActionListener actionListener = new ActionListener() {
    public void onAction(String name, boolean keyPressed, float tpf) {
```

```
    if (name.equals(SHOOT) && !keyPressed) {
      shootCannonBall();
    }
  }
};
```

**3.** In the `simpleInitApp()` method, register a `SHOOT` input mapping for the left mouse button. Register the `SHOOT` action to the `actionListener`.

```
inputManager.addMapping(SHOOT,
    new MouseButtonTrigger(MouseInput.BUTTON_LEFT));
inputManager.addListener(actionListener, SHOOT);
```

Run the code! A left-click now creates a new cannon ball with the given initial velocity. The cannon ball appears in the scene, it flies forward, hits the brick wall, and exerts a physical force on the bricks. Bricks and cannon balls can bounce off one another, and they also bounce off the floor.

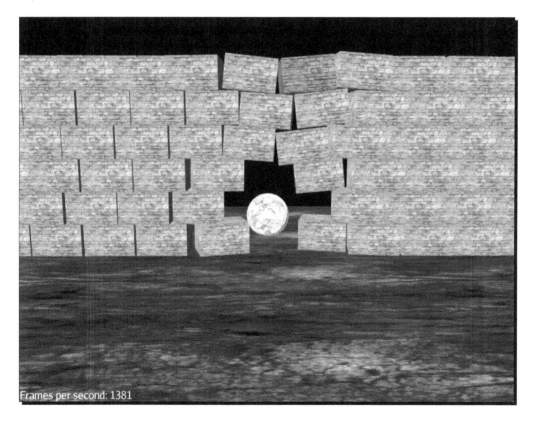

## *What just happened?*

Awesome, you implemented a physical shooting action that lets you tear down a brick wall with a few mouse clicks!

Similar to the bricks, the `RigidBodyControl` constructor generated a default `SphereCollisionShape` for the cannon ball. Since cannon balls are dynamic physical objects, you specify their mass in the constructor.

```
ballPhy = new RigidBodyControl(5f);
```

After each click, the `shootCannonBall()` method creates a new cannon ball object, moves it in front of the camera, and attaches it to the `rootNode`. When you made the bricks appear in the scene, they just sat there, doing their best brick wall impression—but for cannon balls, you have more exciting plans. Since you create cannon balls with an initial linear velocity, they immediately accelerate forward.

The direction and speed of a linear velocity is expressed as the direction and length of a vector. Since you want to shoot the ball from the camera forward, you use the `cam.getDirection()` vector. The returned camera direction vector is normalized; this means it's only 1 world unit short. Since the length corresponds to speed, your cannon ball would be very slow. To increase the speed, multiply the vector by a constant as follows:

```
ballPhy.setLinearVelocity(cam.getDirection().mult(50f));
```

When you shoot a cannon ball, spin a billiard ball, or tilt and push a crate on the floor, you exert physical forces on dynamic objects. The following methods move or rotate physics objects:

| The RigidBodyControl method | Motion |
| --- | --- |
| `setAngularVelocity(v)` | This sets the current rotational speed of the object. The x, y, and z components of the vector are the speed of rotation around the respective axis. (Rotation) |
| `setLinearVelocity(v)` | This sets the current linear speed of this object. (Translation) |
| `applyCentralForce(v)` | This pushes an object over time with an additional moment v, expressed as `Vector3f`, applied to the center. (Translation) |
| `applyForce(v,p)` | This pushes an object over time with additional force v, applied to a non-central point p. (Translation) |
| `applyTorque(v)` | This twists an object over time additionally around its axes. The x, y, and z components of the `Vector3f` v specify the torque around the respective axis. (Rotation) |

| The RigidBodyControl method | Motion |
|---|---|
| `applyTorqueImpulse(v)` | This applies an instantaneous torque v to the object. The x, y, and z components of the `Vector3f` v specify the torque around the respective axis. (Rotation) |
| `applyImpulse(v,p)` | This applies an instantaneous impulse v, expressed as `Vector3f`, to the object at a point p relative to the object. (Translation) |
| `clearForces()` | This cancels all forces and stops all current motion. |

Be aware that a real-time physics simulation takes shortcuts wherever possible to speed up the scene. Some simplifications result in a lack of precision for fast dynamic objects. If your cannon balls fly through obstacles, you can adjust the precision of the simulation by changing the following values:

```
ballPhy.setCcdSweptSphereRadius(.1f);
ballPhy.setCcdMotionThreshold(0.001f);
```

The motion threshold is the amount of motion that has to happen before the physics simulation switches to the continuous motion detection for fast-moving objects. Bullet does not use the full collision shape for continuous collision detection; instead it uses a capsule-like shape ("swept sphere") to simulate the moving object. This approximation allows real-time handling of many objects, but can cause strange behaviors, such as very fast objects passing through one another or getting stuck.

# Time for action – predict the explosion

Play around with each physics property in `PhysicsFallingBricks` to get a feeling for the behavior that they control. Try to predict what happens in each of the following cases:

- Give the floor a mass of more than `0.0f`
- Set the mass of bricks, or cannon balls, to a higher (`50f`) or lower value (`0.5f`)
- Set the cannon balls' velocity to a higher (`100f`) or lower value (`10f`)
- Move `floorGeo` a few world units higher or lower along the y axis
- Set the friction of bricks to a higher value using `brickPhy.setFriction(20f);` or a lower value using `brickPhy.setFriction(0.2f);`
- Set a property (such as `friction`) of a physics control before adding the control to its geometry
- Just for laughs – set the friction of all bricks to zero
- Just for laughs – set the friction of the floor to zero

Run the code with each change and try to explain what is happening. Hint – one case causes an explosion-like impact that collapses the wall, a second one results in a `NullPointerException`—and two are just hilarious.

## What just happened?

Experimenting with the properties shows you that mass has an impact on the intensity of forces. Heavier cannon balls blow bigger holes into the wall, heavier bricks make the wall more sturdy. A floor with a mass is, however, a bad idea. Any object with mass is no longer static and is affected by gravity, causing your whole scene to fall "down" (and get culled).

Velocity has a similar impact on intensity as mass. Faster cannon balls smash harder into the wall, whereas slow balls bounce off the wall weakly. Faster cannon balls, however, are also harder to simulate and may erroneously pass through obstacles.

You also see that if you move the floor lower before positioning the bricks, the bricks simply fall down and land on the floor after they appear in the scene. If the floor is so high that it intersects with the bottom row of bricks, however, you cause a physically impossible situation. The bottom row of bricks will be pushed away vigorously, which makes the wall collapse.

Friction is a positive float value larger than zero. `1.0f` is a good value to start with. Higher friction prevents objects from sliding around, and makes them harder to push. High friction is useful when simulating sticky, rough, uneven surfaces. Friction values between `1.0f` and `0.0f` make objects increasingly slippery, so they slide when pushed. Low friction is useful when simulating ice or slides.

You can modify the following physical properties on a physics control object such as `RigidBodyControl`:

| The RigidBodyControl method | Property |
| --- | --- |
| `setFriction(1f)` | This specifies friction. Rough surfaces have a friction value greater than `1.0f`. Slippery surfaces have a friction between `1.0f` and `0.0f`. |
| `setMass(1f)` | This specifies mass. Dynamic objects have masses greater than `0.0f`. Static immobile obstacles (for example, buildings and terrains) have a mass of `0.0f`. |
| `setRestitution(0.0f)` | This specifies bounciness. To create a rubber object, specify a value greater than `0.0f`. This is CPU-intensive and should be used sparingly. |
| `setPhysicsLocation()` | This positions a dynamic object. Do not use `setLocalTranslation()` or `move()`! |
| `setPhysicsRotation()` | This rotates a dynamic object. Do not use `setLocalRotate()` or `rotate()`! |

| The RigidBodyControl method | Property |
| --- | --- |
| `setGravity(new Vector3f (0f,-10f,0f))` | You can change the individual gravity vector of dynamic objects even after adding them to the physics space. |
| `setCcdMotionThreshold (.1f)` | This is the amount of motion in one physics tick that triggers the continuous motion detection. |

Add the control to its spatial before you set any properties on the control, otherwise the control throws a `NullPointerException` at compile time or runtime.

# Dynamic, static, and kinematic

You can now create static walls and floors, and dynamic objects such as bricks and cannon balls that are affected by forces. Next to static and dynamic objects, the physics simulation supports a third type of physical object, the kinematic object.

A kinematic object is not affected by forces or gravity (similar to a static object), but it can move around and push dynamic objects (similar to other dynamic objects). Typical use cases for kinematic objects in games are airplanes, airships, moving platforms, elevators, drawbridges, and conveyor belts.

## Time for action – an elevator platform

Let's build a scene that uses all three types of physical objects: dynamic, static, and kinematic. The static part of the scene contains a floor (a horizontal box), a slope (a rotated box), and a wall (a vertical box). Later, we add a kinematic moving platform (a cuboid box) and a dynamic ball (a sphere), and then see how they interact.

1.  Make a copy of `Main.java` and name the class `PhysicsKinematic.java`. Remember to also refactor the first line of the `main()` method to the following:

    ```
    PhysicsKinematic app = new PhysicsKinematic();
    ```

2.  Make this a physical game by attaching a `BulletAppState` instance.

    ```
    private BulletAppState bulletAppState;
    @Override
    public void simpleInitApp() {
        bulletAppState = new BulletAppState();
        stateManager.attach(bulletAppState);
        ...
    }
    ```

3. Re-use the materials from `PhysicsFallingBricks`, and initialize them in the `simpleInitApp()` method. As usual, add light sources.

```
private Material brickMat, stoneMat, woodMat;
public void simpleInitApp() {
    ...
    brickMat =
    assetManager.loadMaterial("Materials/brick.j3m");
    stoneMat =
    assetManager.loadMaterial("Materials/pebbles.j3m");
    woodMat  = assetManager.loadMaterial("Materials/bark.j3m");
}
```

4. Initialize the static part of the scene in the `simpleInitApp()` method: a wall, a slope, and the floor. In our example, they are all `Box` geometries resized and rotated into position. Attach them all to a `sceneNode`.

```
private RigidBodyControl scenePhy;
public void simpleInitApp() {
    ...
    Node sceneNode = new Node("Scene");

    /* Create and attach a floor geometry */
    Box floorMesh = new Box(Vector3f.ZERO, 10f, 0.5f, 10f);
    Geometry floorGeo = new Geometry("Floor", floorMesh);
    floorGeo.setMaterial(stoneMat);
    floorGeo.move(0, -.1f, 0);
    sceneNode.attachChild(floorGeo);

    /* Create and attach a slope geometry */
    Box slopeMesh = new Box(Vector3f.ZERO, 6f, 0.1f, 5f);
    Geometry slopeGeo = new Geometry("Slope", slopeMesh);
    slopeGeo.setMaterial(brickMat);
    slopeGeo.rotate(0, 0, FastMath.DEG_TO_RAD * 50);
    slopeGeo.move(4f, 4f, 0);
    sceneNode.attachChild(slopeGeo);

    /* Create and attach a wall geometry */
    Box wallMesh = new Box(Vector3f.ZERO, 5f, 0.4f, 5f);
    Geometry wallGeo = new Geometry("Wall", wallMesh);
    wallGeo.setMaterial(brickMat);
    wallGeo.rotate(0, 0, FastMath.DEG_TO_RAD * 90);
    wallGeo.move(-3.5f, 2, 0);
    sceneNode.attachChild(wallGeo);
    ...
}
```

**5.** Make the `sceneNode` (and everything attached to it) solid by adding a `RigidBodyControl()` with mass zero. Attach the `sceneNode` to the `rootNode`, and add the `RigidBodyControl` to the physics space.

```
private RigidBodyControl scenePhy;
public void simpleInitApp() {
    ...
    scenePhy = new RigidBodyControl(0.0f);
    sceneNode.addControl(scenePhy);
    bulletAppState.getPhysicsSpace().add(floorPhy);
    rootNode.attachChild(sceneNode);
}
```

**6.** Create the kinematic elevator platform. Our simple elevator is a `Box` geometry attached to the `rootNode`. Add a `RigidBodyControl` with a mass of 100 kg to the kinematic `platformGeo`. Set its `setKinematic()` property to `true`. Add `platformPhy` to the physics space as usual.

```
private static final String ELEVATOR = "Elevator";
public void simpleInitApp() {
    ...
    Box platformMesh = new Box(Vector3f.ZERO, 2f, 0.5f, 5f);
    platformGeo = new Geometry(ELEVATOR, platformMesh);
    platformGeo.setMaterial(woodMat);
    platformGeo.move(-1, 2, 0);
    rootNode.attachChild(platformGeo);
    RigidBodyControl platformPhy =
        new RigidBodyControl(100.0f);
    platformGeo.addControl(platformPhy);
    platformPhy.setKinematic(true);
    bulletAppState.getPhysicsSpace().add(platformPhy);
}
```

**7.** Write a test in the `simpleUpdate()` loop that moves the platform up and down. Note that kinematic objects use non-physical methods, such as `move()`.

```
private static final float TOPFLOOR = 6f;
private boolean isPlatformOnTop  = false;
@Override
public void simpleUpdate(float tpf) {
    if (!isPlatformOnTop &&
        platformGeo.getLocalTranslation().getY() < TOPFLOOR) {
        platformGeo.move(0f, tpf, 0f);
    }
```

```
        if (!isPlatformOnTop &&
            platformGeo.getLocalTranslation().getY() >= TOPFLOOR) {
            isPlatformOnTop = true;
        }
        if (isPlatformOnTop &&
            platformGeo.getLocalTranslation().getY() <= .5f) {
            isPlatformOnTop = false;
        }
        if (isPlatformOnTop &&
            platformGeo.getLocalTranslation().getY() > .5f) {
            platformGeo.move(0f, -tpf * 4, 0f);
        }
    }
```

Run the code. You should see a simple scene with an elevator platform moving up and down.

## What just happened?

Physical objects can respond differently to forces, such as gravity or collisions. You have now encountered dynamic, static, and kinematic behavior.

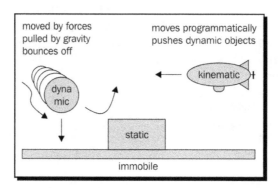

Static objects (such as walls and floors) are immobile solid obstacles. Since static objects never move, they can be positioned in mid-air. No forces affect them; therefore, their mass is irrelevant, and always zero. Dynamic objects bounce off static objects.

```
    floorGeo.setMass(0f);
    floorGeo.setKinematic(false);
```

Dynamic objects (such as balls and bricks) are fully affected by physical forces and must therefore have a mass. When you position a dynamic object in mid-air, gravity makes it fall. A colliding object exerts forces on a dynamic object, and pushes it away. Dynamic objects bounce off dynamic, static, and kinematic objects.

```
ballGeo.setMass(10f);
ballGeo.setKinematic(false);
ballGeo.setPhysicsLocation(new Vector3f(0, 1, 0));
```

Kinematic objects (such as elevator platforms, airplanes, and airships) are solid, but they are not affected by gravity, and do not react to any physical forces. When trying to move kinematic objects through static and other kinematic objects, they can push dynamic objects. The intensity of the kinematic object's effect on dynamic objects depends on the kinematic object's speed and mass.

Remember that you move kinematic objects programmatically (for example, from the update loop) using non-physical methods `setLocalTranslation()` or `move()`.

```
platformGeo.setMass(100f);
platformGeo.setKinematic(true);
platformGeo.move(1f,0f,0f);
```

The following table shows you how you decide which type of solid object to choose:

|  | Static | Dynamic | Kinematic |
| --- | --- | --- | --- |
| Is it moved by forces? (gravity, torque, velocity, and so on) | No | Yes | No |
| Does it only move programmatically? | No | No | Yes |
| Does it have a mass? | No | Yes | Yes |
| Which methods do you use? | `setLocal Translation()`, `move()`, and so on | `setPhysics Location()`, `applyForce()`, and so on | `setLocal Translation()`, `move()`, and so on |
| Examples | Floor, wall, tree, and furniture | Ball, brick, and crate | Elevator, platform, airplane, and airship |

Since they are unaffected by gravity, you can position kinematic objects "in mid-air" and attach special dynamic objects to them. These dynamic objects are called **hinges** and **joints**. You use them for simulating physical pulley chains, rope bridges, or pendulums. You can find more information on this special case on the `jmonkeyengine.org` wiki.

# Time for action – react to collisions

Let's add a dynamic object to the scene to see what happens when it falls onto the platform. You already know how to create a nicely textured sphere and turn it into a physical ball.

Open `PhysicsKinematic.java` again and add the following method:

```
private RigidBodyControl ballPhy;
private static final String BALL = "Ball";
public void dropBall() {
    Sphere ballMesh = new Sphere(32, 32, .75f, true, false);
    ballMesh.setTextureMode(TextureMode.Projected);
    TangentBinormalGenerator.generate(ballMesh);
    Geometry ballGeo = new Geometry(BALL, ballMesh);
    ballGeo.setMaterial(stoneMat);
    rootNode.attachChild(ballGeo);
    /** Create physical ball and add to physics space. */
    ballPhy = new RigidBodyControl(5f);
    ballGeo.addControl(ballPhy);
    bulletAppState.getPhysicsSpace().add(ballPhy);
    ballPhy.setPhysicsLocation(new Vector3f(0, 10, 0));
}
```

Call `dropBall();` from `simpleInitApp()`, and run the app. You should see the ball fall and land on the moving platform. When the platform moves up, it pushes the ball up with it. When the platform goes down, the slightly inert ball is affected by gravity and falls down onto the platform again.

Let's add a listener that detects the collision. This way you can implement how your game responds to a collision.

1. Make `PhysicsKinematic.java` implement the `PhysicsCollisionListener` interface from the `com.jme3.bullet.collision` package.

   ```
   public class PhysicsKinematic extends SimpleApplication
       implements PhysicsCollisionListener { … }
   ```

2. The `PhysicsCollisionListener` interface requires you to implement the `collision()` method. We want to test whether the spatials named BALL and ELEVATOR have collided. Depending on that, we set a Boolean isBallOnPlatform.

   ```
   private boolean isBallOnPlatform = false;
   public void collision(PhysicsCollisionEvent event) {
   ```

```
        if ( (event.getNodeA().getName().equals(BALL)
            && event.getNodeB().getName().equals(ELEVATOR) )
        || (  event.getNodeA().getName().equals(ELEVATOR)
            && event.getNodeB().getName().equals(BALL) ) )
        {
            isBallOnPlatform = true;
        } else {
            isBallOnPlatform = false;
        }
    }
```

3.  In your `simpleInitApp()` method, register the `PhysicsCollisionListener`
    (this class) to the physics space.

    ```
    bulletAppState.getPhysicsSpace().addCollisionListener(this);
    ```

4.  Replace your whole `simpleUpdate()` method with the following variant that tests
    for the `isBallOnPlatform` Boolean before moving the platform:

    ```
    public void simpleUpdate(float tpf) {
        if (isBallOnPlatform &&
                platformGeo.getLocalTranslation().getY() < TOPFLOOR) {
          platformGeo.move(0f, tpf, 0f);
        }
        if (isBallOnPlatform &&
                platformGeo.getLocalTranslation().getY() >= TOPFLOOR)
        {
          isPlatformOnTop = true;
        }
        if (!isBallOnPlatform &&
                platformGeo.getLocalTranslation().getY() > .5f) {
          isPlatformOnTop = false;
          platformGeo.move(0f, -tpf * 4, 0f);
        }
    }
    ```

Run the code. The ball landing on the platform triggers the rising platform. If the ball does
not roll off, the platform now stops on the top floor.

# What just happened?

When the physics simulation detects collisions, it does more than only calculating and exerting forces on the colliding parties. Additionally, it can report properties of the impact as a `PhysicsCollisionEvent` (from the `com.jme3.bullet.collision` package), and let you trigger actions in response. If you have classes that need to be informed about collision events in the physics space, give them access to the `bulletAppState`, and make them implement the `com.jme3.bullet.collision.PhysicsCollisionListener` interface.

```
public class MyClass implements PhysicsCollisionListener {
    public void collision(PhysicsCollisionEvent event) {
        // Test for event.getNodeA().getName() and
        // event.getNodeB().getName(), and implement interaction
    }
}
```

The `collision()` method gives you access to a `PhysicsCollisionEvent` object that contains properties of the event. First, you are interested in the identity of the two nodes that collided, `event.getNodeA()` and `event.getNodeB()`, so you can define the action to trigger when this pair collides. You cannot know which of the two will be node A or node B; always test for either variant. If you want to use properties from the event object, do not pass the event object to other methods, because it is reset when the `collision()` method ends.

 Did you notice that the objects BALL and ELEVATOR are string constants? When you create geometries whose collisions will be relevant for the game, it's a best practice to name them using string constants instead of plain strings. An `equals()` test can fail due to a simple typo—but when you mistype a string constant, the compiler warns you.

When do we use the `com.jme3.bullet.collision.PhysicsCollisionListener` interface, and when not?

- If you just want "balls rolling, bricks falling", you do not need to implement the `PhysicsCollisionListener`. Without it, a collision simply means that physical forces are applied automatically.

- If you want to respond to a `PhysicsCollisionEvent` and trigger a custom action, implement the `PhysicsCollisionListener`. Typical actions include increasing a counter (for example, score points), decreasing a counter (for example, health points), triggering an effect (for example, an explosion), playing a sound (for example, a bang), and countless more, depending on your game.

The PhysicsCollisionEvent gives you access to detailed information about the collision. You already know the event object can identify which nodes have collided. Additionally, you can get details about how they collided; for example, look at the following table:

| The PhysicsCollisionEvent method | Purpose |
| --- | --- |
| getNodeA()<br>getNodeB() | These are the two participants in the collision. You cannot know in advance whether a node will be recorded as A or B, you always have to consider both cases. |
| getAppliedImpulse() | A float value representing the collision's impulse. |
| getCombinedFriction() | A float value representing the collision's friction. |
| getCombinedRestitution() | A float value representing the collision's bounciness. |

After the collision() method ends, the PhysicsCollisionEvent object is cleared. If you still need any of the values, you must assign them to local variables.

# Time for action – timing forces correctly

We want the platform to go down after the ball rolls off, but currently, the ball doesn't have enough momentum to roll off by itself. Let's give it a little push.

1. Open PhysicsKinematic.java again and make it implement the PhysicsTickListener interface.

```
public class PhysicsKinematic extends SimpleApplication
        implements PhysicsCollisionListener, PhysicsTickListener
{…}
```

2. The interface requires you to implement two methods: prePhysicsTick() and physicsTick(). Use the prePhysicsTick() method to apply a pushing force on the ball when the platform reaches the top floor.

```
public void prePhysicsTick(PhysicsSpace space, float tpf) {
        if (isBallOnPlatform && isPlatformOnTop) {
            ballPhy.applyImpulse(new Vector3f(2, 0, 0),
                            new Vector3f(0, 0, 0));
        }
    }
public void physicsTick(PhysicsSpace space, float tpf) {}
```

**3.** Remember to register the `TickListener` (this class) to the physics space.

```
public void simpleInitApp() {
    …
    bulletAppState.getPhysicsSpace().addTickListener(this);
    …
}
```

Run the code. Again, the ball falls onto the platform (`isBallOnPlatform` is true) and triggers the elevator to rise. Now, when the elevator is on top (`isPlatformOnTop` is `true`), the test is `true`, and an impulse pushes the ball off the platform. The platform moves down, while the ball rolls down the slope and lands again on the platform.

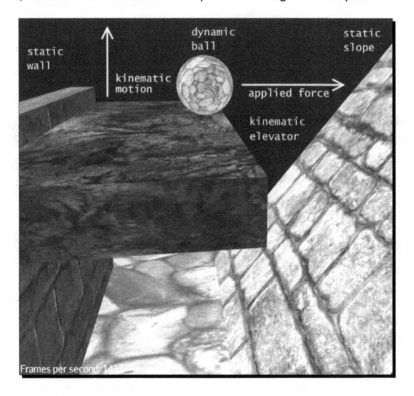

## What just happened?

If you apply forces in the update loop, they can be "out of cycle" with the physics simulation. It will work sometimes, but in random intervals, the simulation will miss calls and forces are not applied. Remember that the jBullet physics simulation is stepped at a framerate of 60 physics ticks per second. Applying forces (or checking for collisions) only makes sense during a physics update, which does not happen in every frame of the update loop. To time forces right, you need to implement the `PhysicsTickListener` interface.

Use `prePhysicsTick()` to apply forces right in time before the next physics step.
Use `physicsTick()` to poll the state right in time after the physics step.

```
public class PhysicsKinematic implements PhysicsTickListener {
  public void prePhysicsTick(PhysicsSpace space, float f){
    // apply forces here
  }
  public void physicsTick(PhysicsSpace space, float f){
    // poll the new state, e.g. test for overlapping objects
  }
}
```

When do we use the `com.jme3.bullet.PhysicsTickListener` interface,
and when not?

- When you apply forces, you must make that call from a `prePhysicsTick()`
  method of `PhysicsTickListener`. The `PhysicsTickListener` makes
  certain all forces are applied in sync with the next physics tick.

- When your game merely polls the current state (for example, location of falling
  bricks) of physical objects, but doesn't apply extra forces, you don't need a
  `PhysicsTickListener`. You can poll the state from anywhere.

# My whole world is falling apart

A physics simulation can be quite a loose cannon. Don't be surprised when physical objects
jitter or are unceremoniously hurled out of the scene. Congratulations, you have created a
physically impossible state! Most likely, you positioned two solid objects too close to each
other. How do you find the source of the problem?

- Activate the physics debug mode to visualize the actual collision shapes. Some
  dynamic objects receive `HullCollisionShapes` by default, which are not
  mesh-accurate. Make certain that no collision shapes overlap. You can render the
  (otherwise invisible) collision shapes as wireframes with the following command:

  `bulletAppState.getPhysicsSpace().enableDebug(assetManager); // on`

  `bulletAppState.getPhysicsSpace().disableDebug()           // off`

- Make sure you do not smash dynamic or static objects into one another by using
  `setLocalTranslation()` or `move()` instead of using a physics-aware method.

- Remember to check unintended overlaps with floor or wall geometries—the whole
  scene has a collision shape to consider too.

# LEET skillz – learn from the pros

Using physics everywhere in a game sounds like a cool idea, but this feature is easily overused. Although physics controls are "put to sleep" while they don't move, the complexity of a world built solely out of dynamic physics controls exceeds your computer's capabilities quite fast.

But other game developers use physics all the time, so why can't you? Their physics simulation is so awesome that whole buildings break apart in real time! Actually, no. Don't let them fool you. Professional video games simply use a clever mix of physics, non-physical kinematics, and visual effects to give you the illusion of a fully physical world.

Unless players are walking around in it, a scene element has no collision shape at all. While an explosion effect obstructs your view, a static model is detached and replaced by (fast rendering, non-physical) debris models. The debris models fly on kinematic (pre-recorded, non-physical) paths before they hit the ground. After the dust settles, a select few pieces—only the ones that the player can reach—receive a physics control. Strategically placed static obstacles ensure that the player does not stumble upon the remaining (non-physical) scenery sets in the background.

In general, don't waste cycles on scene elements that the player will never interact with. Arches in a gothic cathedral may be impressive, but unless you invented a Spiderman versus Bazooka game, no collisions will ever happen up there. Don't give non-interactive geometries expensive physics controls or mesh-accurate collision shapes.

Next time you play an action game, try to spot where the game designers are tricking you into believing that the whole scene is physical, and how they are pretending that all physical objects have individual shapes and sizes. Now that you have started developing games yourself, remember what you learned in this chapter—and look behind the curtain.

## Pop quiz

Which of the following statements about physics properties are true?

1. A moving kinematic object can push dynamic objects, although it uses the non-physical `move()` method.

2. A static physical floor needs a mass and a collision shape to become solid.

3. The main update loop ensures that physical forces are applied to dynamic objects in sync with the simulation.

4. A dynamic physical crate does not need an explicit mass if it uses the default collision shape of the `RigidBodyControl` constructor.

# Have a go hero – rubber balls versus stacked crates

Not all games need a physics simulation. In the Tower Defense project that we started, mobile creeps walk on an even floor in straight lines toward the player base. If you can implement behavior without needing a physics app state, non-physical collision methods (such as ray casting) are preferable, because they leave you more cycles for other game mechanics.

Instead of adding to the Tower Defense game, let's have some fun with the town sample, or another model of your choice.

1. Load a model of your choice, such as `quake3level.zip` or `town.zip`. Make it solid, and add a physical first-person player. Use what you learned in `PhysicsTown`.

   ```
   assetManager.registerLocator(
     "http://jmonkeyengine.googlecode.com/files/quake3level.zip",
     HttpZipLocator.class );
   ```

2. Add some crates to the scene, dynamic `RigidBodys` with a wooden material and a mass. Re-use one `BoxCollisionShape` and `Box` mesh. Use what you learned in `PhysicsFallingBricks`. The physical player can push the crates around in the scene.

3. Allow the player to pick crates. Use the already familiar ray casting algorithm to let the player pick a crate (and deselect any previous crate). Create a copy of the wooden material with an active glow property, and swap materials to mark a crate as selected.

4. Allow the player to stack crates. Assign an input key that applies a constant, central, upward force to the selected crate while the key is pressed (`AnalogListener`). Test the y coordinate of the crate to limit the lifting height for crates.

5. Allow the player to transport crates. Add an elevator platform to the scene that allows the first-person player to get from the ground level to higher floors or rooftops. Use what you learned about kinematic objects and collision listeners.

 Each geometry needs its own instance of a physics control—but it's a best practice to re-use collision shapes and meshes. If you have many geometries of the same size, prepare one collision shape for all of them and pass the shape as first argument into the `RigidBodyControl` constructor. In a warehouse full of dynamic bricks, crates, and barrels, limiting the variety of container sizes can gain you a few frames per second.

Let's add one more type of dynamic object.

1. Add an automatic rubber ball cannon to a central place. Re-use one SphereCollisionShape and Sphere mesh.

2. In PhysicsFallingBricks, you shot cannon balls from the camera position; now, shoot rubber balls from a fixed coordinate in the scene. Use the update loop to track how close the player is to the cannon, and start shooting when he approaches. Accelerate the ball in the direction toward the player.

3. Use the restitution property of the physics control to make the balls bouncy.

 You can determine the distance between two coordinates using float dist = end.distance(start);. You can determine the directional vector from one coordinate to another using Vector3f dir = end.substract(start);.

Just for fun! What happens if you create a BoxCollisionShape and use it in the rubber ball's RigidBodyControl constructors? What happens if you create a SphereCollisionShape and use it in the crates' RigidBodyControl constructors?

# Summary

In this chapter, you have learned how to add realism to your game by making use of simulated physics.

You know how to activate the physics simulation by attaching a BulletAppState to the application. You have learned that you add a physics control instance to each physical geometry, and register the control to the physics space. You know when to use different types of PhysicsControls and CollisionShapes.

You know what static, kinematic, and dynamic physics behavior is, and how these types of physical objects interact. You are aware that overusing physics has a huge performance impact, and you have learned tricks about how to use CPU-intensive features smartly.

 The jBullet physics simulation can also calculate the swinging motions of hinges and joints (useful for chains or rope bridges), and there is also a class that implements typical vehicle behavior (useful for race cars and motorcycles). You can find more details about these specialized use cases of physics on the jmonkeyengine.org wiki.

If you'd start developing now, you could already write a solid, good-looking little game! It's all downhill from here. But don't lay down the book yet; you wouldn't want to miss the shiny enhancements in the next chapter—special effects!

# 7

# Adding Spark to Your Game

*You already know how to take the idea in your head and turn it into an interactive scene with nicely textured models and physical behavior. You are ready to add the final touches and effects to your game. jMonkeyEngine supports two types of effects: particle systems and post-processor filters.*

**Particle systems** *use series of 2D images (sprites) to create the impression of moving swarms and fuzzy clouds, which cannot be visualized by 3D meshes. Particle effects come to the rescue—whether you need fire and smoke, explosions and spells, or butterflies and soap bubbles.*

**Post-processor filters** *work on a larger scale and provide you with screen-wide effects such as focal blurs and blooms. Filter effects make use of the engine's shader architecture and can produce anything from realistic shadows to artistic cartoon styles.*

In this chapter, you will learn some nifty tricks that will make your game more exciting and immersive:

* How to stir up dust and smoke, and let sparks fly
* How to set stuff on fire, and blow everything up
* How to cast shadows in the light and glow in the dark
* How to focus on nearby objects, and blur far-away objects
* How to draw cartoons with no graphic artists

Let's start with particle systems and then proceed to scene processors and filters.

# Particle effects

Meshes can be sculpted, animated, and made translucent—but when a game scene requires smoke, sparks, or flames, then meshes just don't make the cut. When you want to simulate a fuzzy shape in real time, particles are the weapon of choice. A particle system has two secret ingredients: sprites and an emitter. In the following screenshot, you see a particle system that uses a 9-frame sprite animation (left) to simulate spinning flying pieces of debris (right):

The heart of a particle system is the `ParticleEmitter` object (from the `com.jme3.effect` package). The emitter object determines the start location of the effect and stores the texture and animation properties. To add the effect to the scene, you attach a particle emitter to a node under the root node like any other scene object. We'll look at some code samples.

## Time for action – stir up some dust

A speeding car looks faster with rally stripes, but it looks twice as fast when it also stirs up some dust!

1. Make a copy of `Main.java` and name the class `Particle1DustSmoke.java`. Remember to also refactor the first line of the `main()` method to `Particle1DustSmoke app = new Particle1DustSmoke();`.

2. Copy the included file `assets/Effects/smoke.png` into your project's `assets/Effect` directory. It includes a sprite animation of a dust cloud.

3. Create a class field for the `ParticleEmitter` object and initialize the emitter in the `simpleInitApp()` method. Give the emitter a descriptive name and tell it to keep 100 particles of type `Triangle` ready (from the `com.jme3.effect.ParticleMesh.Type` package).

```
private ParticleEmitter dustEmitter;
public void simpleInitApp() {
```

```
dustEmitter = new ParticleEmitter(
  "dust emitter", Type.Triangle, 100);
```

4. Like every visible scene object, an emitter has a material. An effect material is always based on the Common/MatDefs/Misc/Particle.j3md material definition.

```
Material dustMat = new Material(assetManager,
  "Common/MatDefs/Misc/Particle.j3md");
dustEmitter.setMaterial(dustMat);
```

5. Load smoke.png into the Texture property of the material:

```
dustMat.setTexture("Texture",
  assetManager.loadTexture("Effects/smoke.png"));
```

6. When you open smoke.png in an image viewer, you see that the picture contains a 4-frame sprite animation. To help the emitter segment the image correctly, tell it that the image has two columns (ImagesX) and two rows (ImagesY):

```
dustEmitter.setImagesX(2);
dustEmitter.setImagesY(2);
```

7. Make the dust cloud more swirly and random:

```
dustEmitter.setSelectRandomImage(true);
dustEmitter.setRandomAngle(true);
dustEmitter.getParticleInfluencer().setVelocityVariation(1f);
```

8. Attach the emitter to a node, such as the root node:

```
  rootNode.attachChild(dustEmitter);
}
```

9. Since our dust emitter is not attached to a mobile character, it's quite static. Add the following formula to the simpleUpdate() method to make the emitter fly in circles; this motion emphasizes the dust effect for our demo.

```
public void simpleUpdate(float tpf) {
  // make the emitter fly in circles
  angle += tpf;
  angle %= FastMath.TWO_PI;
  float x = FastMath.cos(angle) * 2;
  float y = FastMath.sin(angle) * 2;
  dustEmitter.setLocalTranslation(x, 0, y);
}
```

Run the code. You see a dust devil, swirling back and forth and around. The image on the left shows the four frames used to create the wafting dust plume, shown in the image on the right:

# What just happened?

The emitter object holds the properties of our dusty experiment. The integer value in the constructor specifies the number of particles that this emitter manages. For a dense effect, 50 to 100 particles are a good value to start with.

In a particle system with `Type.Triangle`, each particle is represented as a transparent, textured rectangle made up of two triangles. This is the most common type of particle effect, and it's supported on all platforms.

 The alternative to triangles are point particles with `Type.Point`. Point particles can have textures if you specify `setBoolean("PointSprite",true)` for them. Point sprites are more efficient for large clouds with, say, ten thousand particles, but unfortunately not all platforms render point sprites the same way. This is why they require a lot of extra testing.

Every particle emitter has a material based on the default `Particle.j3md` material definition. In this demo, you replace the material's basic, straight-flying rectangles with swirly, fuzzy shapes, to get a dust effect. The material property `Texture` is the particle texture that you load from your `assets/Effects/` directory.

Remember to use the `setImagesX()` (columns) and `setImagesY()` (rows) methods to specify the number of animation frames in each texture. By default, the animation frames play in order (from left to right, and top to bottom), which looks good for sequential sprite animations, such as butterflies or swirling leaves. The `smoke.png` sprites, however, are not in any particular order, so you use `setSelectRandomImage(true)`.

If you ran the demo now, you'd already see a dense dust cloud. There are several options that enable us to make the emitter more random:

+ By default, the emitter's velocity variation value is `0.0f`, meaning all particles fly in the same direction. Set it to `0.5f` to emit particles within a 180° angle around the initial direction. A velocity variation value of `1.0f` emits particles in all directions (360°).

◆ By default, sprite particles are oriented the way you drew them in the texture. When you set the random angle property to `true`, every sprite is randomly rotated when it is emitted, which makes the dust effect look more varied.

Typically, you attach a mobile emitter to a car, a wizard, an asteroid, a campfire, and so on. You can also attach it to the root node and move it to a fixed location. In this demo, we used the update loop to animate the emitter to fly in a circle. We created a private field `angle` to keep track of the previous position of the orbiting emitter. The `tpf` variable in the update loop keeps track of the time per frame. We use it as pacing factor in the standard circle formula that calculates the emitter's orbit.

# Time for action – sparks

When swords clash so hard that sparks fly, then you know there are heroes at work. Let's create some sparks and make them dash in random directions!

1.  Make a copy of `Main.java` and name the class `Particle2Sparks.java`. Remember to also refactor the first line of the `main()` method to `Particle2Sparks app = new Particle2Sparks();`.

2.  Copy the included file `assets/Effects/spark.png` into your project's `assets/Effect` directory. It includes a sprite animation of sparks.

3.  In the `simpleInitApp()` method, create a spark emitter and attach it to the scene:

    ```
    public void simpleInitApp() {
      ParticleEmitter sparksEmitter = new ParticleEmitter(
        "Spark emitter", Type.Triangle, 60);
      rootNode.attachChild(sparksEmitter);
    ```

4.  Create a material, load the spark texture, and set the material:

    ```
    Material sparkMat = new Material(assetManager,
      "Common/MatDefs/Misc/Particle.j3md");
    sparkMat.setTexture("Texture",
      assetManager.loadTexture("Effects/spark.png"));
    sparksEmitter.setMaterial(sparkMat);
    ```

5.  You see that the spark texture has only one frame. Specify 1 for both the X and Y values of the sprite animation:

    ```
    sparksEmitter.setImagesX(1);
    sparksEmitter.setImagesY(1);
    ```

Modify the dust emitter code until you achieve the desired "sparky" effect:

1. Increase the initial velocity to accelerate the particles upward (along the Y axis) to a speed of 10 world units per second. Since you want the sparks to fly in different directions, you set the velocity variation property to its maximum value, `1.0f`.

```
sparksEmitter.getParticleInfluencer().
  setInitialVelocity(new Vector3f(0, 10, 0));
sparksEmitter.getParticleInfluencer().
  setVelocityVariation(1.0f);
```

2. You tell the hot sparks to fade from yellow to red, using the `com.jme3.math.ColorRGBA` constants:

```
sparksEmitter.setStartColor(ColorRGBA.Yellow);
sparksEmitter.setEndColor(ColorRGBA.Red);
```

3. To make the sparks rain downward, increase the emitter's gravity to, for instance, 50:

```
sparksEmitter.setGravity(0, 50, 0);
```

4. You want the spark particles to face in the direction that they are flying:

```
sparksEmitter.setFacingVelocity(true);
```

5. You adjust the sparks' size to start small, and stay small—here, 0.5f world units:

```
sparksEmitter.setStartSize(.5f);
sparksEmitter.setEndSize(.5f);
```

6. You shorten the particle's maximum and minimum lifetime:

```
    sparksEmitter.setLowLife(.9f);
    sparksEmitter.setHighLife(1.1f);
}
```

Run the example. This emitter produces individual, small, orange sparks that fly quickly, facing in various directions, before they fall and fizzle away, as seen in the screenshot on the right. The one-frame sprite is shown on the left.

## *What just happened?*

You already know about the velocity variation parameter, which makes your sparks fly in vastly different directions. You can also control the `initial velocity` vector to speed up your sparks. Our sparks are exposed to gravity and fall down quickly, facing in the direction of their velocity.

By default, particles are scaled bigger when flying, which creates the illusion of them flying toward the viewer. In this demo, we set the start size and end size properties fields to the same value to achieve the illusion that the particles fly to the sides. The default lifetime of a particle is a random value, between three and seven seconds; for a quick and busy spark effect, you set the high life and low life fields to similar, short values.

You also see that you can set a two-color gradient on particles. White areas in the texture change from the start color (here, yellow) to the end color (here, red). White-gray sparks look metallic, yellow-red ones look like welding sparks, cyan-blue ones look electric—choose whatever suits your game's settings.

## Time for action – fit to burst?

If you have game scenes where bullets or other projectiles hit a target, you may have thought of emphasizing the impact with a short fiery burst.

1.  Make a copy of `Main.java` and name the class `Particle5Burst.java`. Remember to also refactor the first line of the `main()` method to `Particle5Burst app = new Particle5Burst();`.

2.  Copy the included file `assets/Effects/flash.png` into your project's `assets/Effect` directory. It includes a sprite animation of a fiery burst.

3.  Since a burst is short and compact, we create an emitter with only five particles in the `simpleInitApp()` method:

```
public void simpleInitApp() {
    ParticleEmitter burstEmitter = new ParticleEmitter(
        "Burst emitter", Type.Triangle, 5);
    rootNode.attachChild(burstEmitter);
```

4.  The `flash.png` sprite animation contains a random series of 2 x 2 explosive flashes. Set both animation dimensions to 2, and the image order to `random`:

```
Material burstMat = new Material(assetManager,
    "Common/MatDefs/Misc/Particle.j3md");
burstMat.setTexture("Texture",
    assetManager.loadTexture("Effects/flash.png"));
burstEmitter.setImagesX(2);
burstEmitter.setImagesY(2);
burstEmitter.setSelectRandomImage(true);
burstEmitter.setMaterial(burstMat);
```

**5.** Set the burst color's gradient to a fading orange:

```
burstEmitter.setStartColor(new ColorRGBA(
    1f, 0.8f, 0.36f, 1f));
burstEmitter.setEndColor(new ColorRGBA(
    1f, 0.8f, 0.36f, 0f));
```

**6.** The flash particle starts out tiny (.1f), and quickly blows up five times its original size:

```
burstEmitter.setStartSize(.1f);
burstEmitter.setEndSize(5.0f);
```

**7.** This burst is so short and powerful that its particles only exist for .2f seconds, practically weightless:

```
burstEmitter.setGravity(0, 0, 0);
burstEmitter.setLowLife(.2f);
burstEmitter.setHighLife(.2f);
```

**8.** The particles start out flying slightly upward and then in all directions:

```
burstEmitter.getParticleInfluencer().
    setInitialVelocity(new Vector3f(0, 5f, 0));
burstEmitter.getParticleInfluencer().
    setVelocityVariation(1f);
```

**9.** The shape property specifies that particles can start anywhere inside an invisible sphere with a radius of .5f world units:

```
burstEmitter.setShape(
    new EmitterSphereShape(Vector3f.ZERO, .5f));
}
```

Run the sample and you should see layers of orange, fiery flashes. The flashes expand and disappear quickly (the screenshot on the right). The effect is created using the following 4-frame sprite texture (the screenshot on the left):

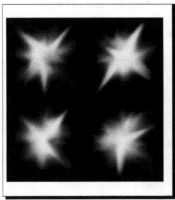 

# What just happened?

The gradient starts out with a custom color defined by its RGBA values: `1f, 0.8f, 0.36f,` and `1f`. The four floats stand for the red, green, blue, and alpha components of the color orange. Note that this gradient does not change colors, but opacity. The alpha value changes from `1f` (opaque orange) to `0f` (transparent orange). The burst fades away.

To emphasize the sudden burst effect, each flash particle starts out very small (`.1f`), and quickly increases to a multiple of its original size (`5.0f`). Increasing the particle size creates the illusion that the explosion is closing in on the viewer.

With a particle life of only `.2f` seconds, this burst is so short and powerful that gravity has no visible impact, so we specify a weightless zero vector. We set the initial velocity to a slightly upward vector (`5f` world units along the Y axis), to give the effect a chance to get away from the ground. We set the `velocity variation` value to fan out to its maximum (`1.0f`) of 360°. The burst's lifetime is so short that the sprites have no time to fly far, but the viewer will notice a random outward jerk.

The last line contains something new. By default, particles are emitted from one spot—the location of the emitter—as if they were emitted from a muzzle. Setting the emitter shape to a sphere (`com.jme3.effect.shapes.EmitterSphereShape`) increases the number of start locations, here to within `.5f` world units from the emitter. This variation makes the explosion look more unpredictable.

## Starting and stopping effects

By default, emitters produce 20 new particles per second as soon as the update loop starts. But effects such as bursts or sparks have a clear start and end. They are triggered by game events—collisions, explosions, or clashing swords. After the event, they disappear.

You pause, start, and stop effects using the following methods:

| Emitter method | Purpose |
| --- | --- |
| `emitter.setParticlesPerSec(0);` | Pause a freshly initialized emitter until you need it. |
| `emitter.setParticlesPerSec(20);`<br>`emitter.emitAllParticles();` | Start playing a 20-particle effect. Typically triggered by a game action or event. |
| `emitter.killAllParticles();` | Stop the effect and remove all flying particles. |

# Time for action – fire!

Let's have a look at a classic fire effect. You can use it in combination with a Point Light, for campfires, torches, or for a wizard's fireball spell.

**1.** Make a copy of `Main.java` and name the class `Particle6Fire.java`. Remember to also refactor the first line of the `main()` method to `Particle6Fire app = new Particle6Fire();`.

**2.** Copy the included file `assets/Effects/flame.png` into your project's `assets/Effect` directory. It includes a sprite animation of flames.

**3.** Initialize the emitter, give it a material based on `Particle.j3md`, and attach it to the scene:

```
public void simpleInitApp() {
    ParticleEmitter fireEmitter = new ParticleEmitter(
        "Emitter", ParticleMesh.Type.Triangle, 30);
    Material fireMat = new Material(assetManager,
        "Common/MatDefs/Misc/Particle.j3md");
    rootNode.attachChild(fireEmitter);
```

**4.** Our fire sprite animation is made up of 2 x 2 random flames:

```
fireMat.setTexture("Texture",
    assetManager.loadTexture("Effects/flame.png"));
fireEmitter.setMaterial(fireMat);
fireEmitter.setImagesX(2);
fireEmitter.setImagesY(2);
fireEmitter.setSelectRandomImage(true);
fireEmitter.setRandomAngle(true);
```

**5.** The color gradient changes from orange to red:

```
fireEmitter.setStartColor(new ColorRGBA(1f, 1f, .5f, 1f));
fireEmitter.setEndColor(new ColorRGBA(1f, 0f, 0f, 0f));
```

**6.** Flames move quickly and seem weightless. They keep blazing in their initial direction (upward along the Y axis) and don't vary much to the sides (`.2f`):

```
fireEmitter.setGravity(0,0,0);
fireEmitter.getParticleInfluencer().
    setVelocityVariation(0.2f);
fireEmitter.getParticleInfluencer().
    setInitialVelocity(new Vector3f(0,3f,0));
```

**7.** Set low and high life to very different values and decrease the size:

```
fireEmitter.setLowLife(0.5f);
fireEmitter.setHighLife(2f);
fireEmitter.setStartSize(1.5f);
fireEmitter.setEndSize(0.05f);
```

Run the sample and watch your cozy fire effect. With the right coloring and particle speed, four flame sprites (the screenshot on the left) create a classical fire effect (the screenshot on the right):

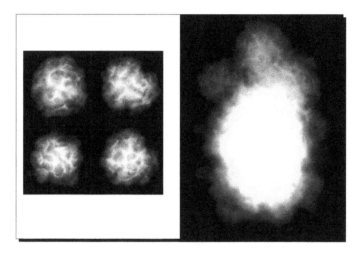

# What just happened?

For the fire's color, you choose a gradient that fades from an opaque orange to a transparent red. A fire starts as a big blaze before it dwindles to tiny flames, so you set the start size (`1.5f`) to a larger value than the end size (`0.05f`). You set gravity to zero to achieve the impression of weightless flames flying upward.

To simulate how most flames flicker away quickly, and only a few lick up above the main blaze, you set the minimum (`0.5f`) and maximum (`2.0f`) lifetime to very different values. You set the initial velocity to an upward vector, and the variation sideways to 72° (0.2f * 360°).

This demo is a basic template for all kinds of fires, from burnt offerings to campfires. Decrease the particle size and maximum life, and you can attach the emitter to a torch or candle. Increase the particle size and lifetime, and you can attach the emitter to a burning building or use it as a forest fire.

## Time for action – design effects in the SDK

SceneComposer in the jMonkeyEngine SDK is a nifty tool to try out different particle settings and preview them in a user-friendly way.

The following screenshot shows the effect preview in the **SceneComposer** window, the spatial in the **SceneExplorer** window, and the **Emitter – Properties** window:

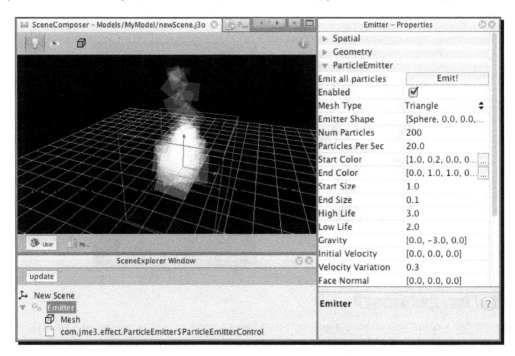

To create your own effect, start with an empty scene in the SDK's project window:

1. Right-click on the assets/Scenes directory and go to **New | Other....**

2. Go to **Scene | Empty jME3 Scene**.

3. Go through the new file wizard and name the effect; for example, FireEffect.j3o.

You find the scene node FireEffect.j3o in your assets/Scenes directory in the **Projects** window.

Let's add a particle emitter:

1. In the **Projects** window, right-click on `FireEffect.j3o` and select **Edit in SceneComposer**. You should see an empty scene in the **SceneComposer** window.

2. Open the **SceneExplorer** window from the **Window** menu.

3. Right-click on the **New Scene** node in the **SceneExplorer** window, and go to **Add Spatial | Particle Emitter**.

You now see the default particle emitter in the **SceneComposer** window.

Let's create the effect material:

1. Click to select the scene's emitter node in the **SceneExplorer** window.

2. Open **Properties** from the **Window** menu. Go to **Properties | Geometry | Material**, and click on **Create j3m** file to create a new `.j3m` material.

3. Select the `Particle.j3md` material definition in the Material Editor.

4. Specify an image as `Texture` in the Material Editor; for example, `Effects/flame.png`.

5. In the Material Editor under **Additional RenderState**, set **Blend** to **Additive**.

6. Click on **Emitter** again and return to the **Properties** window. Make sure to specify the rows (**2**) and columns (**2**) for your chosen texture in the **Image X** and **Image Y** fields!

Your effect now has a custom material.

Let's tweak the color, size, and other properties:

1. Continue to modify the emitter's properties until you're satisfied.

2. Preview the effect in the **SceneComposer** window.

3. Right-click on **Emitter** in the **SceneExplorer** window and choose **Rename...**. Give the emitter a descriptive name; for example, `Fire Effect`.

When you're done, click to select the `.j3o` file in the **Projects** window. Go to **File** in the main menu and click on **Save** to save your changes.

## *What just happened?*

All emitter properties are optional and have default values that you can customize.

The following table lists all emitter properties:

| Emitter property | Description |
|---|---|
| `setParticlesPerSec()`<br>  Default: 20 | The density, how many particles are emitted per second:<br>◆ Set to zero to pause the effect<br>◆ Set to a value greater than zero for a constantly looping effect |
| `setStartSize()`<br>  Default: 0.2f<br>`setEndSize()`<br>  Default: 1.0f | The radius of the scaled particle:<br>◆ Set to the same value for a static cloud effect<br>◆ Set to different values to simulate shrinking (retreating) or growing (approaching) |
| `setStartColor()`<br>  Default: gray<br>`setEndColor()`<br>  Default: transparent | The color of the opaque (non-black) parts of the texture:<br>◆ Set to the same colors for single-colored effects (for example, fog, debris)<br>◆ Set to different colors for a gradient effect (for example, fire, magic spell) |
| `getParticleInfluencer()`<br>  `.setInitialVelocity()`<br>   Default: Vector3f.<br>ZERO | The initial direction and speed of the particles.<br><br>The longer the vector, the faster they fly. |
| `getParticleInfluencer()`<br>`.setVelocityVariation()`<br>  Default: 0.2f = 72° | How much the particles fan out:<br>◆ `0.0f` : Particles fly only in the direction of the initial velocity (for example, laser gun blasts)<br>◆ `0.5f`: Particles emit within 0.5f * 360° = 180° of the initial direction (for example, sparks)<br>◆ `1.0f`: Particles emit in random 360° directions (for example, explosions, butterflies) |
| `setFacingVelocity()`<br>  Default: false | The direction in which particles face while flying; cannot be combined with `setFaceNormal()`:<br>◆ `false`: Particles keep flying, rotated the way they started (for example, insects)<br>◆ `true`: Flying particles pitch in the direction in which they are falling (for example, missiles) |

| Emitter property | Description |
|---|---|
| `setFaceNormal()`<br>  Default: `Vector3f.NAN` | The direction in which particles face while flying; cannot be combined with `setFacingVelocity()`:<br><br>♦ `Vector3f.NAN`: Flying particles face the camera (most commonly used case)<br><br>♦ `Vector3f`: Flying particles are rotated to face the given vector (for example, use `Vector3f.UNIT_Y` to make a horizontal shockwave face upward) |
| `setLowLife()`<br>  Default: `3f`<br><br>`setHighLife()`<br>  Default: `7f` | The fade-out period is set to a random value between high life and low life. High life must be greater than low life.<br><br>♦ Small values make the effect busier; higher values make it steadier.<br><br>♦ Similar values create a regular effect (for example, a fountain). Different values create a distorted effect (for example, fire with individual long flames). |
| `setRotateSpeed()`<br>  Default: `0f` | How much particles spin while flying:<br><br>♦ `0.f`: Particles fly steadily (for example, smoke, insects, controlled projectiles)<br><br>♦ Greater than `0.0f`: Particles spin while flying (for example, debris, shuriken, missiles out of control) |
| `setRandomAngle()`<br>  Default: `false` | Controls whether particles are rotated before they are emitted:<br><br>♦ `true`: Each particle is rotated at a random angle (for example, explosions, debris)<br><br>♦ `false`: Particles fly like you drew them in the texture (for example, insects) |
| `setGravity()`<br>  Default: `Vector3f.`<br>`ZERO` | The simulated gravity of the particles:<br><br>♦ `0,10,0`: Particles are heavy and fall down (for example, debris, sparks)<br><br>♦ `0,-10,0`: Particles are lightweight and fly up (for example, flames)<br><br>♦ `0,0,0`: Particles fly in the direction of their initial velocities (for example, zero-gravity explosions) |
| `setShape(new`<br>  `EmitterSphereShape(`<br>  `Vector3f.ZERO, 2f) )`<br><br>Default:<br>  `EmitterPointShape()` | By default, particles are emitted from a point. You can increase the emitter shape to occupy `EmitterSphereShape` or `EmitterBoxShape`. New particles start anywhere inside the shape, which makes the effect more unpredictable (for example, bursts, spells). |

# Time for action – finding stuff in the scene graph

When you create effects in the SDK, you can add several spatials to one .j3o file. For a campfire, you would add one fire emitter, one smoke emitter, and some wooden logs geometries. After loading the scene, you may want to change the effect properties inside the loaded scene, but how do you access, say, the fire emitter, without a variable?

Use the following approach to find any spatial anywhere in your scene graph:

1. Make a copy of Main.java and name the class LoadEffectFromJ3o. java. Remember to also refactor the first line of the main() method to LoadEffectFromJ3o app = new LoadEffectFromJ3o();.

2. Load the .j3o file containing your effect in the simpleInitApp() method, using assetManager, and attach it:

```
Node myScene =
   (Node)assetManager.loadModel("Scenes/FireEffect.j3o");
rootNode.attachChild(myScene);
```

3. Create a custom com.jme3.scene.SceneGraphVisitorAdapter to define search criteria:

```
SceneGraphVisitorAdapter myEmitterVisitor =
  new SceneGraphVisitorAdapter() {
  @Override
  public void visit(Geometry geom) {
    super.visit(geom);
    searchForEmitter(geom); // trigger custom test
  }
  @Override
  public void visit(Node node) {
    super.visit(node);
    searchForEmitter(node); // trigger custom test
  }

  private void searchForEmitter(Spatial spatial) {
    // specify search criteria, e.g. class, name, properties
    if (spatial instanceof ParticleEmitter) {
      System.out.println("Emitter in "+ spatial.getName());
      // modify the found node:
      ((ParticleEmitter)spatial).setNumParticles(10);
    }
  }
}
```

**4.** Start the search in the `simpleInitApp()` method. You scan `rootNode` for emitters using `myEmitterVisitor`, either depth-first or breadth-first:

```
rootNode.depthFirstTraversal(myEmitterVisitor);
rootNode.breadthFirstTraversal(myEmitterVisitor);
```

Try the code sample on a scene with different search criteria. For example, additionally test for `spatial.getName().equals("Fire Effect")` or `spatial.getName().equals("Smoke Effect")` and change different properties in each emitter.

## *What just happened?*

You created a custom `SceneGraphVisitorAdapters` object that contains specific search criteria, such as a spatial instance of `ParticleEmitter`, and an action, such as `((ParticleEmitter)spatial).setNumParticles(10)`. You must implement the `visit()` method for nodes and geometries. The implementations can be different or the same for both, or simply `return`, depending on whether you search for nodes or geometries, or both. In the previous example, we created a helper method named `searchForEmitter()` that we used for both.

You then applied the visitor to a node, such as `rootNode`. If the spatials in question are children of one special subnode, you save time by starting your search there instead.

> Whether to traverse the graph depth-first or breadth-first, depends on the layout of your scene graph and what you are looking for. If you are searching for geometries, a depth-first search may be more efficient. If you are searching for nodes under the root node, then breadth-first is faster. The two methods return results in different orders: If the action is inherited by child nodes (for example, a transformation), then the order in which you apply changes makes a difference.

You write custom `SceneGraphVisitorAdapters` not just to find lost particle emitters. In general, `SceneGraphVisitorAdapter` is an elegant way to loop over the scene graph and search for spatials by class, name, properties, or controls.

For example, you could create `myAnimationVisitor` that scans spatials for animation controls, and does something with them (here, we simply print them):

```
private void searchForAnimations(Spatial spatial) {
  AnimControl control = spatial.getControl(AnimControl.class);
  if (control != null) {
    for (String anim : control.getAnimationNames()) {
      System.out.println(spatial.getName()+" has animation: "+ anim);
    }
  }
}
```

## Custom effect textures

In this chapter, you used the provided particle textures. You can also create custom particle textures and load them into any material that is based on `Particle.j3md`:

- At minimum, your particle texture has one frame (1 x 1). But effects can have any number of rows and columns, depending on the length of your sprite animation.

- When determining texture size, you must lay out all frames on a regular grid. All frames must be rectangular, non-empty, and have the same size. For example, a 2 x 3 frame animation has two columns and three rows. With a frame size of 128 x 64 pixels each, texture size is 2 * 128 x 3 * 64 = 256 x 192.

- Particle textures are grayscale images with black backgrounds. White is replaced by the color gradient, and black is rendered transparent.

- If you want to play the animation in order (for example, for bats, insects), draw the frames from left to right, and top to bottom. In all other cases (for example, for debris, sparks, smoke, snowflakes) draw the frames in any order.

Look at the included particle textures for examples. The following image shows what the texture for a 3 x 2 frame snowflake effect would look like. Each snowflake is 30 x 30 pixels. Therefore, the total texture size is 90 x 60 pixels.

## Have a go hero – explosion!

A short-circuit causes sparks to rain down on a gunpowder container. The burst of the explosion lights up the night, and the shockwave hurls debris in all directions. The rubble sets on fire, and in the end, all that's left is smoke and embers... Do you accept the challenge to implement an awesome explosion effect, like the one shown in the following screenshot?

An explosion is not limited to a burst of fire. Experiment with what you learned in this chapter and combine several particle effects. You already have sparks, bursts, fire, and smoke. Can you create spinning pieces of debris? A round, horizontally expanding shockwave? A scattered cloud of embers? Create your own textures, or copy the following included textures for inspiration: `Effects/embers.png`, `Effects/debris.png`, and `Effects/shockwave.png`.

Here are some tips:

1. Make a copy of `Main.java` and name the class `Particle7Explosion.java`. Remember to also refactor the first line of the `main()` method to `Particle7Explosion app = new Particle7Explosion();`.

2. Use the jMonkeyEngine SDK to create a `.j3o` file containing the effects. Attach the final effect to the root node and use a visitor to trigger individual emitters. Alternatively, write convenience methods, which initialize individual emitters and their properties, in Java code, and attach each emitter to the root node. Look at the code from previous examples for inspiration.

3. Deactivate the looping behavior in each emitter using `setParticlesPerSec(0)`.

4. Write an update loop timer (or an input listener, if you prefer) that triggers the explosion by calling `emitAllParticles()` on each emitter.

5. Clean up the scene by calling `killAllParticles()` on each emitter.

You begin to see how powerful small-particle systems can become when used together!

# Scene-wide effects

In addition to self-contained particle effects, video games sport impressive scene-wide effects: sunny glows, gloomy shadows, reflections, night-vision goggles, motion blurs, or cartoon shading. These post-processing effects are applied to the rendered scene, in real time. You already saw a post-processing effect in action when you used GlowMap.

By default, post-processing is inactive. You can chain up several effects and apply one processor to the output of the previous one. There are two types of post-processors:

- **SceneProcessor**: This can render scene-wide effects before and after the classic rendering of the scene. You add SceneProcessors to `viewPort` of `SimpleApplication` in the order in which you want them to be rendered. The most common examples of SceneProcessors are drop shadows and reflective water.

- **Filter**: This is a 2D effect that is applied to the buffer after the scene is rendered. A `FilterPostProcessor` is a special `SceneProcessor` that applies several filters to the rendered scene, again, in the order in which you added them. When you want to use filters in your application, add one `FilterPostProcessor` to the `viewPort` of your `SimpleApplication`, and add all filters to it. Examples of filter effects include blurs, fog, bloom, cartoon effects, and fades.

The jMonkeyEngine includes several popular post-processor filters in the `com.jme3.post` package. You find commonly used SceneProcessors under `com.jme3.shadow` and `com.jme3.water`. Check the `jmonkeyengine.org` wiki documentation for the latest post-processor contributions.

Advanced users who are interested in designing their own post-processor filters should check out the jMonkeyEngine sources. Have a look at the `com.jme3.post` and `com.jme3.post.filters` packages and copy `ColorOverlayFilter.java`, a simple example filter that tints every pixel with a color. This Java file references `Overlay.j3md` in `core-data/Common/MatDefs/Post/`. This material definition defines material parameters, and references two custom shaders, `Post.vert` and `Overlay.frag`. Being written in **GLSL (OpenGL Shading Language)**, shader functions have access to, for example, depth and color of all current pixels. Advanced users place their custom `.vert`, `.frag`, and `.j3md` files into the `assets/MatDefs` directory, and use them as described in this chapter.

The following examples demonstrate how you activate `com.jme3.post.SceneProcessors` and `com.jme3.post.FilterPostProcessors` in the `viewPort` of your `SimpleApplication`.

## Time for action – welcome to Dark Town

From the point of view of a 3D engine, shading and lighting are two separate things. You may have noticed that, by default, our walls, bricks, and cannon balls don't cast drop shadows onto the floor or on each other.

This is how you can activate drop shadows using a SceneProcessor:

1. Make a copy of `Main.java` and name the class `ShadowDirectional.java`. Remember to also refactor the first line of the `main()` method to `ShadowDirectional app = new ShadowDirectional()`.

2. Create a directional light source and add it to the scene:

```
public void simpleInitApp() {
   DirectionalLight sun = new DirectionalLight();
   sun.setDirection(new Vector3f(.3f, -0.5f, -0.5f));
   rootNode.addLight(sun);
```

3. Create a `DirectionalLightShadowRenderer` object in the `simpleInitApp()` method. You find it in the `com.jme3.shadow` package. Initialize `DirectionalLightShadowRenderer` and use the `setLight()` method to link it to the global light source:

```
DirectionalLightShadowRenderer dlsr =
   new DirectionalLightShadowRenderer(assetManager, 1024, 2);
dlsr.setLight(sun);
```

4. Add the shadow post-processor to `viewPort` of your `SimpleApplication`:

```
viewPort.addProcessor(dlsr);
```

5. Load a scene in the `simpleInitApp()` method, as in previous demos:

```
assetManager.registerLocator("town.zip", ZipLocator.class);
Spatial sceneGeo = assetManager.loadModel("main.scene");
rootNode.attachChild(sceneGeo);
```

6. If your scene consists of many objects, activate shadows only on objects that require them:

```
rootNode.setShadowMode(ShadowMode.Off);
sceneGeo.setShadowMode(ShadowMode.CastAndReceive);
}
```

Run the code. You should see your scene illuminated and casting drop shadows. Add more objects and switch their shadow modes to `Cast`, `Receive`, `CastAndReceive`, or `Off`, to see the differences. The following screenshot shows drop shadows cast on the floor and neighboring objects:

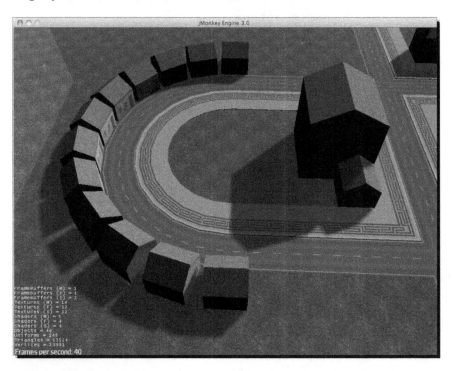

## What just happened?

`DirectionalLightShadowRenderer` depends on a directional light source. The constructor expects as arguments the `assetManager`, a shadow map size, and the number of shadow maps to use:

- Using large shadow maps can slow down performance, but result in more clearly outlined shadows, even for small objects such as a teapot. Shadow map sizes must be powers of two. Typical values are `512`, `1024`, or `2048`.

- Using more shadow maps improves shadow quality—the minimum is `1` and the maximum is `4`. `2` is a good value to start experimenting with.

- You must use `setLight()` on the renderer object to specify a directional light that is attached to the scene.

`DirectionalLightShadowRenderer` uses the **Parallel Split Shadow Mapping** (**PSSM**) technique. It creates several shadow maps and splits the view frustum into several parallel parts. Shadows that are close to the camera get higher-resolution shadows, and areas farther away get less detail. This improves the look of the shadows with almost zero performance loss. If you set the number of maps to 1, the renderer uses one shadow map for the entire scene. This means that every area gets an equal amount of precision on the shadow map, even if the player is not close enough to see it. Using one shadow map wastes resources for large scenes, but works well for small, simple scenes. Games where the camera looks down on a small scene (for example, real-time strategy games with a "bird's eye view") especially benefit from basic drop shadows.

For performance reasons, it's a best practice to only activate shadows on objects that require them. First, you switch off shadow rendering for the entire root node. This prevents all shadow-less objects (the sky, small items, and particle emitters) from wasting GPU resources. Next, you specify the shadow-casting behavior for individual objects: the lowest ground and floors only receive shadows, they don't cast any. Objects high up (for example, airplanes) never receive shadows, but they cast shadows. Many other objects in the main scene cast and receive shadows.

You can choose from the following shadow modes in the `com.jme3.renderer.queue.RenderQueue` package:

| Shadow Mode | Description | Example |
| --- | --- | --- |
| Receive | This node only receives shadows and never casts any.<br><br>Performance impact: medium | Floors, ground, terrains—low objects that no player will ever see from below. |
| Cast | This node only casts shadows and never receives any.<br><br>Performance impact: medium | Lone trees, lone towers, eagles, airships—high or thin objects upon which nothing will ever cast a shadow. |
| CastAndReceive | This node casts and receives shadows.<br><br>Performance impact: high | Common objects such as buildings, walls, characters, projectiles, and vehicles. |
| Off | This node neither casts nor receives shadows.<br><br>Performance impact: low | Particle emitters, sky, ghosts, window panes, far-away background objects, and so on. |

# Time for action – welcome to Dark City

For larger scenes, you should try a `DirectionalLightShadowFilter` object from the `com.jme3.shadow` package.

You can use a copy of `ShadowDirectional.java` for the following exercise:

1. Add a directional light source to the scene:

```
public void simpleInitApp() {
    DirectionalLight sunLight = new DirectionalLight();
    sunLight.setDirection(new Vector3f(.3f, -0.5f, -0.5f));
    rootNode.addLight(sunLight);
```

2. If you re-use code from the `ShadowDirectional.java` class, deactivate the previously created `DirectionalLightShadowRenderer` object, or at least comment out its `addProcessor()` line:

```
// viewPort.addProcessor(dlsr);
```

3. Create a `DirectionalLightShadowFilter` object in the `simpleInitApp()` method. Use the `setLight()` method to specify your scene's directional light source:

```
DirectionalLightShadowFilter dlsf =
    new DirectionalLightShadowFilter(assetManager, 1024, 2);
dlsf.setLight(sun);
dlsf.setEnabled(true);
```

4. Create a `FilterPostProcessor` object (if your scene doesn't already have one), and add the filter to it. As always, add the `FilterPostProcessor` to the `viewPort`:

```
FilterPostProcessor fpp = new FilterPostProcessor(assetManager);
fpp.addFilter(dlsf);
viewPort.addProcessor(fpp);
```

5. Load a scene in the `simpleInitApp()` method, as in previous demos:

```
assetManager.registerLocator("town.zip", ZipLocator.class);
Spatial sceneGeo = assetManager.loadModel("main.scene");
rootNode.attachChild(sceneGeo);
```

6. Again, activate shadows only on objects that require them:

```
    rootNode.setShadowMode(ShadowMode.Off);
    sceneGeo.setShadowMode(ShadowMode.CastAndReceive);
}
```

Run the code. You should see your scene with high-quality drop shadows.

## What just happened?

The shadow quality of `DirectionalLightShadowFilter` is comparable to that offered by `DirectionalLightShadowRenderer`. `DirectionalLightShadowFilter` is generally faster for larger scenes with more than a dozen shadow-receiving objects. Note that `DirectionalLightShadowFilter` ignores the `ShadowMode` property in geometries, which means that all objects in the scene receive shadows.

Eventually, it comes down to the composition of your scene—which of the two shadow implementations creates the effect you want, at the lowest performance cost.

## Time for action – this city needs more gloom

We use ambient occlusion (SSAO) in scenes with no directional sunlight; for example, to simulate a gloomy indoor scene, a narrow street, or a gray, overcast day.

You activate ambient occlusion as follows:

1. Make a copy of `Main.java` and name the class `ShadowSSAO.java`. Remember to also refactor the first line of the `main()` method to `ShadowSSAO app = new ShadowSSAO()`.

2. Add `FilterPostProcessor` as a class field, and initialize it in the `simpleInitApp()` method. Add `FilterPostProcessor` to `viewPort` of your `SimpleApplication`:

   ```
   private FilterPostProcessor fpp;
   public void simpleInitApp() {
     FilterPostProcessor fpp = new FilterPostProces
       sor(assetManager);
     viewPort.addProcessor(fpp);
   ```

3. Create an `SSAOFilter` object (from `com.jme3.post.ssao`), and add it to your `FilterPostProcessor` to activate `SSAOFilter`:

   ```
   SSAOFilter ssaoFilter = new SSAOFilter
     (12.94f,43.93f,.33f,.60f);
   fpp.addFilter(ssaoFilter);
   ```

4. Add at least one ambient light source to the scene:

   ```
   AmbientLight ambientLight = new AmbientLight();
   rootNode.addLight(ambientLight);
   ```

5. Again, load a scene in the `simpleInitApp()` method, as in previous demos:

   ```
   assetManager.registerLocator("town.zip", ZipLocator.class);
   Spatial sceneGeo = assetManager.loadModel("main.scene");
   rootNode.attachChild(sceneGeo);
   }
   ```

Run the code. Your scene should be bathed in gloomy shadows. Despite the lack of actual drop shadows, the edges where objects meet are clearly distinguishable. The following screenshot shows the extra shadows where the tiny house touches the floor, and onto the side of the large building:

## What just happened?

Video games use a simplified **Screen-Space Ambient Occlusion (SSAO)** algorithm, which is not actually physically correct. Nevertheless, SSAO is a good approximation of how light radiates and how occlusion causes extra shading.

Play with the four parameters to get the right effect, depending on how far apart objects, floors, and walls are in your scene:

| Argument | Default | Description |
| --- | --- | --- |
| sampleRadius | 5.1f | The radius of area around a point from where random samples are picked. |
| intensity | 1.2f | The intensity of the occlusion. |
| scale | 0.2f | The distance between occludee and occluders that are still considered to be casting shadows. |
| bias | 0.1f | The width of the occlusion cone considered by the occludee. |

Feel free to combine SSAO with PSSM. As you have seen in *Chapter 5, Creating Materials*, the human brain derives a lot of information from light. If this information is lacking, you keep the player "in the dark," which adds a lot of realism to night and dungeon scenes. Be aware, however, that not every game needs expensive real-time shadows. Activate them only when you need them.

# Time for action – stay focused

In addition to shadows, you can add cool glows and blurs to selected parts of the scene, or pull out all the stops and manipulate the whole scene, as the toon filter does.

The depth-of-field blur effect simulates how objects go in and out of focus when the human eye focuses near and far. The following screenshots focus first on the statue in the foreground, then on the houses in the background, and then on the façade of the building:

This filter needs update loop code to adjust properties depending on where the player is looking. To determine the player's line of sight, we use the familiar ray-casting algorithm.

The following example shows how you activate this cool blur effect:

1.  Make a copy of `Main.java` and name the class `DepthOfFieldBlur.java`. Remember to also refactor the first line of the `main()` method to `DepthOfFieldBlur app = new DepthOfFieldBlur()`.

2.  Add three class fields: one for the scene, one for `FilterPostProcessor`, and one for the depth-of-field blur filter (from the `com.jme3.post.filters` package):

    ```
    private Spatial sceneGeo;
    private FilterPostProcessor fpp;
    private DepthOfFieldFilter dofFilter;
    ```

3. Initialize these objects in the `simpleInitApp()` method. Add the `FilterPostProcessor` object to the `viewPort`, and add the `DepthOfFieldFilter` to the `FilterPostProcessor`:

```
public void simpleInitApp() {
    fpp = new FilterPostProcessor(assetManager);
    viewPort.addProcessor(fpp);
    dofFilter = new DepthOfFieldFilter();
    fpp.addFilter(dofFilter);
```

4. Load and attach a scene, and add a light source:

```
assetManager.registerLocator("town.zip", ZipLocator.class);
sceneGeo = assetManager.loadModel("main.scene");
rootNode.attachChild(sceneGeo);

DirectionalLight sunLight = new DirectionalLight();
sunLight.setDirection(new Vector3f(0.3f, -0.5f, -0.5f));
rootNode.addLight(sunLight);
}
```

We need to determine what the player is looking at in the scene, so we can update the focus distance. We use the following ray-casting code in `simpleUpdate()`:

1. Cast a ray from the camera location forward, in the view direction. This is the direction in which the player is looking:

```
public void simpleUpdate(float tpf) {
    Ray ray = new Ray(cam.getLocation(), cam.getDirection());
```

2. Reset the collision results:

```
CollisionResults results = new CollisionResults();
```

3. Collect the new collision results between the ray and the `sceneGeo` scene:

```
int numCollisions = sceneGeo.collideWith(ray, results);
```

4. If the result is greater than 0, the player is focusing on the scene: get the distance between collision point and camera, and adjust the focus distance:

```
if (numCollisions > 0) {
    CollisionResult hit = results.getClosestCollision();
    dofFilter.setFocusDistance(hit.getDistance() / 10.0f);
}
```

Run the code. The scene is clear in the center where the player is focusing. Everything else, closer or farther away, seems slightly out of focus.

# What just happened?

The `DepthOfFieldFilter` constructor is initialized with default values for its three arguments: focus distance, focus range, and blur scale. In use cases such as this demo, you only set the focus distance and leave the rest of the parameters untouched.

Focus range is the radius around the focus distance where the objects begin to go out of focus. If you set the blur scale to values greater than the default value, `1f` (for example, `4f`), the blurriness increases and the player seems to see the scene through the eyes of a drugged or dizzy character, which can be a desired effect.

We use `DepthOfFieldFilter` in first-person games where players navigate through scenes that have a lot of depth. It works great with wide landscapes with hiding places, or vast halls with small details that the player may want to focus on.

## Time for action – this city needs more glow

You already know a way to add glows: the `GlowMap` and `GlowColor` parameters in materials. A bloom filter results in the same halo-like glow, but it is applied scene-wide.

Let's apply a glow to our scene:

1. Make a copy of `Main.java` and name the class `BloomGlow.java`. Remember to also refactor the first line of the `main()` method to `BloomGlow app = new BloomGlow()`.

2. Add three class fields: one for the scene, one for the `FilterPostProcessor`, and one for the bloom filter (from the `com.jme3.post.filters` package):

   ```
   private Spatial sceneGeo;
   private FilterPostProcessor fpp;
   private BloomFilter bloom;
   ```

3. Initialize `bloom` and `fpp` in the `simpleInitApp()` method. Add the `FilterPostProcessor` to the `viewPort`, and add the `BloomFilter` to the `FilterPostProcessor`:

   ```
   public void simpleInitApp() {
     fpp = new FilterPostProcessor(assetManager);
     viewPort.addProcessor(fpp);

     bloom = new BloomFilter();
     fpp.addFilter(bloom);
   ```

4. Load and attach a scene of your choice, and add a light source:

   ```
   assetManager.registerLocator("town.zip", ZipLocator.class);
   sceneGeo = assetManager.loadModel("main.scene");
   ```

```
        rootNode.attachChild(sceneGeo);

        DirectionalLight sunLight = new DirectionalLight();
        sunLight.setDirection(new Vector3f(0.3f, -0.5f, -0.5f));
        rootNode.addLight(sunLight);
    }
```

Run the code and note how the light changed. The following example screenshot zooms in on a glowing teapot in a Bloom-enhanced scene:

## What just happened?

The `BloomFilter` constructor is initialized with good default values. You can adjust the following `Bloom` parameters to make the scene look more the way you want:

| Method | Default | Description |
|---|---|---|
| setBlurScale() | 1.5f | Control the blurriness of the bloom effect. Using values too high causes artifacts. |
| setExposurePower() | 5.0f | Intensify the glow color. |
| setExposureCutOff() | 0.0f | Set the glow threshold. 0f means everything glows; values closer to 1f allow only bright areas to glow. |
| setBloomIntensity() | 2.0f | Increase the brightness. |
| setDownSamplingFactor() | 2.0f | Increase the blur range. |

Activate the glow effect temporarily, for a sunrise, or to emphasize an important scene: when the powerful sorcerer reveals himself, when the hero reaches "the Promised Land"—or when the player is knocked out by a ninja.

# Time for action — toons and artistic effects

CartoonEdge, Posterization, and CrossHatch (from the com.jme3.post.filters package) are three examples of artistic filters. In contrast to the other photo-realistic filters, artistic filters make the 3D scene look flat and untextured, as if painted or printed.

The following screenshot shows how a toon shader makes the fiercest dinosaur look cute:

The toon effect is activated just like any other filter:

1.  Make a copy of Main.java and name the class Cartoon.java. Remember to also refactor the first line of the main() method to Cartoon app = new Cartoon().

2.  Add three class fields: one for the scene, one for the FilterPostProcessor, and one for the CartoonEdgeFilter (from the com.jme3.post.filters package):

    ```
    private Spatial sceneGeo;
    private FilterPostProcessor fpp;
    private CartoonEdgeFilter toon;
    ```

3.  Initialize fpp and toon in the simpleInitApp() method. Add the FilterPostProcessor to the viewPort, and add the CartoonEdgeFilter to the FilterPostProcessor:

    ```
    public void simpleInitApp() {
      fpp = new FilterPostProcessor(assetManager);
      viewPort.addProcessor(fpp);

      toon = new CartoonEdgeFilter();
      fpp.addFilter(toon);
    ```

**4.** Load and attach a scene or model of your choice, and add a light source:

```
assetManager.registerLocator("town.zip", ZipLocator.class);
sceneGeo = assetManager.loadModel("main.scene");
rootNode.attachChild(sceneGeo);

DirectionalLight sunLight = new DirectionalLight();
sunLight.setDirection(new Vector3f(0.3f, -0.5f, -0.5f));
rootNode.addLight(sunLight);
}
```

**5.** Adjust the material of all Phong-illuminated geometries in the scene:

```
public void makeToonish(Spatial spatial) {
  if (spatial instanceof Node) {
    Node n = (Node) spatial;
    for (Spatial child : n.getChildren()) {
      makeToonish(child);
    }
  } else if (spatial instanceof Geometry) {
    Geometry g = (Geometry) spatial;
    Material m = g.getMaterial();
    if (m.getMaterialDef().getName().equals
      ("Phong Lighting")) {
      Texture t = assetManager.loadTexture(
        "Textures/ColorRamp/toon.png");
      m.setTexture("ColorRamp", t);
      m.setBoolean("VertexLighting", true);
      m.setBoolean("UseMaterialColors", true);
      m.setColor("Specular", ColorRGBA.Black);
      m.setColor("Diffuse", ColorRGBA.White);
    }
  }
}
```

**6.** Apply the `makeToonish()` method in your `simpleInitApp()` method. For example, apply it to the root node after attaching the scene:

```
makeToonish(rootNode);
```

Run the code. You should see your scene rendered with fake "two-dimensional" comic book materials and outlined with black edges.

## What just happened?

Apart from activating the filter as usual, the trick with the toon shader is changing the color ramp of the materials of all geometries in the scene:

- Enable color ramp lighting and set the `ColorRamp` argument to a simple color ramp. The included `assets/Textures/ColorRamp/toon.png` contains a simple three-step grayscale gradient. The color ramp creates the reduction in colors that is typical for cartoons.
- Disable specular colors because cartoon surfaces do not shine.
- Set all diffuse colors to white, to make everything equally bright.
- Enable vertex lighting in the material to make colors look like simple gradients. This also disables bump mapping to make objects look flatter.

Although this filter makes the scene look very simple and flat, do not expect to use this approach to make a game use as few GPU resources as a 2D game would! The engine must still render the whole scene in 3D. The post-processor filters work very hard to remove the depth and material information from the buffers again, which has almost the same performance impact as using photo-realistic filters.

## Have a go hero

Open your Tower Defense game once more, and decorate it with your favorite effects! You could also use the following tips:

- Accompany every shot with a glow, a burst, and a shockwave
- Accompany the defeat of a creep with debris and smoke
- Accompany the destruction of the player base with a huge explosion
- Add drop shadows and ambient occlusion shadows to the scene

# Summary

You can now spice up games with small particle effects, and enhance the whole scene by applying post-processor filters. Specifically, you learned:

- How to configure particle emitters to look like smoke, fire, or sparks
- How to combine particle emitters to create complex effects, such as explosions
- How to make a scene cast shadows in the light and glow in the dark
- How to add focal depth to a wide scene
- How to turn any 3D scene into a cartoon

Other very common scenarios for post-processor filters include environmental effects such as waving fog, glittering water, and scattered sunlight. These effects are somewhat specialized (not every 3D game needs them), so they get a chapter of their own. To stay with the "nature" theme (and to give your sunlight something to shine upon) the following chapter covers terrains and skies. Come on, let's take a hike!

# 8

# Creating Landscapes

*Many of your adventures have taken you through gloomy dungeons, endless warehouses, and claustrophobic space ship corridors. You stumbled through dark hallways wondering whether you would ever see the light of day again. It's nice to be a fearless hero and all, but can the whole world-saving business not happen outdoors just once in a while? It can!*

*Maybe what your game needs is a meandering landscape under an awesome sky. Flood the scene with a good dose of sunlight (or moonlight) or shroud it in mysterious fog. Decorate it with trees and bushes and throw in a body of water for good measure. And off you go, this time across the rock-strewn desert, through wild jungles, into the overgrown city ruins.*

In this chapter, you learn how to create a landscape with:

- ◆ Terrains and trees
- ◆ Sky and sunlight
- ◆ Fog and water

Ready to go for a hike?

## Welcome to Earth

Another cool feature that makes it worthwhile to install the jMonkeyEngine SDK is the Terrain Editor, nicknamed TerraMonkey. This tool allows you to create terrains easily and save them in the .j3o format.

# Time for action – climbing a hill

Let's create a scene and add a terrain spatial to it. Open the jMonkeyEngine SDK and create a `.j3o` file.

1. Open the **Project Assets** node in the SDK. Right-click on the **Scenes** node, and choose **New | Other...**.

2. In the **New File** wizard, select the **Scene** category to create an **Empty jME3 Scene**.

3. Name the scene `myTerrain.j3o`. The wizard saves the scene to the **Scenes** directory, and opens the empty scene in the **SceneComposer**.

4. Open the **SceneExplorer** from the **Windows** menu.

5. In the **SceneExplorer**, right-click on the **New Scene** node, and choose **Add Spatial...** | **Terrain**. The **Terrain** wizard opens.

You use the **Terrain** wizard to generate a terrain mesh.

1. Specify the terrain's **Total Size** (for example, 256) and **Patch Size** (for example, 64). Both values must be powers of two. Click on **Next**.

2. Under **Heightmap**, choose **Flat** to start with a flat landscape.

3. Specify the size of the **AlphaMap** of the terrain material (for example, 256). The value has to be a power of two. The larger the alphamap, the more detailed your terrain's textures can be. You cannot change this value later.

4. Click **Finish** to generate the terrain.

5. Click on the **Edit Terrain** toolbar button (the icon looks like three mountains).

The terrain mesh appears in the Terrain Editor.

The Terrain Editor uses the `SceneComposer` to preview the scene. When you load a scene in the `SceneComposer` and the screen stays black, click on the light bulb button. This activates a light source so that the materials can be rendered.

If the model is lacking textures, click on the cube button to visualize the scene as a wireframe.

If you still see nothing, drag the mouse with the right or left button pressed to move around in the scene to make certain that you are not too far above or below the terrain to see it.

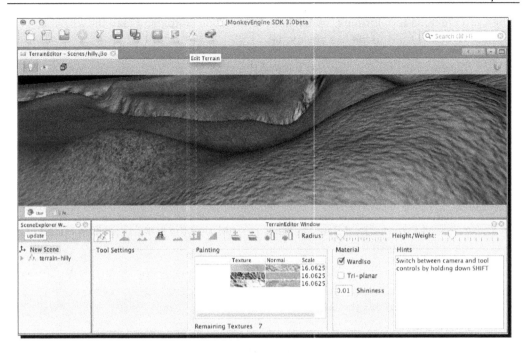

Now you can use the *terraforming* buttons in the Terrain Editor to modify the terrain. Click to activate one of the tools and drag the mouse over the terrain to sculpt it. Just like a paintbrush, you can specify the radius and weight (intensity) of the terraforming tools, so you can sculpt larger or smaller chunks of the terrain. You have the following tools at your disposal:

- **Raise or lower**: Pull up hills or push down valleys
- **Smooth or rough**: Soften edges or make surfaces more uneven
- **Level or slope**: Create level plateaus or create slanted slopes

Have a go and terraform some hills! Don't worry about textures for now; we'll look at them soon.

 In the SceneComposer window, press the right mouse button to set the 3D cursor, and press the left mouse button to select an object. Drag the left mouse button to rotate, and drag the right mouse button to move the scene. Use the **Monkey Head** menu to position the camera above, below, to the left or right, in front of, or behind the model.

When you are done terraforming, switch back to the Code Editor, and load the `assets/Scenes/myTerrain.j3o` file like any model.

1.  Make a copy of `Main.java` and name the class `TerrainFromScene.java`. Remember to also refactor the first line of the `main()` method to the following:

    ```
    TerrainFromScene app = new TerrainFromScene();
    ```

2.  Load the scene, and attach it to the `rootNode`.

    ```
    public void simpleInitApp() {
        Spatial terrainGeo =
            assetManager.loadModel("Scenes/myTerrain.j3o");
        rootNode.attachChild(terrainGeo);
    ```

3.  Add a light source. By default, terrains created with the SDK use an illuminated material similar to `Lighting.j3md`.

    ```
    DirectionalLight sun = new DirectionalLight();
    sun.setDirection(new Vector3f(-0.39f, -0.32f, -0.74f));
    rootNode.addLight(sun);
    }
    ```

Run the code sample. Use the W, A, S, and D keys to fly over your terrain and look at it from different angles.

## What just happened?

Congrats, you created a terrain mesh, and you didn't even need Blender! Granted, manually sculpting a terrain in a model editor gives you full artistic freedom, especially if your landscape includes overhangs, ledges, or caves. But storing the position of every pixel in the model uses up a lot of memory. Rendering large terrains in one piece is very inefficient, and likely to slow down your game.

For a real-time game, you want a faster-loading, more compact solution. While you are terraforming, the jMonkeyEngine SDK does a lot of work in the background for you. TerraMonkey saves a top-down view of your terrain in a format called heightmap. Similar to a topographical hiking map, a `heightmap` reduces a 3D terrain to a flat 2D array of sampled height values. When loading the terrain data, the engine extrapolates missing height values between the sampled coordinates, and recreates the 3D mesh.

In the following screenshots, compare the rendered 3D terrain (middle) to the corresponding 2D topographic map (left) and 2D heightmap (right).

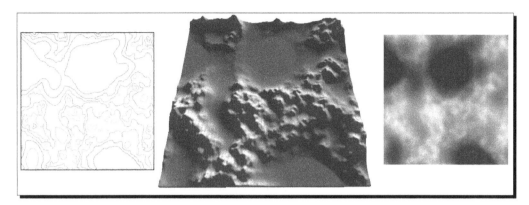

A standard heightmap uses height values between 0 to 255, where 0 represents the lowest valleys and 255 the highest mountains. These values are relative. Whether the highest elevation in your scene is a 1 world unit high mole hill, or a 1,000 world units high mountain peak solely depends on how you scale the terrain.

Using a 256-step interval has the advantage that a heightmap can be nicely visualized as an 8-bit grayscale image. The valleys (down to 0) are black, the mountains (up to 255) are white, and the slopes in between are gray. Editing a 2D heightmap in a graphic editor is easier than sculpting a 3D mesh in a model editor. You see that a heightmap is a user-friendly and memory-efficient way to store elevation data.

## Time for action – let there be grass

After you terraformed the landscape, you want to texture areas as grass, rock, sand, stone, soil, pebbles, pavement—or whatever ground your game's world requires.

Right-click on your terrain file and choose **Edit Terrain**, and then perform the following steps:

1.  Click on the **Add Texture Layer** button (a green plus sign) in the Terrain Editor. This lets you add a texture that will be used as a diffuse map. For example, add a grass or rock texture from the provided assets/Textures/Terrain directory.

2.  Optionally, add the corresponding NormalMap of the DiffuseMap.

3.  Click on the **Paint Texture on Terrain** button (looks like a spray can) in the Terrain Editor.

4. Click to select the texture that you want to paint.

5. Adjust the radius and weight of the paint brush to apply textures with broader or finer strokes.

6. Drag the mouse to texture the terrain.

This process is called **texture splatting**. Repeat it for each texture on your terrain; for example, rock or grass. Similarly, you can remove textures using the **Erase Texture** button.

## What just happened?

Again, many things happened in the background as the SDK created several texture layers for you. This user-friendly way of free-form painting is called texture splatting. The jMonkeyEngine provides you with two material definitions that support texture splatting: Terrain.j3md and TerrainLighting.j3md from Common/MatDefs/Terrain.

Do you remember that we specified an alphamap size in the Terrain wizard? An **alphamap** is one of the secret ingredients of materials that support texture splatting. For each texture that you paint onto the terrain, the Terrain Editor paints one color on the alphamap. An alphamap supports up to four splat textures—represented by the red, green, blue, and alpha channels (RGBA color).

Splat textures work similar to blue screen backgrounds (chroma key) on TV. While you are painting the first texture on the terrain, the Terrain Editor is drawing red pixels into the alphamap. When the engine renders the terrain, it replaces these red pixels with your first texture. Green pixels are replaced by the second texture, and blue pixels by the third. This abstraction allows you to swap out whole textures later. You are beginning to see how nifty texture splatting is!

Here you see an example of a grayscale heightmap (left) and a simple alphamap (middle) with red, green, and blue channels. The engine generates the terrain from the heightmap, and replaces the colored pixels with the textures that you assigned (right).

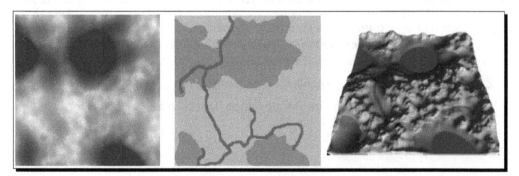

# Time for action – splat goes the texture

You see how easy it is to create and texture a terrain in the SDK—but you can of course achieve the same with hand-drawn textures and hand-written Java code.

First, we create a heightmap for our terrain by performing the following steps:

1.  Create a grayscale PNG image in a graphic editor of your choice. The size must be a square power of two; for example, 512 px x 512 px.

2.  Use a spray or brush tool to outline the terrain's elevation in grayscales, where white represents high and black low.

3.  Save the heightmap as `assets/Textures/Terrain/heightmap.png`.

Next, we draw the alphamap that specifies where the grass, rock, and road textures go.

1.  Create an empty 32-bit RGBA color image. The size must be a square power of two; for example, 512 px x 512 px.

2.  Open `assets/Textures/Terrain/heightmap.png`, copy its content, and paste it into your empty RGB image. We want to use the heightmap as a template for the alphamap.

3.  Choose a wide brush and paint over the heightmap as shown in the preceding example. Paint dark valleys pure red and paint light mountains pure green. Then choose a thin brush and paint a pure blue winding road through the valleys and over mountain passes. Make sure to cover the gray heightmap completely, so only colors are left.

4.  Save the image as PNG under `assets/Textures/Terrain/alphamap.png`.

We now have a simple custom alphamap that defines where the three texture layers go. Let's write code that creates a material using this alphamap and three textures.

1.  Make a copy of `Main.java` and name the class `TerrainSimple.java`. Remember to also refactor the first line of the `main()` method to the following:

    ```
    TerrainSimple app = new TerrainSimple();
    ```

2.  Create a material based on `Terrain.j3md`.

    ```
    public void simpleInitApp() {
      terrainMat = new Material(assetManager,
        "Common/MatDefs/Terrain/Terrain.j3md");
    ```

3.  Load your `alphamap.png` into the `Alpha` layer of the material.

    ```
    terrainMat.setTexture("Alpha", assetManager.loadTexture(
      "Textures/Terrain/alphamap.png"));
    ```

4. `Terrain.j3md` **supports three textures. Load grass, rock, and road textures into layers** `Tex1` **(red),** `Tex2` **(green), and** `Tex3` **(blue). Optionally, specify a texture scale.**

```
// Grass texture for the splatting material
Texture grass = assetManager.loadTexture(
  "Textures/Terrain/grass.jpg");
grass.setWrap(WrapMode.Repeat);
terrainMat.setTexture("Tex1", grass);
terrainMat.setFloat("Tex1Scale", 32);

// Rock texture for the splatting material
Texture rock = assetManager.loadTexture(
  "Textures/Terrain/rock.png");
rock.setWrap(WrapMode.Repeat);
terrainMat.setTexture("Tex2", rock);
terrainMat.setFloat("Tex2Scale", 64);

// Road texture for the splatting material
Texture road = assetManager.loadTexture(
  "Textures/Terrain/road.png");
road.setWrap(WrapMode.Repeat);
terrainMat.setTexture("Tex3", road);
terrainMat.setFloat("Tex3Scale", 16);
```

The texture splatting material is ready.

Let's proceed to load the heightmap and create a terrain mesh from it.

1. Load the heightmap image as a texture.

```
Texture heightMapImage = assetManager.loadTexture(
    "Textures/Terrain/heightmap.png" );
```

2. Create an `AbstractHeightMap` object (from the `com.jme3.terrain.heightmap` package) from the texture.

```
AbstractHeightMap heightmap = null;
try {
  heightmap = new ImageBasedHeightMap(
      heightMapImage.getImage(), 0.5f );
  heightmap.load();
} catch (Exception e) { e.printStackTrace(); }
```

3. Create a `TerrainQuad` object (from the `com.jme3.terrain.geomipmap` package). A `TerrainQuad` is a type of node optimized for terrain meshes.

```
TerrainQuad terrain = new TerrainQuad(
    "terrain", 65, 513, heightmap.getHeightMap() );
```

**4.** Apply the previously created material to the terrain node. Finally, attach the terrain to the `rootNode`.

```
terrain.setMaterial(terrainMat);
rootNode.attachChild(terrain);
```

**5.** Optionally, speed up the `flyCam` and move the camera into a position from where you get a good look at the terrain.

```
flyCam.setMoveSpeed(100);
cam.setLocation(new Vector3f(0, 512, 512));
cam.lookAt(Vector3f.ZERO, Vector3f.UNIT_Y);
```

Run the code. You do not need a light source this time since `Terrain.j3md` is a simple, unshaded material.

## What just happened?

This simple example demonstrates the steps that the SDK performs in the background when you create a terrain. You see that you can create and texture terrains manually if you need more artistic control, or if you generate landscapes procedurally from code.

The `ImageBasedHeightMap` constructor expects an image file and a float value.

- The image is the grayscale heightmap. Remember that the image size must be a square power of two.
- The float value (here `0.5f`) is a dampening value that smoothes the terrain.
- Use the `heightmap.load()` method to initialize the heightmap object.
- Optionally, call `heightmap.smooth(0.9f);` after `heightmap.load()` to avoid bumps and stairsteps on the generated terrain.

The `TerrainQuad` constructor expects a node name, terrain patch size in pixels, size of the heightmap in pixels, and lastly the raw heightmap data as a float array.

- The patch size is a value used to break down a large terrain mesh into smaller chunks that can be culled efficiently if out of sight. Obviously, the patch size must be smaller than the heightmap size: for example, 64 px x 64 px is a good terrain patch size for a 512 px x 512 px terrain. This value must be a power of two, plus one, so we specify `65` (64 + 1).
- The next argument is the size of the heightmap in pixels. Again, this must be a power of two, plus one. Our image file is 512 px x 512 px, so specify `513` here.
- The last argument is the raw heightmap data: this data is stored in a 2D float array that you simply get using `heightmap.getHeightMap()`.

Next, let's have a closer look at the Java side of texture splatting.

Using the `Terrain.j3md` definition demonstrated here is the simplest method to texture a terrain. This material definition supports three diffuse map textures with texture scales. Typically, you set `setWrap(WrapMode.Repeat);` on each tiled texture. If the repetitiveness becomes too visible, decrease the texture scale; if small blades of grass appear as big as twigs, increase the texture scale. The `Terrain.j3md` material's diffuse maps are named `Tex1` (red), `Tex2` (green), and `Tex3` (blue). The texture scale properties are `Tex1Scale`, `Tex2Scale`, and `Tex3Scale`.

Internally, the Terrain Editor follows the same approach as shown in the `Terrain.j3md` example, but it uses the more advanced `TerrainLighting.j3md` material definition. `TerrainLighting.j3md` combines the texture-splatting features of `Terrain.j3md` with the Phong lighting support of the already familiar `Lighting.j3md`, and can produce very beautiful landscapes. `TerrainLighting.j3md` supports multiple diffuse and normal maps (for example, `DiffuseMap_1`, `DiffuseMap_1_scale`, and `NormalMap_1`), in addition to material colors (`Ambient`, `Diffuse`, `Specular`, and `GlowColor`), `Shininess`, `GlowMap`, and `SpecularMap`. As always, remember to add a light source.

The following screenshot shows a rendered terrain with Phong illumination. The trail, rocks, and grass were added using texture splatting.

Typically, you use the SDK to create terrains with materials based on `TerrainLighting.j3md`. Advanced users may sometimes want to write Java code that sets these material properties procedurally, similar to how we just did for `Terrain.j3md` in `chapter08.TerrainSimple.java`. A code sample (`chapter08.TerrainLighting.java`) is included with this book. If you are curious, look up the material properties in the jMonkeyEngine source or on the `jmonkeyengine.org` wiki. Or simply type `TerraMonkey` into the SDK's search box to open the built-in documentation.

Did you know that if you draw your textures and alphamaps by hand as described here, you can use materials based on `Terrain.j3md` and `TerrainLighting.j3md` on any geometry? These two material definitions let you apply free-form texture splatting on any model—not only terrains.

# But wait, there's more

Now you know the basics and can start adding terrains to your games. The following terrain features are optional, but it's good to know they exist.

## Time for action – up hill and down dale

We have seen how to generate a terrain from a heightmap using `ImageBasedHeightMap` or the SDK. This type of terrain is the one that you have most control over, and you will probably use it most often. jMonkeyEngine can also generate a random heightmap if you need a quick and dirty solution.

Perform the following steps to generate a simple random heightmap for a hilly terrain:

1.  Return to your copy of `TerrainSimple.java`.

2.  Comment out the line that generates the `ImageBasedHeightMap`.

3.  Add a line that generates a `HillHeightMap`.

    ```
    AbstractHeightMap heightmap = null;
    try {
      // heightmap = new ImageBasedHeightMap(
      //     heightMapImage.getImage(), .5f );
    heightmap = new HillHeightMap(1025,500,50,100,(byte)3);
      heightmap.load();
    } catch (Exception e) { e.printStackTrace(); }
    ```

4.  Keep the rest of the code.

Run the code. You see a random terrain with lots of round hills. Don't be surprised if the texture-splatting material that you re-used from the heightmap-based terrain is static, and obviously will not fit the random shape of the new hilly terrain very well.

## What just happened?

The `HillHeightMap` constructor expects the following arguments:

- The size of the heightmap to generate (here 1,025 px x 1,025 px)
- The number of hills (here 600) on the heightmap
- The minimum and maximum radius of the hills (here 50 to 100)
- A random seed (here `(byte)3`) that initializes the randomizer—different seeds result in different landscapes

> In a previous tutorial, you already used the jMonkeyEngine SDK's Terrain wizard to generate a flat terrain for terraforming. You can also use it to generate the hill- and image-based heightmaps that we just demonstrated.
>
> The `SceneComposer` is not a replacement for a 3D model editor, but you can generate terrains, preview models, arrange scenes, and save them. Even if you decide to use another IDE for coding, it's worth keeping the jMonkeyEngine SDK as a handy tool to create scenes in the `.j3o` format.

Whichever terrain you generate, heightmaps have pros and cons to consider. Their shape is restricted to a fixed grid of height samples. A heightmap-based ground cannot have any holes or concave spaces, which makes caves impossible; similarly, if you need ledges, you must attach them as extra models.

At the same time, its uniformity is also the heightmap's main strength. It allows the scene graph to use optimizations (such as quadtrees) to adjust the **level of detail** (**LOD**) efficiently, and to cull non-visible parts of the terrain. A heightmap-based terrain does not only render faster than a mesh of equal size but also collision detection is quicker against a 2D array than against a 3D mesh.

## Time for action – go fast and vast

Vast terrains can render quite slowly, especially if you waste cycles calculating vertices that the player doesn't even see.

We can activate an optimization called LOD by performing the following steps:

1. Return to your copy of `TerrainSimple.java`.

2. Create a `TerrainLodControl` (from the `com.jme3.terrain.geomipmap` package) and add it to the terrain spatial.

```
TerrainQuad terrain =
    new TerrainQuad("terrain", 65, 513, heightmap.getHeightMap());
TerrainLodControl lodControl =
    new TerrainLodControl(terrain, getCamera());
terrain.addControl(lodControl);
terrain.setMaterial(terrainMat);
rootNode.attachChild(terrain);
```

Run the code and move high up and closer again. Watch the change in the level of detail based on how far away each terrain patch is from the camera.

## What just happened?

The `TerrainLodControl` tracks the camera position to determine which patches of the terrain are near or far from the user's point of view. The terrain patches that are close to the camera are rendered in full detail. The patches that are far away from the camera are drawn with reduced quality, since the user is not able to spot the details anyway. This optimization is called **LOD**. Pass the constructor the camera of `SimpleApplication`, and the terrain node as arguments.

Even with LOD activated, one problem of meshes is a loss of detail at steep, almost vertical slopes. The mesh gets stretched, and especially on terrains, distorted textures result in unnatural-looking cliffs. To alleviate this aesthetic issue, you can use the material definition's optional tri-planar mapping support. Be aware that tri-planar mapping has enough impact on performance that it should only be used if your gameplay hinges on well-textured steep terrains.

To activate it, set the `useTriPlanarMapping` property on the material object to `true`.

```
terrainMat = new Material(assetManager,
    "Common/MatDefs/Terrain/Terrain.j3md");
terrainMat.setBoolean("useTriPlanarMapping", true);
```

While we are speaking of steep slopes, one issue with 3D scenes in general, and terrains in particular, is the hard edge where the model or terrain ends—followed by a sudden abyss. For the player, stumbling upon a hard, unnatural cliff puts a major damper on game immersion. When designing the terrain, plan ahead to cover up the edge with natural obstacles, such as walls, mountainsides, or dense thicket. Design the barriers to be inconspicuous and clearly non-interactive, so players do not wrongly assume surmounting these obstacles was part of the game.

> If you are fed up with having to sprinkle obstacles over the map to keep players from falling over the edge, look at the `TerrainGrid` examples that are included in the JMETests project. A `TerrainGrid` provides you with a randomized endless terrain that automatically extends itself to wherever the camera moves.

# Time for action – plant a tree

Placing a tree on flat ground is easy: you know the y coordinate of the ground plane.

Let's try placing a tree on a hilly terrain.

1. Make a copy of `TerrainSimple.java` and name the class `Trees.java`. Remember to also refactor the first line of the `main()` method to the following:

   ```
   Trees app = new Trees();
   ```

2. Keep the code that creates `HillHeightMap(1025, 1000, 50, 100, (byte) 3)`.

3. Load a tree model from the assets folder included with this book.

   ```
   public void simpleInitApp() {
     Spatial treeGeo = assetManager.loadModel(
       "Models/Tree/Tree.j3o");
     treeGeo.scale(5); // make tree bigger
     treeGeo.setQueueBucket(Bucket.Transparent);
     // transparent leaves
     rootNode.attachChild(treeGeo);
   ```

4. Place the tree at `(-30,y,-30)` on the terrain.

   ```
     Vector3f treeLoc = new Vector3f(-30,0,-30);
   treeLoc.setY( terrain.getLocalTranslation().getY() );
     treeGeo.setLocalTranslation(treeLoc);
   }
   ```

Run the code. You should see the tree standing on the flat ground, surrounded by hills. As long as (-30,y,-30) is on the flat part of your terrain, this code works.

But what if you want to place models on the hilly parts of the randomly generated terrain? You wouldn't want the tree to end up underground, flying in midair, or stuck inside a hill.

With randomly generated heightmaps, you have no chance of guessing where the hills and the planes are. This is why the TerrainQuad object provides you with an accessor to determine the y coordinate for any given x and z coordinate on the terrain.

Let's plant a tree at (0,y,-30) on a random terrain.

1.  Return to Trees.java.
2.  Keep the code that loads the tree model and the terrain.
3.  Place the tree at the position (-30,y,-30). Change the line that sets the tree's y coordinate as follows:

```
Vector3f treeLoc = new Vector3f(0,0,-30);
treeLoc.setY(terrain.getHeight(
        new Vector2f( treeLoc.x, treeLoc.z ) ) );
treeGeo.setLocalTranslation(treeLoc);
```

Run the code. The tree stands on the hill.

## *What just happened?*

The `getHeight()` method returns the height (y coordinate) of the `TerrainQuad` at the given x and z coordinates.

Load some models, `Sphere` or `Box` shapes, and experiment. You will notice that spheres and boxes seem to sink into the ground. You have to add half the box's or sphere's height to the y coordinate to position them correctly.

The difference between the shapes and the tree model is the geometry's origins. The origin of a box or sphere is its center. The origin of the tree model is at its roots. So when you place the tree, you set the position of the tree roots. When you place the box, you set the position of the center of the crate.

Who decides where a geometry's origin is? It simply depends on how the artist positioned the model relative to the 3D editor's origin before exporting it! How do you tell where a model's origin is? Open the model in a 3D scene editor (such as the jMonkeyEngine SDK's `SceneComposer`) and find the local origin marker. For example, when you right-click and edit the tree model in the SDK's `SceneComposer`, you see the tree's origin is marked at its root.

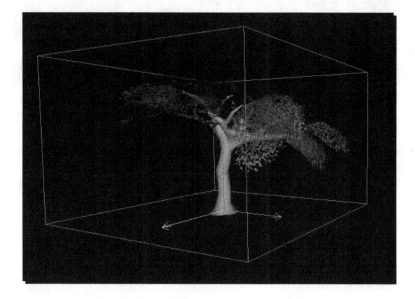

In contrast, a box geometry's location is relative to its center. You have to add half the box's height (its extend) to prevent the box from being half sunk into the ground.

# Not even the sky is the limit

In our first few demos, the background of the scene was always plainly colored—black or blue. Not very realistic, but acceptable if the indoor player only catches a glimpse of something blue through the blinds anyway. Now that the game scene is no longer set underground or indoors, you face the question of how to design a natural background.

The horizon is so far away—it might as well be a flat backdrop on a theatre stage. In fact, the sky in video games is just that: a flat, pre-rendered image. You can find free sky images online, but typically, you design custom skies that fit your game's atmosphere.

Don't create a large 3D model filled with skyscrapers and mountains as background. A huge model may look pretty; rendering it will, however, slow down your game at runtime. It's also a waste of your artist's time, especially if the player will never see these models close up.

Scenery generators (such as Bryce or Terragen) are graphic tools that specialize in creating great-looking panoramic images that are lightweight enough to be used as backgrounds in video games.

## Time for action – nothing but blue sky

The following image shows a simple example of six images that make up a game's background panorama: you see the top (blue sky), the bottom (the ground), and four sides (a snow-covered mountain at the horizon).

The trick with skies is that you project these six textures onto the insides of a gigantic cube that encompasses your whole scene. This popular approach of faking a background is called **environment mapping**. When we use a six-image CubeMap to simulate a sky, we refer to the box as **SkyBox**.

You can create your own SkyBox from a vacation photo or poster in a graphic editor:

1. Take six matching square snapshots of a panoramic view: one in each of the cardinal directions, plus one up, and one down.

2. Use the tools of your graphic editor to make the seams of the photos match.

3. Save them as six individual PNG files. Name them South, East, Up, Down, and so on.

To create a SkyBox, keep your six images ready, or use the ones provided with this book in assets/Textures/Sky/Lagoon for now. The jMonkeyEngine SDK creates special SkyBox objects that you can load into your game just like any other model.

Open the jMonkeyEngine SDK and create an empty scene by performing the following steps:

1. Open **Project Assets**, right-click on the **Scenes** node, and choose **New | Other...**.

2. In the **New File** Wizard, select the **Scene** category to create an **Empty jME3 Scene**.

3. Name the scene mySky.j3o. The wizard saves it to the **Scenes** directory. The empty scene opens in the **SceneComposer**.

Just like you used scene objects as containers for terrains, you can use this one as a container for a SkyBox.

1. Open the **SceneExplorer** from the Windows menu.

2. Right-click on the **New Scene** node in the **SceneExplorer**, and choose **Add Spatial...** | **SkyBox**.

3. Use the **SkyBox** wizard to load your sky images. Typically, you choose **Multiple Textures** and then browse to six images. For this exercise, you can use the Lagoon picture set included in the assets/Textures/Sky/Lagoon/ directory.

4. Click **Finish** to create the SkyBox spatial.

The following screenshot shows the jMonkeyEngine SDK after creating a SkyBox. Drag the mouse with the middle mouse button pressed to turn and look at the SkyBox from all sides.

The mySky.j3o object now contains a sky. Use the AssetManager to load the sky into a scene like any other model:

**1.** Make a copy of Main.java and name the class Sky.java. Remember to also refactor the first line of the main() method to the following:

```
Sky app = new Sky();
```

**2.** Load the sky spatial from the mySky.j3o file.

```
public void simpleInitApp() {
    Spatial mySky = assetManager.loadModel("Scenes/mySky.j3o");
    rootNode.attachChild(mySky);
}
```

Run the code and look at your SkyBox.

## *What just happened?*

The implementation of a SkyBox relies a bit on smoke and mirrors.

- The SkyBox is added to a special `Sky` bucket in the rendering queue. The depth of geometries in this bucket is set to infinity. This ensures that the sky always appears behind everything else.

- The SkyBox automatically follows the camera location. When the player moves, the SkyBox moves too. Just like the horizon, you will never reach it.

- The `SkyBox` does not follow camera rotation. When the player turns, the orientation of SkyBox stays fixed, just like a real horizon would.

- The `CullMode` of SkyBox is set to `Never`, which ensures it is always visible.

This combination of clever 3D graphic tricks creates the impression of a horizon—a vast landscape that is infinitely distant. We can see that SkyBoxes are the most efficient way to simulate a vast panoramic background.

This method only has a few disadvantages that we must work around: the cube maps used in SkyBoxes do not support animations, so they don't support floating clouds, or trees waving in the breeze. Also, if you attach overlapping 3D objects to the `Sky` bucket, don't expect them to render correctly—infinitely distant objects skip depth testing.

## Time for action – sky factory

The SkyBox wizard is handy if you need a sky in a `.j3o` file. But of course you can also procedurally create your SkyBox in Java code, using the jMonkeyEngine's `com.jme3.util. SkyFactory` package.

*1.* Return to `Sky.java`.

*2.* Comment out the `assetManager` line that loads the `mySky.j3o` model.

```
//Spatial mySky = assetManager.loadModel("Scenes/mySky.j3o");
```

*3.* Replace it by the following code that loads the six images:

```
Texture west  = assetManager.loadTexture(
    "Textures/Sky/Lagoon/lagoon_west.jpg");
Texture east  = assetManager.loadTexture(
    "Textures/Sky/Lagoon/lagoon_east.jpg");
Texture north = assetManager.loadTexture(
    "Textures/Sky/Lagoon/lagoon_north.jpg");
Texture south = assetManager.loadTexture(
```

```
    "Textures/Sky/Lagoon/lagoon_south.jpg");
Texture up = assetManager.loadTexture(
    "Textures/Sky/Lagoon/lagoon_up.jpg");
Texture down  = assetManager.loadTexture(
    "Textures/Sky/Lagoon/lagoon_down.jpg");
```

**4.** Use the `createSky()` method of `SkyFactory` to create the spatial:

```
Spatial sky = SkyFactory.createSky(assetManager,
    west, east, north, south, up, down);
```

**5.** Keep the line that attaches the sky spatial.

```
rootNode.attachChild(sky);
```

Run the code. The result should look the same as attaching `mySky.j3o` to the `rootNode`.

## What just happened?

The visual tool in the jMonkeyEngine SDK is quite nifty, but there are situations where we want to have full control over the scene elements that we generate. In this case, you can use the `com.jme3.util.SkyFactory` class to create a sky spatial out of six images directly in your code. The order of the sky image arguments in the `createSky()` constructor is always `assetManager, west, east, north, south, up,` and `down`.

> If you don't recall the order of arguments of a method or constructor, call up your IDE's javadoc support. If you use the jMonkeyEngine SDK, javadoc is already preconfigured. Place the cursor after the opening bracket; for example, `SkyFactory.createSky(|`
>
> Now press *Ctrl + Space bar* to open a handy javadoc pop up that shows the arguments that this method expects. Use the arrow keys and press *Return* to select one of the options, and the SDK generates example code. Fill in the arguments, and press *Tab* to jump to the next argument. Press *Ctrl + ;* to add a semicolon to the end of the line.

Instead of six individual cube map files, some applications export a single sky texture. One compressed **DDS (DirectDraw Surface)** file can contain the whole cube map. The jMonkeyEngine's `com.jme3.util.SkyFactory` class also supports loading DDS SkyBoxes as follows:

```
Spatial sky = SkyFactory.createSky( assetManager,
    "Textures/Sky/Bright/BrightSky.dds", false);
rootNode.attachChild(sky);
```

The Boolean `false` specifies that this is a cube map and not a `SphereMap`.

## Time for action – fog of war

If you have ever walked through unfamiliar terrain when it was foggy, you know the eerie feeling. Shadows scurry at the edge of your vision and monsters seem to lurk behind every tree. Isn't that just the atmosphere that you need for your game?

Thanks to the post-processor, adding fog to a scene is very easy:

*1.* Make a copy of `Main.java` and name the class `Fog.java`. Remember to also refactor the first line of the `main()` method to the following:

```
Fog app = new Fog();
```

*2.* Load a scene model or terrain of your choice. Re-use code from the previous examples. Remember to add a light.

*3.* Create one `FilterPostProcessor` per game, and a `FogFilter` (from the `com.jme3.post` package).

```
private FilterPostProcessor fpp;
private FogFilter fogFilter;
```

*4.* In the `simpleInitApp()` method, initialize the `FilterPostProcessor`, and add it to the `viewPort`.

```
public void simpleInitApp() {
    fpp = new FilterPostProcessor(assetManager);
    viewPort.addProcessor(fpp);
    //Initialize the FogFilter and
    //add it to the FilterPostProcesor.
    fogFilter = new FogFilter();
    fogFilter.setFogDistance(155);
    fogFilter.setFogDensity(2.0f);
    fpp.addFilter(fogFilter);
}
```

Run the code. The following screenshot shows the same town scene once with fog, and once in the sunlight:

## What just happened?

You can specify values for `FogFilter` settings to change the fog's starting distance (relative to the camera), and the density of the fog.

```
fogFilter.setFogDistance(155);
fogFilter.setFogDensity(2.0f);
```

Use these methods whenever you want fog to appear (for example, when the player approaches a swamp, stormy seas, or a spooky graveyard) or disappear (for example, when the player approaches a safe haven).

You can also change the fog color for various effects: white fog during the day, gray fog at dusk or dawn, or black fog to simulate night. A warm fog color (a light orange or light yellow) can add a lot to the atmosphere of a hot dusty desert, a burning apocalyptic world, or a volcano cave. A cold fog color (light blue or light green) can emphasize the chilly, wet atmosphere of a thunderstorm, a murky forest, or an underwater scene.

```
fog.setFogColor(new ColorRGBA(0.9f, 0.9f, 0.9f, 1.0f));
```

Fog is popularly used to cover up the horizon or sky. In a world constantly wrapped in fog, you easily get around not having a SkyBox.

# Catch the sun

When sunlight passes through gaps in the tree canopy, shines in through a window, or radiates from behind mountaintops, it often appears as a light cone or even individual beams. We refer to this atmospheric effect colloquially as god beams—the technical term for them is crepuscular rays.

In 3D graphics, light scattering is simulated with a technique called volumetric lighting. The beams are rendered as transparent cones of light. The jMonkeyEngine offers support for these cool light beams in the `com.jme3.post.filters.LightScatteringFilter` class.

## Time for action – let the sun shine in

The light scattering filter is another example of an effect that uses the post-processor that we are already familiar with from a previous chapter.

**1.** Make a copy of `Main.java` and name the class `SunLight.java`. Remember to also refactor the first line of the `main()` method to the following:

```
SunLight app = new SunLight();
```

**2.** Specify the direction of the sunlight as a vector.

```
private Vector3f lightDir = new Vector3f(-0.39f, -0.32f,
-0.74f);
```

**3.** Create one `FilterPostProcessor` per game, and a `LightScatteringFilter`.

```
private FilterPostProcessor fpp;
private LightScatteringFilter sunLightFilter;
```

**4.** Use the `lightDir` vector to create a `DirectionalLight` and add it to the `rootNode`.

```
public void simpleInitApp() {
    DirectionalLight sun = new DirectionalLight();
    sun.setDirection(lightDir);
    sun.setColor(ColorRGBA.White.clone().multLocal(2));
    rootNode.addLight(sun);
```

**5.** Initialize the `FilterPostProcessor` and add it to the `viewPort`.

```
fpp = new FilterPostProcessor(assetManager);
viewPort.addProcessor(fpp);
```

**6.** Initialize the `LightScatteringFilter` and add it to the `FilterPostProcesor`.

```
sunLightFilter = new LightScatteringFilter
(lightDir.mult(-3000));
fpp.addFilter(sunLightFilter);
```

7. Continue in the `simpleInitApp()` method to load a SkyBox, and a scene model or terrain of your choice. Re-use the code from the previous examples.

8. Finally, look into the sun.

```
cam.lookAtDirection(lightDir.negate(),
Vector3f.UNIT_Y);
}
```

Run the code sample. Use the WASD keys to walk around and get a hill or building between you and the sun. Note how the light beams become brighter and surround the obstacle.

## What just happened?

The `LightScatteringFilter` expects one argument—the position of the main light source. A `DirectionalLight`, however, does not actually have a location in the 3D scene. It only has a direction, because it simulates parallel light emitted from a great (near infinite) distance.

You can easily extrapolate a light position from a light direction by multiplying the direction vector with a large scalar. We just pretend that the sun is at a point -3,000 world units away. Note that if you use SkyBox that includes a graphical sun, you need to choose a light direction vector that matches where the sun is depicted on your SkyBox graphic.

To make the sun brighter, we multiply the light color by a scalar. Here we multiply `ColorRGBA.White` by 2.

The following screenshot shows the blinding rays of sunlight that appear when the player looks into the sun behind a mountain.

# Still waters run deep

Water is one of the more difficult things to render well. You can't simulate an ocean by creating an animated mesh, or a battalion of particle emitters. If your code does not calculate all the light reflections and refractions perfectly, the water simulation is bound to look like either melting plastic or leaking mercury.

The jMonkeyEngine comes prepackaged with two different ready-made water effects for your scenes: `SimpleWaterProcessor` and `WaterFilter`.

## Time for action – simple water

A correctly simulated water surface reflects the scene around it—or to be more precise, it reflects everything attached to a specific scene node that you supply.

1. Make a copy of `Main.java` and name the class `WaterSimple.java`. Remember to also refactor the first line of the `main()` method to the following:

```
WaterSimple app = new WaterSimple();
```

2. Create a class field for the node grouping the reflected scene.

```
private Node reflectedScene;
```

3. Create a class field for the light's direction.

```
private Vector3f lightDir =
    new Vector3f(-0.39f, -0.32f, -0.74f);
```

4. Initialize a `DirectionalLight`.

```
public void simpleInitApp() {
    DirectionalLight dl = new DirectionalLight();
    dl.setDirection(lightDir);
    rootNode.addLight(dl);
```

5. Initialize the `reflectedScene` node and attach it to the `rootNode`.

```
reflectedScene = new Node("Scene");
rootNode.attachChild(reflectedScene);
```

6. Add some scene elements, such as a sky and at least one geometry. Attach both to the `reflectedScene` node.

```
reflectedScene.attachChild(SkyFactory.createSky(assetManager,
    "Textures/Sky/Bright/BrightSky.dds", false));
Material boxMat = new Material(assetManager,
    "Common/MatDefs/Light/Lighting.j3md");
```

```
boxMat.setTexture("DiffuseMap",
    assetManager.loadTexture("Interface/Monkey.png"));
Box boxMesh = new Box(2, 2, 2);
Geometry boxGeo = new Geometry("Box", boxMesh);
boxGeo.setMaterial(boxMat);
reflectedScene.attachChild(boxGeo);
```

7. Create a `SceneProcessor` for the water effect and add it to the `viewPort`. The water reflects sunlight, and everything attached to the `reflectedScene` node.

```
SimpleWaterProcessor waterProcessor =
    new SimpleWaterProcessor(assetManager);
waterProcessor.setReflectionScene(reflectedScene);
waterProcessor.setLightPosition(lightDir.mult(-3000));
viewPort.addProcessor(waterProcessor);
```

8. Create a 100 x 100 world units big flat geometry as water surface. Apply the "magic" water material that you get from the water post-processor.

```
Spatial waterPlane =
    waterProcessor.createWaterGeometry(100,100);
    waterPlane.setMaterial(waterProcessor.getMaterial());
    waterPlane.setLocalTranslation(-50, 0, 50);
    rootNode.attachChild(waterPlane);
```

Run the code and watch the waves! Note how the geometry as well as the sky reflect.

## What just happened?

The com.jme3.water.SimpleWaterProcessor class provides a basic water effect. It is clearly recognizable as water, and it simulates waves and reflections. It renders quickly enough for a large scene—but you can also scale several water geometries down to fit into fountains, drinking troughs, or puddles.

Some important things to remember:

- Attach the sky and scene elements to the reflectedScene node, and not directly to the rootNode. When you create the water post-processor, you have to supply the reflectedScene node as an argument. Everything attached to this node is reflected by the water.

- Attach the water plane itself to the rootNode, and not to the reflectedScene node. We don't want the water surface to be reflected in itself (try it, it looks weird).

Since the implementation of the SimpleWaterProcessor is literally quite simple, it comes with a few downsides:

- The waves don't really stand out in the third dimension.

- The WaterPlane is single sided. Seen from below, the water surface becomes invisible, which breaks the immersion for the player.

- The WaterPlane has a visible edge that you need to cover up with a model or within the shape of the terrain.

These caveats are not an issue if you use this effect only on small bodies of water, where you can make certain that the player has no opportunity to dive into the water.

## Time for action – take a swim

Beautifully designed 3D landscapes invite the player to explore and interact. You couldn't hold it against a player if he or she tried to take a closer look at your water. Maybe a body of water is an important element in your game. Maybe some parts of the game story are even set underwater. For these cases, we need to pull out all the stops and show off what the engine is capable of, by using the com.jme3.water.WaterFilter class.

1. Make a copy of WaterSimple.java and name the class WaterTerrainSky.java. Remember to also refactor the first line of the main() method to the following:

   ```
   WaterTerrainSky app = new WaterTerrainSky();
   ```

2. Keep the class field for the node that groups the reflected scene.

   ```
   private Node reflectedScene;
   ```

**3.** Keep the class field for the light direction.

```
private Vector3f lightDir = new Vector3f
(-2.9f, -1.2f, -5.8f);
```

**4.** Keep the `DirectionalLight` in `simpleInitApp()`.

**5.** Keep the `reflectedScene` node and attach it to the `rootNode`.

```
reflectedScene = new Node("Scene");
rootNode.attachChild(reflectedScene);
```

**6.** Keep the attached scene elements, such as a sky and a geometry or terrain. Attach them to the `reflectedScene` node.

**7.** Remove the code from `simpleInitApp()` that initializes the `SimpleWater` and `WaterPlane`. Replace it with the following code that creates a `WaterFilter` instead:

```
FilterPostProcessor fpp = new FilterPostProcessor(assetManager);
viewPort.addProcessor(fpp);
WaterFilter water = new WaterFilter(reflectedScene, lightDir);
fpp.addFilter(water);
```

Run the code. Don't you just want to jump in and take a swim? Go ahead! The `WaterFilter` does not only simulate the surface but also includes an underwater filter!

## *What just happened?*

The `WaterFilter` simulates waves, foam, reflections, and refractions of the water surface. Underwater light reflections cause a typical scattered pattern on the sea floor: this optical effect is called **caustics**. When light passes through a curved transparent object—such as water or glass—it is reflected and refracted many times.

The `WaterFilter` constructor depends on the `reflectedScene` and the light direction of the main directional light. This filter has countless optional settings that you can configure. The defaults, however, already produce very nice results.

Let's have a look at the most commonly used settings:

| The WaterFilter method | Purpose |
| --- | --- |
| `setLightColor(ColorRGBA. White );` `setLightDirection(lightDir);` | Set these two to the same values as your main light source's color and direction. |
| `setSunScale(3);` | This specifies the size of the reflection of the sun. |
| `setWindDirection(new Vector2f(0.0f, -1.0f) );` | Set this to `Vector2f.ZERO` for calm water, and to larger vectors for flowing water. |
| `setWaveScale(0.005f);` `setMaxAmplitude(1);` | This specifies how big the waves are. The smaller the wave scale, the wider the waves are. The bigger the amplitude, the higher the waves are. |
| `setWaterTransparency(.1f);` | This specifies how muddy (`1f`) or clear (`.01f`) the water is. |
| `setWaterColor(new ColorRGBA(.1f,.3f,.5f,1f));` `setDeepWaterColor(new ColorRGBA(0f,0f,.1f,1f));` | These specify the gradient of the water's color from the upper layer to the deepest layers. |
| `setWaterHeight(0.0f);` | This specifies the height (y) of the water plane in the scene. Change this value procedurally in the update loop to simulate tides. |

Caustics add a lot of realism to an underwater scene, but calculating them in real time is prohibitively CPU intensive. Since 3D game engines must favor cheap and fast solutions over physical correctness, jMonkeyEngine internally simulates underwater caustics using simple transparent splat textures. The outcome looks just as good, and leaves you enough resources to add other filters to your scene.

Let's speak about adding other filters. The `WaterFilter` goes extremely well in combination with the other post-processor effects that we already know. Why not add a `LightScatteringFilter`, `DepthOfFieldFilter`, and `BloomFilter` to improve the scene?

## Pop quiz

Q1. What do you need to make the most of texture splatting with a material based on `TerrainLighting.j3md` or `TerrainLighting.j3md`?

1. Specular color, ambient color, diffuse color, alphamaps, and any mesh.
2. Diffuse maps, normal maps, scale, and a terrain mesh.
3. Specular color, ambient color, diffuse color, and a terrain mesh.
4. Diffuse maps, normal maps, alphamaps, scale, and any mesh.

## Have a go hero

Create a cool-looking environment for your Tower Defense game. Decide whether you want to go for a science-fiction themed alien planet, a modern terrestrial war-zone, a medieval fantasy battleground, or a futuristic post-apocalyptic world—whatever genre tickles your fancy.

◆ Use the SDK to terraform some hills for your towers to stand on, and a valley for your player's base to hide in. Scale and move the terrain so that the creeps now approach through the valley entrance. Texture the terrain with materials that fit your chosen genre.

◆ Design a cool background panorama for your game genre and turn it into a SkyBox. Are you going for a bright, dark, or colorful sky? Adjust the ambient light color to a warm, neutral, or cold color accordingly.

◆ What would your terrain look like if it was shrouded by fog, with only a few light beams shining through the clouds? (Position the light source not quite opposite to the camera.)

◆ What would your terrain look like if it was set on a lonely island surrounded by the turbulent sea?

Combine the effects and see how they change the atmosphere of your game completely—although the game mechanics stay the same.

# Summary

In this chapter, we learned how to create natural-looking landscapes.

We can generate terrains with plains, hills, and valleys. The sky in our scenes is not just a blue background color any more, but a real horizon with a cloudy atmosphere. We can add realistic-looking water with waves, foam, reflections, and caustics. We know how to enhance the atmosphere of a scene by adding environmental effects such as sunbeams and fog.

As a side effect, we also learned what a heightmap, cube map, and texture splatting is. With what we now know, our scenes look nothing less than professional. But do they also sound professional? The next chapter demonstrates how we can enhance the immersion even more by adding audio.

# 9
# Making Yourself Heard

*You have come very far on your adventurous journey: you have mastered the creation of interactive scenes, you have the power to control physical forces, and you know how to fine-tune materials and visual effects. Your game world is looking pretty good already. But suddenly your spider sense tingles. Did the birds stop singing? Is there danger ahead? An experienced explorer knows what is missing: sound effects. As always, the mighty* `SimpleApplication` *is your friend and gives you access to a preconfigured* `AudioRenderer` *object.* `AudioRenderer` *supports the widely-used* **Open Audio Library** *(OpenAL) interface that is exposed by the* **Lightweight Java Game Library** *(LWJGL).*

In this chapter, you will learn how to complete your game, by adding the following:

- ◆ Ambient sounds, GUI beeps, and music
- ◆ Positional sound and directional sound

Time to switch on the surround system (or grab your headphones) and make some noise!

# Please roar into the microphone now

To record and edit sound files, you need an audio editor. Similar to graphic and model editors, countless options exist, both free and proprietary.

> The jMonkeyEngine team recommends Audacity, which you get for free (http://audacity.sourceforge.net). This user-friendly software is open source, and provides you with a solid set of sound recording, editing, and conversion tools.

You can choose any audio software that is able to export sounds in the supported file formats: jMonkeyEngine supports **Ogg Vorbis** audio compression inside .ogg file containers, and uncompressed **PCM audio** in .wav file containers.

| Format | Description | Usage |
|---|---|---|
| Waveform .wav | A raw format with a bigger file size and better quality. | Save short exclamations and noises (steps, clunks, beeps, voices, cries, and so on in this uncompressed format). |
| Ogg Vorbis .ogg | A compressed format with a smaller file size and some loss of quality. Decompression may take extra time on low-performance devices. | Compress longer clips such as music or ambient noise loops. |

For noises and speech, we recommend saving disk space by exporting sounds with a bitrate of 96 kbps. If you don't know which of the two formats to choose, we recommend Ogg Vorbis.

> If you don't have time to track down your friendly neighborhood T-Rex for that perfect "roar!", have a look at the appendix for websites where you can download free audio samples.

When you are done with recording and editing, you save your sounds in the subdirectories of your project's assets/Sounds directory, as you do with textures and models.

# Ambient sounds! They are everywhere!

In 3D games, objects are scene nodes, lights are light nodes, and similarly, sounds are audio nodes. You find audio nodes in the com.jme3.audio.* package.

# Time for action – add ambient sound

Let's create an audio node in the `simpleInitApp()` method, and play it:

**1.** Make a copy of `Main.java` and name the class `BackgroundSounds.java`. Remember to also refactor the first line of the `main()` method to `BackgroundSounds app = new BackgroundSounds();`.

**2.** Copy the `River.ogg` sound file into the `assets/Sounds/Environment/` directory.

**3.** Use the `simpleInitApp()` method to load the sound into an audio node:

```
public void simpleInitApp() {
AudioNode natureAudio = new AudioNode(
assetManager, "Sounds/Environment/River.ogg");
```

**4.** Specify properties of the sound; for example, set the volume to 5. 10 is loudest, 0 is silent.

```
natureAudio.setVolume(5);
```

**5.** Switch the sound to play continuously by setting the looping property to `true`. Note that if you ran the application now, you would not hear anything yet.

```
natureAudio.setLooping(true);
```

**6.** Call the `play()` method on the `AudioNode` to start playing the sound:

```
natureAudio.play();
}
```

Run the application. You should hear the continuous sound of a river. Since this is a looping sound, it plays continuously until you quit the application or call the `stop()` method on the `AudioNode`.

## What just happened?

Atmospheric music and background noises—such as chirping birds and cicadas in the wilderness, dripping water in a dungeon, or the ubiquitous clunking of machines in a factory—are ambient sounds. Ambient sounds are relatively quiet, they do not emanate from any specific location, and their volume stays the same independent of the player's distance. Ambient sound stands in contrast to 3D sound that seems to have an identifiable location in the scene (we will look into positional audio later).

The main purpose of ubiquitous ambient loops is to support the player's immersion in the scene: your underground maze may *look* forbidding, but together with the sound of dripping water, it also *feels* chilly. And there's nothing like some cracks and whispers to turn an abandoned office model into a regular Arkham Asylum...

User interface feedback noises—such as beeps and blips when the user selects an item or switches weapons—can also fall into the category of position-less ambient sounds. GUI sounds, however, are typically short, while ambient sounds can be quite long. Let's have a look at how jMonkeyEngine handles longer and shorter sounds; you can choose to either pre-buffer or stream sounds.

## Time for action – to pre-buffer or to stream?

Try the following code to see the difference between the two ways of loading audio files. Use the Boolean parameter in the `AudioNode` constructor to switch streaming on (`true`) or off (`false`).

1. Make a copy of `Main.java` and name the class `BufferedVsStreamed.java`. Remember to also refactor the first line of the `main()` method to `BufferedVsStreamedapp = new BufferedVsStreamed();`.

2. `Nature.ogg` is a large file (650 kb), so you decide to stream it using the following code:

```
public void simpleInitApp() {
    AudioNode natureAudio = new AudioNode(assetManager,
        "Sounds/Environment/Nature.ogg", true); // streaming=true
    natureAudio.setVolume(5);
    natureAudio.play(); // play as stream
```

3. `Footsteps.ogg` is a small file (25 kb), so you decide to pre-buffer it using the following code:

```
    AudioNode stepsAudio = new AudioNode(assetManager,
        "Sounds/Effects/Footsteps.ogg", false); // streaming=false
    stepsAudio.setVolume(2);
    stepsAudio.setLooping(true);
    stepsAudio.play(); // play prebuffered
}
```

When you run this sample, you should hear continuous nature sounds in the background, together with a looping sound of footsteps. If you call `setLooping(false)` on the pre-buffered steps sound, you only hear one set of steps before the sound stops.

## What just happened?

jMonkeyEngine has two ways of handling audio: you can pre-buffer or stream sound files. For the user, either mode sounds the same; the only difference lies in loading speed and memory consumption.

Pre-buffering means that jMonkeyEngine loads the whole file into memory before it starts playing:

```
AudioNode stepsAudio = new AudioNode(assetManager,
    "Sounds/Effects/Footsteps.ogg", false);
    // no streaming = prebuffered
```

The default constructor pre-buffers new Audio Nodes—this is the one you will use the most:

```
AudioNode stepsAudio = new AudioNode(assetManager,
    "Sounds/Effects/Footsteps.ogg"); // default = prebuffered
```

In contrast, when you stream audio, you do not have to worry how much memory a large sound file uses, or how long it takes to load. A streamed sound can start playing without being fully loaded:

```
AudioNode natureAudio = new AudioNode(assetManager,
    "Sounds/Environment/Nature.ogg", true); // streaming is active
```

The only caveat is that you cannot use `setLooping(true)` to loop a sound stream.

 If you want to loop streaming audio, use `getStatus()` in the update loop to test whether the stream is still `Playing`. As soon as the status is `Stopped`, `play()` the stream again.

The ambient sounds that we just discussed typically start playing when you load the scene. In contrast, let's look at a more situational use of sound next—the sound of a weapon.

## Time for action – push a button to receive *BAM*

Let's look at a code sample where the user's mouse click triggers a gunshot. The click also triggers related attack actions, such as identifying the target and determining the damage, which we already covered in previous chapters.

This is how you play a gunshot sound after a click:

1.  Make a copy of `Main.java` and name the class `AudioTrigger.java`. Remember to also refactor the first line of the `main()` method to `AudioTrigger app = new AudioTrigger();`.

2.  Copy the provided file `Sounds/Effects/Gun.wav` into your project's `Sounds/ Effects/` directory.

3.  Create a private class field for the audio node:

    ```
    private AudioNode gunAudio;
    ```

4.  Initialize the audio node in the `simpleInitApp()` method. You want it to play the `Gun.wav` sound. It's a short sound, so we use the default constructor that pre-buffers the audio:

    ```
    public void simpleInitApp() {
      gunAudio = new AudioNode( assetManager,
        "Sounds/Effects/Gun.wav");
    ```

5.  Declare an input mapping for a gunshot: map the left mouse button to the action named `Shoot`, and add it to the `actionListener` that you will create next:

    ```
    inputManager.addMapping("Shoot",
      new MouseButtonTrigger(MouseInput.BUTTON_LEFT));
    inputManager.addListener(actionListener, "Shoot");
    }
    ```

6.  Create the `ActionListener` and test for the `Shoot` action. The action plays the gunshot sound once. (You can trigger additional target picking actions here, as shown in *Chapter 3, Interacting with the User.*):

    ```
    private ActionListener actionListener =
      new ActionListener() {
    @Override
      public void onAction(String name, boolean keyPressed, float tpf)
      {
        if (name.equals("Shoot") && !keyPressed) {
          gunAudio.play();
          // additional target picking and damage code goes here…
        }
      }
    };
    ```

7.  Run the code sample. If you kept the template code, you will see a blue cube in an empty scene. Left-click to trigger the sound of a gunshot.

## *What just happened?*

Next to ambient sound, you use audio to give the user feedback about an action and its outcome. When players click to fire a weapon, they either hear the bang of a successful shot, or the disappointing clack of an empty cartridge. When the projectile reaches the enemy, players can tell by the sound effect whether they hit or missed.

User interfaces also swoosh, buzz, and blip when players switch weapons, ready spells, or activate their night-vision goggles. Here too, the user receives auditory feedback about a status change. In all these cases, one particular sound is triggered by one particular action. You can call the `play()`, `pause()`, and `stop()` methods anywhere in your code where you have access to the particular audio node—for example, from an action listener or an update loop.

# Basic sound APIs

The following table is an overview of the most common getters and setters that you use with audio nodes:

| Audio node method | Usage |
|---|---|
| `play()`<br>`playInstance()` | Starts playing an audio node. |
| `pause()` | A paused node continues playing where it left off. |
| `stop()` | Stopping the node rewinds it. |
| `getStatus()` | Returns the status: `Status.Playing`, `Status.Paused`, or `Status.Stopped`. |
| `setVolume(5.0f)` | Sets the volume gain. `1.0f` is the default volume, `2.0f` is twice as loud, `10.0f` is 10 times as loud, and so on. Set this to `0.0f` to mute the sound. |
| `setPitch(1.0f)` | Makes the sound play in a higher or lower pitch. The standard pitch is `1.0f`. A pitch of `2.0f` is one octave higher, a pitch of `0.5f` is one octave lower. |
| `setTimeOffset(1.0f)` | Fast-forwards by a specified number of seconds into the sound. Use this to skip the beginning of a sound before playing. By default, there is no offset (that is, `0.0f` seconds). |
| `setLooping(true)` | Activates looping in pre-buffered sounds. When the sound plays, it repeats from the beginning, until it is stopped. |

Both `play()` and `playInstance()` start rendering the audio, but they are used in different situations:

| play() | playInstance() |
| --- | --- |
| Use `play()` if you expect to be using getters and setters on this sound node while it's playing. | Use `playInstance()` if you want to fire off a new instance of the sound. You cannot use getters and setters while it is playing, because the audio node is not a reference to the temporary copy. |
| Calling `play()` on one audio node twice will not play the same sound on top of itself. | Calling `playInstance()` on one audio node twice plays two copies simultaneously, each with current parameters. |
| A looping sound plays repeatedly when you call `play()`. | A looping sound plays only once when you call `playInstance()`. |
| Use `play()` on audio streams. | You cannot use `playInstance()` on audio streams. |

For example, you could set an audio node's position, call `playInstance()`, change its position, and call `playInstance()` again. Now you have the same audio node playing simultaneously from two different positions. You see that `playInstance()` is an efficient solution for playing possibly overlapping sounds, such as footsteps or gunshots.

You must convert sounds to mono format (one channel) if you intend to use them for positional or directional sound. 3D effects do not work if the base sound file is already stereo. For non-positional sounds such as ambient music, background noises, or interface beeps that don't use reverberation, stereo (two channels) is a great choice.

# Something's coming from behind!

Ambient sounds are noises "in headspace": they have no location in the 3D scene and seem to be coming from everywhere and nowhere. You can attach non-positional audio nodes to another node in the 3D scene, but it is not a requirement. In contrast, you want other sounds to emanate from one particular spot.

The humming of the motor should emanate from the passing race car itself; hearing the steps of the guard approach from the right gives you the split second needed to dodge to the left; and the monster sneaking up on you in the dark is a lot scarier when you hear it breathe right behind your chair; hearing the ocean roar to your right and leaves rustling to your left helps you navigate the terrain.

3D sounds have a position in 3D space, therefore you must attach these positional audio nodes to (a node attached to) the root node. You need two things to render 3D audio:

◆ An attached audio node representing the position or direction of the sound

◆ The `AudioListener` representing the position and rotation of the "player's ears"

`SimpleApplication` provides you with a preconfigured `AudioListener` object. In a game with a third-person perspective, you make the `AudioListener` follow the avatar's location and rotation. In a game with a first-person perspective, you make the `AudioListener` follow the camera's location and rotation.

## Time for action – positional audio

We create a looping positional audio node, and attach it to a parent node that is positioned at the origin.

The following sample code introduces you to a simple case of positional audio.

**1.** Make a copy of `Main.java` and name the class `PositionalSound.java`. Remember to also refactor the first line of the `main()` method to `PositionalSound app = new PositionalSound();`.

**2.** Copy the provided file `Sounds/Environment/River.ogg` into your project's `Sounds/Environment/` directory.

**3.** In the `simpleInitApp()` method, attach some filler content (a node and a cube geometry) to the scene graph so you have a point of reference:

```
public void simpleInitApp() {
  // Create a node for the object the sound belongs to
  Node riverbedNode = new Node("Riverbed");
  riverbedNode.setLocalTranslation(Vector3f.ZERO);
  rootNode.attachChild(riverbedNode);
  // Attach a geometry to the scene node (just a blue cube)
  Box riverbedMesh = new Box(Vector3f.ZERO, 1, 1, 1);
  Geometry riverbedGeo = new Geometry(
    "marks audio source", riverbedMesh);
  Material riverbedMat = new Material(assetManager,
    "Common/MatDefs/Misc/Unshaded.j3md");
  riverbedMat.setColor("Color", ColorRGBA.Blue);
  riverbedGeo.setMaterial(riverbedMat);
  riverbedNode.attachChild(riverbedGeo);
```

Still in the `simpleInitApp()` method, you initialize and configure a positional audio node:

```
AudioNode riverAudio = new AudioNode(assetManager,
    "Sounds/Environment/River.ogg");
riverAudio.setPositional(true);    // Use 3D audio
riverAudio.setRefDistance(10f);    // Distance of 50% volume
riverAudio.setMaxDistance(1000f);  // Stops going quieter
riverAudio.setVolume(1);           // Default volume
riverAudio.setLooping(true);       // play continuously
```

**4.** Attach the positional sound to its scene node, and start playing:

```
riverbedNode.attachChild(riverAudio);
riverAudio.play();
}
```

**5.** Use the update loop to make the default `AudioListener` (the first-person player's ear) follow the camera:

```
public void simpleUpdate(float tpf) {
    listener.setLocation(cam.getLocation());
    listener.setRotation(cam.getRotation());
}
```

Put on your headphones and run the code. You should see a blue cube, and you should hear the sound of water emanating from it. Use the keys *W* and *S* to move along the Z axis. The sound becomes louder when you approach the cube, and grows more and more quiet the farther you move from it. Use the mouse to turn, or use the keys *A* and *D* to move sideways, along the X axis. Note that you can hear the sound coming from the left or right, respectively.

You can think of positional audio nodes as the auditory equivalent of point lights. A point light is a light source at a location, emanating light in all directions. A positional audio node is a sound source at a location, emanating sound in all directions.

## *What just happened?*

By default, the "player's ears" are located at the origin. To let mobile players hear sound from their changing points of reference, you must move the `AudioListener` object with the camera (or the third-person player avatar, respectively). You do this as part of the update loop:

```
listener.setLocation(cam.getLocation());
listener.setRotation(cam.getRotation());
```

You see that a positional audio node has the following special properties:

| Audio node property | Purpose |
| --- | --- |
| `setPositional(true)` | Set this Boolean parameter to true to turn this audio node from an ambient sound in headspace to a positional audio node. |
| `setRefDistance(10f)` | The reference distance defines at what distance from the source (in world units) the volume has decreased to 50 percent (assuming exponential fall-off). |
| `setMaxDistance(1000f)` | The maximum attenuation distance specifies how far from the source (in world units) the sound stops growing more quiet. |
| `getLocalTranslation()` | The position of the audio node in the 3D scene. This property is inherited from the parent node. |

# A closer look at volume fall-off

The two properties `RefDistance` and `MaxDistance` influence the volume fall-off at a distance. Play with the values in the `PositionalSound.java` code sample to get a feeling of how it works.

The following list gives you an idea how different values influence the volume fall-off. This list uses `10f` as an example of a small value, and `1000f` as an example of a large value. The actual values, of course, depend on the size of your scene.

- With `RefDistance=10f` and `MaxDistance=1000f`, sound is loudest up close, and its volume fades out—this is the most commonly used case
- With `RefDistance=1000f` and `MaxDistance=10f`, sound remains loud from a distance, and its volume remains constant at almost 100 percent
- With `RefDistance=1000f` and `MaxDistance=1000f`, sound remains loud from a distance, and its volume never falls below 50 percent
- With `RefDistance=10f` and `MaxDistance=10f`, sound is loudest up close, and its volume never falls below 50 percent

 If you set `RefDistance` and `MaxDistance` to the same value, the volume remains constant and never falls below 50 percent of its original value. Since sounds typically fade at a distance, the most natural and commonly used case is to use a low value for `RefDistance` and a very high value for `MaxDistance`.

When you configure your audio nodes, you may wonder what the best values are so that your audio fades out naturally as the player walks farther away from a positional node. You know that the volume becomes half as loud when the listeners double their distance from the sound source (the dashed fall-off curve in the following graphic).

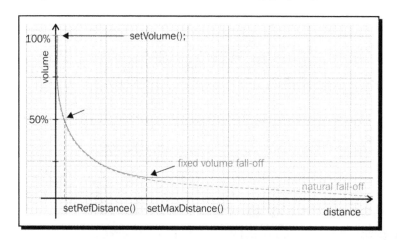

By specifying RefDistance (and optionally, MaxDistance) you control how fast the volume fades (the vertical dotted lines in the above graphic). The start point is the original volume.

RefDistance is the reference distance (in world units) after which the sound has lost half of its original volume. For ambient sounds that maintain the same volume throughout the scene, set RefDistance to a high value—it makes the fall-off curve flatter. For geographically limited sounds that fade out quickly, set RefDistance to a small value—this makes the fall-off curve steeper.

MaxDistance is the distance (in world units) after which the audio does not fade any quieter. No matter how far players move away, they can still hear the sound at a constant volume. Of course, this does not happen in nature. Ambient sounds are audible everywhere, so you set MaxDistance to a low value—this fixes the sound fall-off early, at a well audible volume. For sounds that fade quickly and that can only be heard when up close, set MaxDistance to a high value—this fixes the sound fall-off late, when the volume is practically inaudible.

In jMonkeyEngine, 3D sound can be positional or directional. Let's have a look at what we mean by directional.

# Time for action – I spy with my little ear

In real life, sound can be occluded (behind closed doors in another room) or obstructed (in the same room, but behind the couch).

The `audioRenderer` of `SimpleApplication`, however, does not take the scene's walls into account when rendering audio. This means that when you attach audio nodes to a scene, the sound is audible through obstacles. For loud gunshots or ambient sounds in a forest, this may be acceptable. But often, gameplay requires you to hide a sound: you do not want all players to hear the zombies right away—not before they have entered the abandoned warehouse and it's too late.

The sample code given next introduces you to a simple case of directional audio.

1.  Make a copy of `PositionalSound.java` and name the class `DirectionalSound.java`. Remember to also refactor the first line of the `main()` method to `DirectionalSound app = new DirectionalSound();`.

2.  Copy the provided file `Sounds/Environment/Ocean Waves.ogg` into your project's `Sounds/Environment/` directory.

3.  In the `simpleInitApp()` method, keep the filler content (a node and a cube geometry) in the scene graph so you have a point of reference:

    ```
    public void simpleInitApp() {
      Node beachNode = new Node("sound source node");
      beachNode.setLocalTranslation(1, 1, 1);
      rootNode.attachChild(beachNode);

      Box beachMesh = new Box(1, 1, 1);
      Geometry beachGeo = new Geometry(
        "Sound source visuals", beachMesh);
      Material beachMat = new Material(assetManager,
        "Common/MatDefs/Misc/Unshaded.j3md");
      beachMat.setColor("Color", ColorRGBA.Blue);
      beachGeo.setMaterial(beachMat);
      beachNode.attachChild(beachGeo);
    ```

4.  As before, initialize and configure a positional audio node in `simpleInitApp()`:

    ```
    AudioNode beachAudio = new AudioNode(assetManager,
      "Sounds/Environment/Ocean Waves.ogg");
    beachAudio.setLooping(true);
    beachAudio.setPositional(true);
    ```

A directional audio node is a type of positional audio node with additional properties that specify the sound cone:

```
beachAudio.setDirectional(true);
beachAudio.setInnerAngle(50);
beachAudio.setOuterAngle(120);
beachAudio.setDirection(new Vector3f(0, 0, 1));
```

**5.** Attach the sound to its parent node and start playing:

```
beachNode.attachChild(beachAudio);
beachAudio.play();
}
```

**6.** As with any 3D audio node, use the update loop to make the audio listener follow the camera:

```
public void simpleUpdate(float tpf) {
    listener.setLocation(cam.getLocation());
    listener.setRotation(cam.getRotation());
}
```

Run the sample code. The "sound cone" starts at the cube and points toward the camera, so you are standing in it when hearing the sound. As in the positional example, use the *W*, *A*, *S*, and *D* keys to move around in the scene, and experience the change in volume. If you move too far to the left or right, the sound stops completely—you have left the sound cone.

You can think of directional audio nodes as the auditory equivalent of spot lights. A spot light is a light source at a location, emanating a cone of light in one direction. A directional audio node is a sound source at a location, emanating a cone of sound in one direction.

## What just happened?

To work around the lack of real occlusion, video games use "sound cones" or "directional" audio nodes—a concept that does not exist in real life. By default, a directional audio node broadcasts at 360°, which makes its behavior identical to a positional node. You specify the angle and direction of the sound cone. This way you simulate sound occlusion and control who hears what from where.

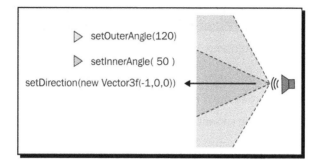

The sound emanates from the audio node's position. It is loudest within the inner cone. It is still audible within the outer cone. The sound is not audible outside these two cones.

When you lay out a room whose sounds are occluded and cannot be heard outside, place several directional audio nodes in the corners. Rotate them so they broadcast their sound toward the center of the room.

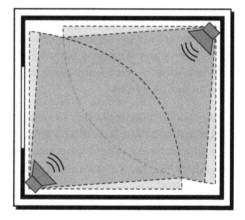

Adjust the outer and inner cones to angles less than 90° so that no sound trickles through the four walls. Adjust `MaxDistance` and `RefDistance` to make certain that the sound falls off before it reaches the walls of the room.

## Pop quiz – audio nodes

Q1. Which of the following statements is false?

1. A directional audio node must always be positional.

2. A directional audio node must not be positional.

3. A positional audio node cannot play sound files that are stereo.

4. A directional audio node cannot play sound files that are stereo.

# Sound environments

The audio in jump-n-run, maze, or platform games is often just beeps, bangs, and boings. Shooters, action, and stealth games, however, have higher standards as far as immersion is concerned. They are typically set in realistic environments such as cities, space stations, castles, or wilderness.

Just like humans recognize an object's material by the way it reflects light, we intuitively gain information about our environment by how sound propagates. In real life, you can tell from afar whether footsteps stem from the narrow echoing hallway, or from the muffled carpeted room next to it. When one player patrols inside a warehouse, and the other sneaks around outdoors, their footsteps should sound different.

Games also often play the same sounds repeatedly: you hear your avatar's footsteps while exploring the haunted castle, the bangs of weapons discharging, or the avatar's gasp when he jumps from a ledge—over and over. Make sure to introduce some variation to avoid boring your players. Using the different audio environments discussed in this section is an example of variation that you can introduce.

To increase variety, collect various recordings of a repetitive sound (such as footsteps), and normalize the volume. Number the variations (`1.ogg`, `2.ogg`, `3.ogg`) and save them into one directory (for example, `assets/Sounds/footsteps/`). Write a custom method that picks a numbered file at random from the given directory and plays it.

# Time for action – using default sound environments

jMonkeyEngine provides you with predefined audio environments in the `com.jme3.audio.Environment` package.

The following example plays one sound repeatedly in several different environments so you can hear the difference:

**1.** Make a copy of `Main.java` and name the class `AudioEnvironments.java`. Remember to also refactor the first line of the `main()` method to `AudioEnvironments app = new AudioEnvironments();`.

**2.** Copy the provided file `Sounds/Effects/Bang.wav` into your project's `Sounds/Effects/` directory.

**3.** Keep the code that attaches a blue cube as point of reference.

**4.** Create two class fields: one audio node, and one audio environment. Initialize the environment to the predefined value `AcousticLab`:

```
private AudioNode stepsAudio;
private Environment env = Environment.AcousticLab;
```

**5.** In the `simpleInitApp()` method, initialize SimpleApplication's default `audioRenderer` to use your custom environment:

```
public void simpleInitApp() {
   audioRenderer.setEnvironment(env);
```

**6.** Initialize a looping audio node that plays a bang sound, and start playing:

```
stepsAudio = new AudioNode(assetManager,
   "Sounds/Effects/Bang.wav");
     stepsAudio.setVolume(1);
     stepsAudio.setLooping(true);
     stepsAudio.play();
}
```

**7.** Again, use the `simpleUpdate()` loop to keep the position of the listener up-to-date while the player moves the camera through the scene. Additionally, move the bang sound with the camera.

```
public void simpleUpdate(float tpf) {
   listener.setLocation(cam.getLocation());
   listener.setRotation(cam.getRotation());
   stepsAudio.setLocalTranslation(cam.getLocation());
```

**8.** Finally, use the `simpleUpdate()` loop to change the environment depending on the position of the camera, as if the first-person player was stepping from one room into another while moving:

```
float x = cam.getLocation().getX();
  float z = cam.getLocation().getZ();
  if (x > 0 && z > 0 && env != Environment.Dungeon) {
    System.out.println("Playing in environment Dungeon");
    env = Environment.Dungeon;
  } else if (x > 0 && z < 0 && env != Environment.Cavern) {
    System.out.println("Playing in environment Cavern");
    env = Environment.Cavern;
  } else if (x < 0 && z < 0 && env != Environment.Closet) {
    System.out.println("Playing in environment Closet");
    env = Environment.Closet;
  } else if (x < 0 && z > 0 && env != Environment.Garage) {
    System.out.println("Playing in environment Garage");
    env = Environment.Garage;
  }
  audioRenderer.setEnvironment(env);
}
```

**9.** Run the code sample. You should see the blue cube and hear a looping bang sound. Use the *W*, *A*, *S*, and *D* keys to move the camera around the cube. The "bang!" should sound noticeably different in the four quadrants.

## What just happened?

The update loop tests whether the camera is left, right, in front of, or behind the blue cube. In each quadrant, it switches to a different sound environment. You can choose from preset environments such as Garage, Cavern, Closet, or Dungeon.

```
audioRenderer.setEnvironment(Environment.Dungeon);
```

By default, audio nodes have an audio property called reverberation:

```
stepsAudio.setReverbEnabled(true);
```

Reverb is a kind of echo that emphasizes different sound environments to enhance the game's atmosphere: you can hear the hard nakedness of the narrow walls of the dungeon, compared to the muffled openness of the vast snow plain outside. Environments are also great as part of the challenge of chasing and being chased—hearing opponents approach, and passing them unheard.

To experience full 3D audio, connect your PC to a 5.1 or 7.1 surround sound system. The sound system levels and delays the audio signal over several channels to simulate sounds echoing from different directions and surfaces. Not all PC hardware support these OpenAL effects, however. Check your terminal for the warning message `OpenAL EFX not available! Audio effects won't work.`

For advanced digital signal processing and hardware-accelerated sound effects, jMonkeyEngine also supports custom **Environmental Audio Extensions (EAX)**. EAX audio presets are used in many AAA games, such as Doom 3 and Prey. This book cannot go deeper into the details of custom audio environment configurations. If you are interested, read the `jMonkeyEngine.org` documentation wiki for examples of audio environment presets.

## Time for action – underwater

Do you remember the beautiful underwater effects that we recently discussed, with waves and sunbeams? You can increase the immersion of an underwater scene by dampening all sounds while the camera is under water.

**1.** Make a copy of `WaterTerrainSky.java` and name the class `UnderWaterAudio.java`. Remember to also refactor the first line of the `main()` method to `UnderWaterAudioapp = new UnderWaterAudio();`.

**2.** Keep all code of the water-terrain-sky simulation.

**3.** Add the following class fields for the audio node and the environmental effect:
```
private AudioNode wavesAudio;
private LowPassFilter underWaterAudioFilter =
  new LowPassFilter(0.5f, 0.1f);
private LowPassFilter aboveWaterAudioFilter =
  new LowPassFilter(1f, 1f);
```

**4.** Create a Boolean class field to track whether the player is above or under the water surface, so you can toggle the audio filter on and off:
```
private boolean wasUnderwater = false;
```

**5.** Keep the code in the `simpleInitApp()` method, and add the following to initialize the sound:
```
public void simpleInitApp() {
  …
  wavesAudio = new AudioNode(assetManager,
    "Sounds/Environment/Ocean Waves.ogg");
```

```
        wavesAudio.setLooping(true);
        wavesAudio.setPositional(false);
        wavesAudio.play();
        rootNode.attachChild(wavesAudio);
    }
```

6.  In the update loop, we regularly "test the waters" by comparing the camera position to the water height. Then we toggle to the appropriate sound filter.

```
public void simpleUpdate(float tpf) {
    //update the AudioListener
    listener.setLocation(cam.getLocation());
    listener.setRotation(cam.getRotation());
    // whether underwater or not depends on camera position
    if (water.isUnderWater() && !wasUnderwater ) {
        // activate underwater sound effect
        wavesAudio.stop();
        wasUnderwater = true;
        wavesAudio.setDryFilter(underWaterAudioFilter);
        wavesAudio.play();
    } else if (!water.isUnderWater() && wasUnderwater ) {
        // deactivate underwater sound effect
        wavesAudio.stop();
        wasUnderwater = false;
        wavesAudio.play();
        wavesAudio.setDryFilter(aboveWaterAudioFilter);
    }
}
```

## What just happened?

In order to muffle all underwater sound, we make use of a special audio filter called `LowPassFilter`. This audio filter cuts off all high frequencies and lets only low frequencies pass. This is basically what happens to sound under water.

Our custom `LowPassFilter` reduces the volume by 50 percent (`0.5f`) and muffles 90 percent of the high frequencies—because only the lowest 10 percent (`0.1f`) of frequencies pass:

```
LowPassFilter underWaterAudioFilter = new LowPassFilter(0.5f, 0.1f);
```

The second `LowPassFilter`, on the other hand, resets the sound environment back to normal. It lets 100 percent (`1.0f`) of high frequencies pass, and it does not decrease the volume (`1.0f`):

```
LowPassFilter aboveWaterAudioFilter = new LowPassFilter(1f, 1f);
```

The code in the update loop uses `water.isUnderWater()` to compare the camera position to the current water height. Depending on the outcome, it stops the sound loop, and restarts it with the appropriate `LowPassFilter` applied. We set the `wasUnderwater` Boolean parameter to ensure that we don't unnecessarily switch to the same state repeatedly.

## Have a go hero

Going back to our Tower Defense game, there are some obvious spots where you can add audio:

- The tapping footsteps of creeps coming closer.

  Create a positional audio node in the `CreepControl` class (pass the `AssetManager` as object an argument in a custom constructor) and play the sound after the control has calculated the creep's next step.

- The sound of towers shooting lasers or cannon balls (depending on your choice of genre).

  Create a positional audio node in `TowerControl` (pass the `AssetManager` object as an argument in a custom constructor) and play the sound after the control has calculated the tower's next attack.

- The crunching noise of the player base crumbling under the attack of approaching creeps.

  Trigger this sound in `CreepControl` after testing whether the creep has reached the player base in the update loop.

- A sound in headspace expressing "you win!" or "you lose!". This can be an emotional short jingle or melody, or a recorded voice. This sound is triggered in `GamePlayAppState.java` after testing the player's health in the update loop.

- A short theme music in headspace that plays at the beginning and end.

# Summary

What you learned in this chapter increased the immersion of your game, because now you address the two main human senses: seeing and hearing.

Specifically, you learned the difference between ambient sounds in headspace and 3D audio, the difference between playing sounds and instances of sounds, the difference between streaming and pre-buffering, and the differences between environments such as underwater and dungeons.

You are now ready to develop a desktop game, congratulations! The final chapters give you an overview of optional, but interesting, game development topics. We also share lots of best practices on how to build and deploy the actual game application.

# 10
# Showing Your Game to the World

*You are coming close to the end of your journey. When you look back, you realize a whole new world has emerged in your wake: you populated your little creation with buildings and characters; you made the world interactive and it came alive; your creatures make themselves heard through sound effects, and seen through visual effects; and you command your world's innermost physical forces. Pretty awesome, don't you think?*

*All the while, you ran and tested your game in your development environment—typically, inside the jMonkeyEngine SDK. When your game has reached its first major milestone, your last step is to package it up so it is easy for your customers to run—outside the SDK.*

In this chapter, you will learn how to get ready for the release day:

 ◆ Save and load display settings
 ◆ Save and load games
 ◆ Deploy the game as a desktop, Web Start, applet, or a mobile application

If you use the jMonkeyEngine SDK, choosing a deployment type is only a matter of checking a box in the project properties. If you use any other development environment, consult the manual included with that software.

## Customizing display settings

Every game that is based on `SimpleApplication` lets you specify application settings and defaults.

# Time for action – the name of the game

Obviously, you must specify the display options for your game, before starting the
application. Here is a simple example: the default window title is jMonkey Engine 3.0;
let's change this display setting to the name of your game:

*1.* Make a copy of `Main.java` and name the class `SettingsTest.java`. Remember
to also refactor the first line of the `main()` method to `SettingsTest app = new
SettingsTest();`.

*2.* Go to the `main()` method of `SettingsTest` and add a new `AppSettings` object:

```
public static void main(String[] args) {
    AppSettings settings = new AppSettings(true); //  create
```

*3.* Use setters to specify one or more options. In this example, we set the game's
window title:

```
settings.setTitle("My Cool Game");              // modify
```

*4.* Activate the new `settings` object before calling `app.start()`:

```
SettingsTest app = new SettingsTest();
app.setSettings(settings);                      // activate
app.start();
}
```

When you run the code, your jMonkeyEngine window title is set to `My Cool Game`.

## What just happened?

You see that you use setters on a custom `AppSettings` instance to store your game's
display settings. You have two options:

◆ To initialize all options with jMonkeyEngine-defined default values, use:

```
AppSettings settings = new AppSettings(true);
```

◆ To initialize all options with user-defined settings from the previous launch, use:

```
AppSettings settings = new AppSettings(false);
```

Let's look at some more examples of commonly used display settings.

# Time for action – make a big splash (screen)

By default, every game based on `SimpleApplication` presents the user with a built-in **Select display settings** dialog at the start of the game. This window lets the user specify the minimum set of display settings. The users can choose a screen resolution, color depth, vertical syncing, whether they want anti-aliasing, and whether they want to run the game in a window or in full-screen mode.

1.  Create an image file in PNG or JPG format with a recommended minimum width of 600 pixels. Name the file; for example, `logo.png`.
2.  Save `logo.png` to the `assets/Interface/` directory.
3.  Load your custom splash screen into the settings:

```
public static void main(String[] args) {
  AppSettings settings = new AppSettings(true);
  settings.setTitle("My Cool Game");
  settings.setSettingsDialogImage("Interface/logo.png");
  SettingsTest app = new SettingsTest();
  app.setSettings(settings);
  app.start();
}
```

When you start the application now, the splash screen shows your custom `logo.png` image.

## What just happened?

When you use the built-in **Select display settings** dialog, you should supply your own splash screen image. If you do not provide a custom image, the dialog displays the built-in jMonkeyEngine splash screen (`/com/jme3/app/Monkey.png`).

As an alternative to using the built-in settings dialog, you can also create a whole custom window. In this case, you deactivate the built-in `Select display settings` dialog on the app object before calling `app.start()` in the `main()` method:

```
public static void main(String[] args) {
  AppSettings settings = new AppSettings(true);

  /* Create a custom dialog and specify settings here... */

  SettingsTest app = new SettingsTest();
  app.setShowSettings(false); // skip built-in dialog
  app.setSettings(settings);  // activate custom settings
  app.start();
}
```

To create your custom splash screen, you can use either standard Swing windows, or an integrated solution, such as the Nifty GUI framework. Note the following difference:

◆ If you use a Swing window, you set it to `visible` before calling `app.start()`

◆ If you use Nifty GUI, you load your custom screens after calling `app.start()`

Visit the `jMonkeyEngine.org` documentation wiki for more information on Nifty GUI integration.

## Time for action – window seat or full screen?

By default, your game runs in a window of its own, and the user can move this window by dragging the title bar. In this case, you should customize the title bar and specify a resolution.

1. Copy application icons in various sizes to your project's `Interface/icons` directory.

2. Add the following code in your game's `main()` class:

```
public static void main(String[] args) {
  AppSettings settings = new AppSettings(true);
  settings.setResolution(1024,768);
  settings.setTitle("My Cool Game");

  try {
    Class<Main> myclass = Main.class;
    settings.setIcons(new BufferedImage[]{
      ImageIO.read(myclass.getResourceAsStream(
        "/Interface/icons/SmartMonkey256.png")),
      ImageIO.read(myclass.getResourceAsStream(
        "/Interface/icons/SmartMonkey128.png")),
      ImageIO.read(myclass.getResourceAsStream(
        "/Interface/icons/SmartMonkey32.png")),
      ImageIO.read(myclass.getResourceAsStream(
        "/Interface/icons/SmartMonkey16.png")),});
    } catch (IOException ex) {
    Logger.getLogger(Main.class.getName()).
      log(Level.WARNING,
      "Failed to load application icon.", ex);
  }

  SettingsTest app = new SettingsTest();
  app.setSettings(settings);
  app.start();
}
```

When you run this code, your application opens with a resolution of 1024 x 768, your custom window title, and application icon (depending on the operating system).

Other game developers prefer the game window to fill the whole screen. For example, you can switch to a 1025 x 768 full-screen mode using the following alternative setting:

```
public static void main(String[] args) {
  AppSettings settings = new AppSettings(true);
  settings.setResolution(1024,768);
  settings.setFullscreen(true);
  SettingsTest app = new SettingsTest();
  app.setShowSettings(false); // skip built-in dialog
  app.setSettings(settings);
  app.start();
}
```

This code sample opens the application window without a title bar, hence you do not specify a window title.

## What just happened?

It is possible that your game's GUI layout imposes a restriction on the screen resolution of the game. For example, if you allow the user to resize the window, a more complex GUI may become unwieldy, or a HUD may not have enough space to display its information. If that is the case in your game, specify a fixed recommended screen resolution. If you do not specify a resolution, and the user does not change the resolution in the built-in **Select display settings** dialog, the game window opens with a default width and height of 640 x 480.

If you choose the full-screen option, be aware that the user is not able to see the title bar or system menus while the game is running. This means it is not obvious to the user how to quit, or return to the desktop. The default `SimpleApplication` is set up so that pressing the *Esc* key stops the application without saving changes. Remember to provide a key mapping that saves the game state and calls `app.stop()` so the user can exit the full-screen view gracefully.

This example shows how you customize the application icon that is displayed in the title bar and in the application switcher (not available in Mac OS). Optimally, you supply icons in the four most commonly used sizes: 256 x 256, 128 x 128, 32 x 32, and 16 x 16. Note that `setIcons()` has no impact on the application icon on the desktop!

# Time for action – fine-tuning video settings

You can let your users choose video settings, or you can predefine settings that you recommend.

Try the following example:

```
public static void main(String[] args) {
    AppSettings settings = new AppSettings(true);
    settings.setVSync(true);
    settings.setFrequency(60);
    settings.setFramerate(30);
    settings.setSamples(4);
    SettingsTest app = new SettingsTest();
    app.setShowSettings(false); // skip default dialog
    app.setSettings(settings);
    app.start();
}
```

When you run your sample application with these video settings, you should notice softer edges, and less CPU/GPU usage.

## What just happened?

To improve video quality, consider activating vertical synchronization (vsync). Vertical synchronization prevents screen tearing—an annoying video glitch where part of a frame lags behind and shows the previous frame. Use vsync to cap the frame rate to the monitor's refresh rate, typically 60, 75, or 120 fps (frames per second), depending on the display used. The default is 60 fps. Vsync is deactivated by default, which is acceptable for slower machines, or during the development phase.

When no upper limit is imposed on the video frame rate, your game runs as fast as possible. The downside of an unlimited frame rate is that it uses as much of the GPU and CPU as it can, leaving hardly any resources for other open applications. Here are some guidelines:

- A refresh rate of 60 fps results in fluent rendering for the human eye. If your game does not perform any intensive calculations, and you want to free up the CPU for other applications, you can even set the frame rate to half as much (30 fps).

- There is no use in setting the frame rate to a higher value than the screen frequency; you would just be wasting cycles. On the other hand, if the frame rate goes below 30 fps, the video will look choppy. You want to avoid either extremes jMonkeyEngine supports multisample anti-aliasing, a rendering technique that improves video quality by smoothing rough edges. By default, multisample anti-aliasing is inactive (that is, it uses zero samples). Without anti-aliasing, the game renders faster, but you may see hard, stair-stepping edges. Typically, you set multisampling to use two or four samples. (If you specify a sample value higher than what the user's graphic card supports, the game will crash with an `LWJGLException` that you have to catch and handle.) Anti-aliasing results in softer edges, but the extra calculations may slow down game performance. Again, you need to find a compromise between good looks and speed.

> If you are using a `FilterPostProcessor`, do not set the global sample value (here 4) on the settings object only; also set it on the post-processor object:
>
> ```
> FilterPostProcessor fpp = new FilterPostProcesso
> r(assetManager);
>
> fpp.setNumSamples(4);
> ```

## Time for action – window, canvas, or headless?

Every jMonkeyEngine game has a so-called context type. The context type specifies whether the game opens an OpenGL window, renders on a canvas, or runs "headless"—without drawing anything to the screen.

**1.** You switch the context type in your `main()` method when you `app.start()` the application:

```
public static void main(String[] args) {
   AppSettings settings = new AppSettings(true);
   settings.setTitle("My Cool Game");
   SettingsTest app = new SettingsTest();
   app.setSettings(settings);
   app.start(JmeContext.Type.Headless); // switch context type
}
```

**2.** Run this code.

The game loop executes in a so-called headless context; this means no video is rendered. We'll look at examples where you would switch context types.

## What just happened?

By default, a `SimpleApplication` displays a window, runs the main loop, and renders the scene. But it is also possible to use jMonkeyEngine for purposes other than desktop games.

Maybe you are coding the headless server part of a networked game, where the server runs the main loop, but does not do any rendering. Or you want to visualize 3D data in the canvas of an applet. Or you may use jMonkeyEngine to send the rendered image to a custom buffer, and pass the buffer onto another application. In all of these cases, you switch the context type.

The jMonkeyEngine supports the following context types (`com.jme3.system.JmeContext.Type`):

- `JmeContext.Type.Display`: The application runs the main loop, and renders either full screen or in a window of its own. This is the default. Use this for mobile, desktop, or Web Start games, and for the clients of networked games.

- `JmeContext.Type.Canvas`: The application renders embedded in a Swing canvas. Use this canvas for applets, or if you embed jMonkeyEngine graphics inside a custom Swing GUI.

- `JmeContext.Type.Headless`: The application runs and processes the main loop. It does not open any window, does not listen to input, and does neither calculate nor render any audio/video. Use this context type to run the server of a network game.

- `JmeContext.Type.OffscreenSurface`: The application runs and calculates the main loop. It calculates the visual data in a frame buffer, but it does not open any window and does not listen to any user input. Advanced developers can use `renderer.readFrameBuffer()` to save visual content as a screenshot or video, or to send it over the network.

## Time for action – reload settings

Let's assume you want to use `settings.setResolution()` to change the resolution while playing a cut scene. If the game is already running, changing `application settings` has no effect, unless you reload them.

1. Make a copy of `Main.java` and name the class `ReloadSettings.java`. Remember to also refactor the first line of the `main()` method to `ReloadSettings app = new ReloadSettings();`.

**2.** Add the following temporary variable and code to the `simpleUpdate()` method:

```
float temp;
public void simpleUpdate(float tpf) {
  // a trivial 2-second timer
  temp+=tpf;
  if( temp>2 ) { restartDemo(); temp=0; }
}
```

**3.** Add the following custom demo method:

```
private void restartDemo() {
  settings.setResolution(
    FastMath.nextRandomInt(100, 800),
    FastMath.nextRandomInt(100, 800) ); // a random resolution
  this.restart(); // reload settings
}
```

When you run this code, the application closes and reopens its window every two seconds, with a random resolution.

## What just happened?

Typically, you apply display settings in the `main()` method before starting the application. This demo shows how you change `AppSettings` while the game is already running. The `simpleUpdate()` loop uses the `tpf` variable (time per frame in seconds) as a trivial timer. Every two seconds, it calls `settings.setResolution()` to set the height and width to two random numbers. Then it calls `this.restart()` on the `SimpleApplication` to activate the modified settings.

Here's another example: by default, a game based on `SimpleApplication` listens to user input coming in through the mouse and keyboard. During an elaborate cut scene, however, you want your jMonkeyEngine application to be non-interactive. In this case, you temporarily deactivate the input listeners by calling `settings.setUseInput(false)` and call `this.restart()`. After the cut scene, you reactivate the input listeners by calling `settings.setUseInput(true);` and `this.restart()`.

# SimpleApplication options

In contrast to video and input settings that have to be specified *before* the game window opens, there are also application settings that only become relevant *after* the application has been initialized. You change the application behaviors, described in the following sections, inside the `simpleInitApp()` method of your game.

# Time for action – time for a pause

By default, `SimpleApplication` pauses the update loop whenever the window loses focus, that is, the player switches to another application. For multiplayer or real-time applications, pausing one of the players is not even an option. For such games, you need to deactivate the default pausing behavior in the `simpleInitApp()` method:

1.  Make a copy of `Main.java` and name the class `FocusTest.java`. Remember to also refactor the first line of the `main()` method to `FocusTest app = new FocusTest();`.

2.  In `simpleInitApp()`, change the application behavior as follows:

    ```
    public void simpleInitApp() {
      setPauseOnLostFocus(false);
    }
    ```

3.  In the `simpleUpdate()` loop, add the following sample code:

    ```
    public void simpleUpdate(float tpf) {
      rootNode.rotate(tpf,tpf,tpf);
    }
    ```

When you run the application, the blue cube rotates. When you switch to the desktop, the cube should continue rotating.

Remove the `setPauseOnLostFocus()` line (or set it to `true`) and run the sample again. When you switch to the desktop now, the cube should stop rotating.

## What just happened?

Single-player games allow users to pause the game and switch to other applications, without having to quit what they are playing. When the user switches applications, the game loses focus. In this situation, users expect the enemy AI (artificial intelligence) to stop attacking the player. On the other hand, users would not be surprised if the AI made good use of the idle time and continued calculating its next move. Users would not expect the AI to keep walking while paused. On the other hand, they would not be surprised to see "idle" animation loops (paused characters breathe, look around, or shuffle their feet).

In the trivial case, pausing a game merely disables the update loop. User-friendly games maintain a `paused` Boolean parameter and offer a pause key. Implementing idle animations is a good way to show the player that the game is indeed merely paused, and not frozen.

Most importantly, you must implement how pausing affects your custom loops. What precisely happens to music, NPCs, or other timed game mechanics (such as "poison" or "health regeneration") when the player switches to another application?

To implement pausing, define a `setEnabled()` toggle method for each custom `Control` and `AppState` class, and call it, if paused. Since every game is different, you need to evaluate and define individually what `enabled` and `disabled` mean for that particular `Control` or `AppState` class.

# Time for action – hide statistics and FPS

Every `SimpleApplication` displays the current frames per second (FPS) and some mesh statistics, in the bottom-left corner. Before releasing your game, you should hide these displays as follows:

1. Make a copy of `Main.java` and name the class `HideStatistics.java`. Remember to also refactor the first line of the `main()` method to `HideStatistics app = new HideStatistics();`.

2. In `simpleInitApp()`, call the following method to hide the FPS value:
   ```
   setDisplayFps(false);
   ```

3. In `simpleInitApp()`, call the following method to hide the debug statistics:
   ```
   setDisplayStatView(false);
   ```

Run the application with either of the application settings, and note the difference.

## What just happened?

By default, a jMonkeyEngine game displays debug information. You can track how many textures and vertices are in use, and how many frames per second are rendered. This kind of information is very valuable during development and debugging, to detect memory leaks and inefficient implementations. For your release build, however, you deactivate these debug displays so you don't break the user's immersion.

Some games offer a debug mode so users can gather information and submit better bug reports. If you want to reactivate the statistics and FPS displays, use the following calls:

```
setDisplayFps(true);
setDisplayStatView(true);
```

# Save, load, and be merry

Whether the boss is coming, or the notebook is running out of batteries—there are reasons why users quit the game while it is running. In these cases, they typically did not intend to abandon the game. When they run it the next time, they expect their character to appear at the same spot where they left it, with all its equipment and points. Since every game is different, you have to implement custom code to save (persist) and load (restore) a game.

# Time for action – save and load game data

To save a node, you call the `save()` method on an instance of the `com.jme3.export.binary.BinaryExporter` class. To restore the node, call the `load()` method on an instance of the `com.jme3.export.binary.BinaryImporter` class.

The following code snippet shows how you save a node as a binary file by overriding the `stop()` method of `SimpleApplication`:

**1.** Make a copy of `Main.java` and name the class `SaveAndLoad.java`. Remember to also refactor the first line of the `main()` method to `SaveAndLoad app = new SaveAndLoad();`.

**2.** Override the `stop()` method to save the game:

```
@Override
public void stop() {
  String userHome = System.getProperty("user.home");
  BinaryExporter exporter = BinaryExporter.getInstance();
  File file = new File(userHome+"/mycoolgame/savedgame.j3o");
  try {
    exporter.save(rootNode, file);
  } catch (IOException ex) {
    Logger.getLogger(SaveAndLoad.class.getName()).
      log(Level.SEVERE,
      "Failed to save node!", ex);
  }
  super.stop();
}
```

**3.** Add the following code that loads the saved file back into the scene when you initialize the next game in the `simpleInitApp()` method:

```
@Override
public void simpleInitApp() {
  /* Load any scene, e.g. attach a cube. */
  String userHome = System.getProperty("user.home");
  BinaryImporter importer = BinaryImporter.getInstance();
  importer.setAssetManager(assetManager);
  File file = new File(userHome+"/mycoolgame/savedgame.j3o");
  try {
    Node sceneNode = (Node)importer.load(file);
    sceneNode.setName("My restored node");
    rootNode.attachChild(sceneNode);
  } catch (IOException ex) {
    Logger.getLogger(SaveAndLoad.class.getName()).
      log(Level.SEVERE,"Could not load saved
      node.", ex);
  }
```

Run the code sample, and press *Esc* to stop the application. Verify that a file named `mycoolgame/savedgame.j3o` was created in your user directory. When you run the code a second time, the application restores the saved game from this file, if it exists.

## What just happened?

jMonkeyEngine's `BinaryExporter` saves files in a custom format with the suffix `.j3o`. If you have stored user data in a node, this data is automatically serialized, and deserialized too, which is quite handy. Saving user data works out of the box with all serializable Java datatypes such as ints, floats, Strings, and arrays. If you stored custom Java objects as user data, make sure these objects implement the `com.jme3.export.Savable` interface, and override the write (`exporter`) and read (`importer`) methods.

Before saving, verify that you have identified a directory for which your application has write permissions. Typically, you store saved games in a new directory under `System.getProperty("user.home")`.

In sandbox games, where everything changes all the time, you can save the whole root Node, as shown in this simple demo. Consider, however, that this results in a huge file. If you have static content that you can simply restore using `AssetManager`, detach it before saving the root node and remaining changed nodes. When you restore the root node later, remember to reattach the static content too.

## Time for action – save and load display settings

You save the scene to a binary `.j3o` file, and similarly, you save display settings to an XML file. The next time your users run the game, you want to present them with their previously selected display settings.

1. Return to your `AppSettings.java` file.
2. In your `main()` method, load previously saved settings, if they exist; configure a new settings objects if it doesn't exist:

```
public static void main(String[] args) {
  AppSettings settings = new AppSettings(true);
  try {
    settings.load("com.foo.MyCoolGame");
  } catch (BackingStoreException ex2) {
      Logger.getLogger(AppSettingsDemo.class.
      getName()).log(Level.WARNING,
      "failed to load settings, reverting to defaults", ex);
    settings.setTitle("My Cool Game"); // init defaults here…
  }
```

**3.** Then continue to save your settings:

```
AppSettingsDemo app = new AppSettingsDemo();
try {
  settings.save("com.foo.MyCoolGame");
} catch (BackingStoreException ex) {
  Logger.getLogger(AppSettingsDemo.
    class.getName()).log(Level.WARNING,
    "failed to save settings", ex);
}
app.setSettings(settings);
app.start();
}
```

## What just happened?

Saving and loading settings this way is especially useful if you create a custom options screen that lets users configure and save video settings in a user-friendly way. Make sure you provide the unique name of your jMonkeyEngine application as a `String` argument. The unique name typically looks like your main class' package name; for example, `com.foo.MyCoolGame`.

On Windows, the preferences are saved under the following registry key:

`HKEY_CURRENT_USER\Software\JavaSoft\Prefs\com\foo\MyCoolGame`

On Linux, the preferences are saved in an XML file, in the user's home directory:

`$HOME/.java/.userPrefs/com/foo/MyCoolGame`

On Mac OS X, the preferences are saved in an XML file, in the user's home directory:

`$HOME/Library/Preferences/com.foo.MyCoolGame.plist`

# Pre-release checklist

Your application is now built and ready to be shipped to customers. Before you start the shipping process, it's time to go through a checklist to catch common omissions and to remind yourself of certain best practices:

- Verify that media assets are up-to-date:
  - Convert all models to `.j3o` format
  - Update all code to load models only in `.j3o` format
  - Verify that no code is left that tries to load `Blender.blend`, `Ogre.xml`, or `Wavefront.obj` files

◆ Save storage space and loading time:

❑ For desktop games, compress textures to DXT; for web games, compress textures to JPG

❑ Update all code to load the compressed textures

❑ Verify that no code is left that loads uncompressed textures

◆ Adhere to best practices:

❑ Activate compressed packaging to reduce the size of the application. You find this option in the **Project Properties** window inside **Build | Packaging**.

❑ Switch off fine logging output and make the application print only "severe" messages to the console. Add the following to your `simpleInitApp()` method: `AppLogger.getLogger("").setLevel(Level.SEVERE);`.

❑ For applets and Web Start applications only: decide whether to certify the authenticity of your application. Purchasing a certificate from a certificate authority is only necessary if you want your company name to appear under the `Vendor` part of the security confirmation dialog in the browser. A Web Start game can run without a certificate, but you will have to inform your users how to react positively to the quite discouraging default security warning.

❑ Prepare a `Read Me` file. Inform your customers of the requirements: they need a 1 GHz CPU or better, and a graphic card that supports OpenGL 2.0 or higher. They need to have the Java Virtual Machine (JVM) installed. The JVM is preinstalled on many operating systems; otherwise remind them to download the JVM for free from `http://www.java.com`. Just to be clear: your users do not need the jMonkeyEngine SDK to run the game.

❑ Prepare marketing materials that convince your audience in 30 seconds (a so-called "elevator pitch"). Keep promotional art ready, such as cool screenshots and short thematic video clips. Look for social networking and gaming sites that allow you to share links and videos and advertise your game. Include the game's name, slogan, how to obtain it, and your contact info.

# Release checklist

Now that you have specified settings and know how to save and load your game, it's time to decide how to deploy it. The default build script generated by the jMonkeyEngine SDK for your project assists you with common deployment options.

The default deployment type for Java is **Java archive** (**JAR**). A JAR file contains an executable desktop application that runs on Windows, Mac OS, and Linux. In order to be able to simply double-click and run JAR files, the user must have his system configured to allow that, or the user must know how to run JAR files from the command line. Since not all users know how to launch JAR files, you typically need to provide a more user-friendly option.

Whether you release your game as a Web Start application, Android mobile game, desktop application, or as a browser applet, you have to consider the pros and cons of each option:

| Distribution | Pros | Cons |
| --- | --- | --- |
| Desktop Launcher (for Windows (.exe), for Mac (.app), for Linux (.jar, .sh) | This is a typical desktop application that a user double-clicks, and it starts running. The jMonkeyEngine SDK can create launchers for these three operating systems. | You need to offer several separate, platform-dependent downloads. |
| Web Start (.jnlp) | To start the game, the user browses to a URL and downloads it into a cache. The game then runs outside the web browser. Easy process for the user, no installer required. The user always downloads the most recent version. You can also allow them to play the game offline. | The first time the user downloads the game, it takes a while, as opposed to running the app from a local drive. Unsigned Web Start applications have restrictions (cannot save to or read from disk). |
| Browser applet (.html+.jar) | The user plays the game in a web page in the browser. Applets are a quick, user-friendly solution for small browser games. | You need a host with enough bandwidth. Applets only run in the browser, not offline. Unsigned Web Start applications have restrictions (cannot save to or read from disk). The browser imposes restrictions on game navigation (game cannot capture the mouse). |

| Distribution | Pros | Cons |
|---|---|---|
| Mobile (.apk) | The user installs the game from the Google Play Store. Alternatively, the user downloads and installs the APK file using a USB cable and an Android file explorer. | Most mobile devices do not support post-processor effects, so you need to offer a way to disable or replace them. You have to provide input settings that work without keyboard. |

No matter which method you choose, Java desktop and browser applications work on all major operating systems (MS Windows, Mac OS, and Linux) that have the JVM installed.

## Time for action – build the final release

By default, the jMonkeyEngine SDK builds a JAR file, but possibly, you have decided on another deployment method. Now, it is only a matter of selecting a checkbox in the jMonkeyEngine project properties to build your executables.

Right-click on the project in the SDK to open the **Properties** window. Go to the **Application** section and choose among the following deployment choices: **Web Start**, **Applet**, **Mobile**, and **Desktop**.

For Web Start applications:

1. Check the **Enable Web Start** checkbox.
2. Choose **Codebase: Local Execution**.
3. (Optional) Specify a desktop icon for this application.
4. (Optional) Check the **Allow Offline** checkbox.
5. Check the **Application descriptor** checkbox.
6. Click on **OK**.
7. Right-click on the project and choose **Clean and Build**. The executable appears in the dist directory.
8. Upload all files from the dist directory to your web server.
9. Tell your users to browse to the file dist/launch.html to start the game.

For applets:

1. Check the **Create Applet** checkbox.
2. Click on **OK**.

3. Right-click on the project and choose **Clean and Build**. The executable appears in the `dist` directory.

4. Upload all files from the `dist` directory to your web server.

5. Tell your users to browse to the file `dist/Applet/run-applet.html` to start the game.

For mobile applications:

1. If you use this option for the first time, specify your Android SDK folder.

2. Check the **Enable Android Deployment** checkbox.

3. Select an Android target.

4. Enter the main class.

5. Click on **OK**.

6. A folder named `mobile` appears in your project directory. This folder contains the complete Android project, with settings to run the application using AndroidHarness.

7. Restart the jMonkeyEngine SDK. A new `Mobile Files` node appears in the **Project** window. It lets you edit the `MainActivitity.java`, the `AndroidManifest.xml`, and `build.properties` files.

8. Right-click on the project and choose **Clean and Build**. The executable appears in the `dist` directory.

9. Tell your users to install the `dist/MyCoolGame.apk` file on their Android device to start the game. Typically, this means you submit it to the Google Play Store.

For desktop applications:

1. Check the platforms that you want to build launchers for: **Windows**, **Mac OS**, and **Linux**.

2. Click on **OK**.

3. Right-click on the project and choose **Clean and Build**. The executables appear in the `dist` directory.

4. Upload the zipped files, or distribute them on a medium.

5. Tell Windows users to double-click on the `MyGame.exe` file to start the game. Tell Mac users to double-click on the `MyGame.app` file to start the game. Tell Linux users to execute the `MyGame.sh` file to run the `MyGame.jar` file.

Note that the jMonkeyEngine SDK allows you to select several deployment options at the same time. The distributable files are all placed in the `dist` directory. Verify that you distribute the right files to the right audience.

You can customize the `.sh` and `.html` launcher files after they have been generated. However, remember to keep backup copies of any customized launcher files: the SDK deletes and regenerates the `dist` directory every time you build.

## What just happened?

We have now built the final release. We discussed procedures for building executables using different deployment choices, such as Web Start, Applet, Mobile, and Desktop.

# Summary

We have reached the end of the development cycle! Now you know:

◆  How to specify, load, and save display and application settings

◆  How to load and save games

◆  How to deploy the application to various platforms

Time to ship! In *Appendix A, What's Next?*, you will get a quick overview of all the other interesting possibilities offered by jMonkeyEngine that we haven't discussed yet.

# A
# What's Next?

*Now that you know how to write and publish a jMonkeyEngine-based application, it's your turn to design and implement a game! You probably already have an idea in your head; if not, join the jmonkeyengine.org forum and get inspiration from your fellow game developers. Alas, there is no bullet-proof algorithm to generate and calibrate the perfect game idea, so this book cannot help you with that part of the task. This short final chapter can, however, teach you how to avoid well-known design traps.*

Read on for some closing advice on how to make gameplay fun:

- ◆ How to delight players with challenging choices
- ◆ How to keep things balanced and still exciting
- ◆ How to enable players to make the most of their newly found super-powers
- ◆ How to smooth the learning curve
- ◆ How to create a polished game concept

Okay, let's look deeper into this mysterious "fun" thing, shall we?

## Hey, this game is fun!

Think of your favorite games. Why did you enjoy playing them? Probably because they piqued your curiosity and gave you a feeling of success. Why did you stop playing others? Because they were boring or frustrating.

Unsurprisingly, criteria such as "special effects not colorful enough" or "cartoon characters not crazy enough" rank quite low among the reasons why not to play a game. These factors are the least of your worries when designing a fun game. But how do you find out whether your game idea is "fun"? Let's see what the experts say. Here is a quote by *Raph Koster* from "*A Theory of Fun for Game Design*":

> *"A fun game is the one that offers an interesting challenge to the player and makes him want to play the game until the challenge is conquered. But, the trick is to make the challenge not too hard (it will cause frustration) or too easy (it will cause boredom), so that the player can keep on playing."*

A challenge becomes interesting if players feel they have a choice and control over the outcome. If the challenge is "not too hard, nor too easy", it is balanced. What we mean by interesting and balanced will become quite clear when you will look at a few examples.

Put your game idea to the test and answer the following questions:

◆ Does your game have an item such as a "+50 Bazooka of Deadly Deadliness", a weapon with no disadvantages and which is so powerful that there is no reason to own any other? If yes, then you have deprived players of the fun of choosing the optimal equipment.

 Get rid of no-brainer choices that are automatically successful. If you must have a killer item, balance the game by providing several similarly powerful items, each with a built-in disadvantage (one-time use only or 50 percent chance it may backfire).

◆ Does your game exclusively generate enemies that are of equal strength as the player? Then you have deprived your players of the fun of taking smart risks. Make sure your game does not encourage arbitrary behavior—in this case, "I attack whomever I meet with no consequences."

 Offer players the choice among more and less challenging tasks. For example, they can choose to compete against a single stronger or equal opponent, or a group of equal or weaker opponents. This way, your players get a better feeling for their own progress.

◆ Does your game have lots of weak items that cannot be sold or used, and whose only purpose is to add volume to a pile of loot? If yes, you have deprived your players of the fun of identifying valuable items.

Either get rid of boring, useless filler items, or add situations where choosing a seemingly weak item turns out to be an advantage. For example, give a bonus if players use non-magic daggers against an enemy that is immune to magic.

You see that challenges are only meaningful if players face choices that noticeably influence the outcome of the challenge. How does your game idea fare regarding these important criteria?

# Some dos and don'ts

During the game, you want to give players the feeling that they made the right choices, outsmarted the system, and pulled the strings in their own favor. There are no hard rules, but let's look at some examples how you maintain enjoyable gameplay:

- **Fairness is not the same as balance**: Although well-balanced game mechanics include a weakness behind every strength, they avoid perfect symmetry. In a perfectly fair game (such as rock-paper-scissors) choices are arbitrary. You should offer a counterattack for every attack, but you distribute these resources unevenly. In other words, let the players know that "the counter-card is somewhere in the deck", but not whether it is in their opponent's hand this round. "I can prepare a counterspell for each type of magic, but which spell type will the opponent cast?" "I can wear armor against every weapon type, but will the opponent pick the sniper rifle or the shotgun?" The opponent faces the same conundrum, and that keeps the battle balanced and interesting.

- **Predictable events are boring, random events are frustrating**: Let players take a stab at figuring out the probabilities behind the game mechanics. The opportunity to weigh the success of various strategies lets players tweak probabilities in their favor and prove their smarts.

- **Valuable resources must be limited**: By definition, more valuable resources (health, ammo, equipment, and skills) must be more costly to obtain. Each choice comes at a different price—everything costs money, time, or carrying capacity. Limited resources force the player to make interesting economic and logistic decisions. Cheap, fast, or strong? Pick two!

- **Life is not black and white**: Create emotional complexity by making players face inner conflicts. Going beyond the basic contrast of "either good or evil" forces players to make interesting moral decisions. "Should I risk harming my team, if I can nuke the enemy?" "Should I risk helping the enemy if it also saves my team?"

You will find the perfect balance for your game by running lots of play tests and gathering player feedback. Over time, players will teach themselves "every trick in the book" and their strategies grow more and more successful. They worked hard for it, and the learning process is fun because winning brings a sense of well-earned achievement.

# Superpowers – Go!

Consider a case when your game idea poses an interesting, balanced challenge, but your test players quit before the fun begins. Time to give your user interface a makeover. Bad usability is a major reason why players abandon otherwise promising games.

Consider that the player's expectations toward a user interface are quite high. Video games promise nothing less than super-human powers. Player avatars are strong, fast, and dexterous; they fly, climb, dive, and ride everything from helicopter to pterodactyl. All of that, plus infinite lives. What's not to like?

Well, your players also pay a price. A video game only provides a subset of visual and auditory information; the player's choice of actions is severely limited by the game mechanics; and some sensory information (smell, touch, pain, balance, and proprioception) is missing completely.

Why not invite some jmonkeyengine.org forum members to test your milestone builds? Tweak parameters until you're certain that your user interface does no longer throw a monkey wrench in the player's works.

An unclear interface frustrates players because they misjudge situations. Unresponsive input methods make players stumble over their own feet. Without a sense of pain, they cannot feel the intensity of the shockwave or the heat of the lava and run blindly into danger. Give your players a fair chance. If, for example, the troll leader is stronger than its minions, reflect that in the intensity of the NPC's special effects.

Conversely, don't sprinkle meaningless effects all over the game world. Distracting players away from meaningful elements can easily backfire and cause frustration. If you play natural sounds in the background, for example, make the birds fall silent right before a monster appears. Players will quickly learn to associate "birdsong" with peace and "silence" with danger—as a nice side-effect, all those random pauses in the bird loops really keep them on their toes.

Use audio and visual hints wisely to convey information. If you use effects and symbols consistently, players learn to trust them, and they get an extra feeling of success when they assess a situation correctly.

A good user interface uses sound and visuals to show players whether a decision has taken them closer to their goal, or further away from it. You want to enable players to detect an unsuccessful strategy fast and try a different approach: for example, "Walking on rocks: good. Walking on lava: bad." If players can't tell why they just lost hitpoints (or lives), it's nothing but frustrating. If they understand the danger, they feel empowered to avoid it next time.

# Keep it simple

Games such as "Go" and "Tetris" prove that a game idea can be successful with relatively few rules. On the other end of the spectrum, some games get bogged down in an avalanche of rules that hinder adoption and eventually kill gameplay. Do you want to read a 50-page booklet and watch an hour-long training video before you can survive even a day in this brave new world? Nah, you want to jump right in and explore!

If your game mechanics need a lot of explanation, try to smooth a steep learning curve by providing players with an interactive in-game tutorial. Optimally, the in-game tutorial is a simplified version of playing the game itself. Design levels so that they expose players slowly to new examples of the game mechanics, one rule after the other. Point out each pattern and give them opportunity to recognize it in context. When they understand the basics, expose them to combinations of patterns. In doing so, you teach the rules implicitly and players can get started right away—which lessens the need for long, explicit handbooks.

For example, the first four dungeons introduce the player to the four different elements of your fantasy world. While traveling through Snowingham, Volcania, Snakepit, and Teslaville, the player is introduced to ice, fire, poison, and lightning. In each dungeon, the player learns how to identify, attack, and defend with one of the elements. Thus prepared, the player ventures on to medium levels. Here he encounters enemies who are immune to more than one element, or who can use combinations of elemental attacks. Since the player is already trained to identify individual elements, he now merely needs to combine what he has learned.

In-game tutorials can take on a variety of forms. Sometimes they come in the guise of an easier, preliminary level that can be skipped or fast-forwarded by experienced players. Many games offer in-game help as tooltips, or arrows that point lost beginners in the right direction. Other games repeat hints over several levels, as it is nicely done in the increasingly more difficult puzzle combinations of the Portal series.

# Polishing off the last pages

Popular games such as Portal (physics puzzle), Super Mario Bros (jump and run), Legend of Zelda (adventure with minigames), or Halo (action) look quite different on the outside, but they have one thing in common. They were successful because they had "polish".

In a polished game, everything is of one piece. The rules and game interactions provide a consistent experience. The game provides all details needed for the solution, and leaves no plot holes that distract from the solution (also known as the "Chekov's Gun" principle). Players are never pulled out of the immersion. Whether a move is illegal or legal, there is an obvious in-game reason, no wordy explanations required.

Be careful not to water down your fun game idea by making one game "do everything, but better". Gameplay does not progressively become better every time you add another cool gimmick. Ask your test players what helped them most, and what misled them most. Polish your game by identifying the fun areas and putting them in front and center. Drop distractions.

Different types of challenges appeal to different players. Optimally, you focus on one type of challenge. Here are some common examples:

- Some games require hand-eye coordination and fast reflexes
- Other games can only be solved with patience and logic
- In some games you must find the perfect strategy and tactics
- Other games can only be won with lateral thinking or pattern recognition

Similar to Charlie Sheen, different players consider different achievements "winning". Here are a few common groups of players who you may encounter:

- Some players enjoy employing their reflexes in faction wars and coordinated teams. They expect to compete (and win) in duels against human players, with whichever weapon they collect during a match. Slow-paced brainteasers and predictable "artificially dumb" NPCs bore them to tears.

- Other players enjoy taking on a role and training an avatar's skills. They expect to excel themselves every time they progress through another increasingly difficult quest. Game elements that cannot be measured, compared, and "min-maxed" do not appeal to them. Neither do they care about hand-eye coordination—after all, that's what the avatar trained Dexterity for!

- Yet other players enjoy solo adventures, exploration, and brainteasers. They want to beat the game designers by solving a handcrafted puzzle. The last thing these players want is fellow human players spoiling the solution; nor do skills by proxy of an avatar have any value to them. Who needs an avatar if they can use their own problem-solving skills?

These are just exaggerated examples; the point is that games present vastly different challenges that do not mix well. Don't succumb to the temptation of squeezing too many types of challenges into one game. If you attempt to fulfill contradictory requirements, you risk losing the interest of all target groups. Or, as the famous saying by *Antoine de Saint-Exupéry* goes:

> *Perfection is achieved, not when there is nothing more to add, but when there is nothing left to take away.*

# Summary

That's it! You now know how to use the jMonkeyEngine to develop a Java 3D game, you are aware of the most common pitfalls of game design, and you know the best practices for how to avoid them.

The Appendix B, Additional Resources for Fellow jMonkeys contain more information about the jMonkeyEngine SDK, how to set up the jMonkeyEngine without the SDK, and many links to game resources, where you can find free assets, tools, and tutorials.

Need help? Join the jmonkeyengine.org forum; you are always welcome to ask questions. And (interesting fact!) now that you've read this book, you are also qualified to answer questions!

# B

# Additional Resources for Fellow jMonkeys

*You already know that the jMonkeyEngine SDK is a software development kit that contains handy tools for game developers.* The SDK has many more unique game development tools that are worth knowing.

In the previous chapters, you already heard about the main features of the SDK:

- Project creation wizard, including fully preconfigured classpath and deployment settings
- 3D model importer and converter
- SceneComposer and SceneExplorer
- Material Editor
- Bitmap Font Creator plugin
- The SkyBox wizard
- Terrain Editor
- Particle Effect Editor

 Press *Ctrl + I*, or type a keyword into the search box in the top right of the SDK to search the built-in help and documentation (*Ctrl + I*). Even when offline, you always have access to documentation, code samples, and best practices (shortcut is *F1*)!

You can access the following features from the **Windows** and **Tools** menus in the SDK. This book cannot cover all advanced features in detail, so let's just look at a quick outline of what you can expect:

- **Post-Processor Filter Editor**: This window lets you configure and preview several post-processor filters together in a scene, and package the code into one easily loadable asset file.

- **Nifty GUI 1.3 Editor**: An editor and previewer that makes the development of Nifty GUIs easier. It includes templates and a Swing-to-Nifty converter.

- **Internationalization Wizard**: This user-friendly tool for translators creates and integrates standard `Bundle.properties` files into your project. In these files, you specify the strings in your code that you want to localize.

- **AssetPack Browser**: This browser lets you create AssetPacks and share your 3D models with your team or other community members. The SDK comes preloaded with the WorldForge AssetPack that includes many free-to-use 3D models.

- **The NeoTexture plugin**: This user-friendly plugin lets you design procedural textures visually.

> You heard of a cool SDK feature, but you cannot find it in your SDK's Window or Tools menu. Then you may be missing a plugin. Installing plugins is very easy. Open **Tools | Plugins** from the SDK menu, and go to the **Available Plugins** tab. Check the boxes to choose plugins, click on **Install**, and restart the SDK, if prompted.

Just like any **Integrated Development Environment** (**IDE**), the jMonkeyEngine SDK offers an advanced code editor, several file and project creation wizards, and integrated teamwork tools.

The following are useful features that you as a (hopefully) future SDK user should be aware of:

- The code editor makes your code more readable, thanks to automatic highlighting and formatting for Java, XML, .j3o, .j3m, and .j3md files. For many file types, the editor also offers code completion (*Ctrl + Space bar*), boilerplate code generation, and refactoring.

- File wizards and templates assist you in creating Java classes, Java packages, and jMonkey files such as materials (.j3m), scenes (.j3o), FilterPostProcessors (.j3f), and Nifty GUI's screens, procedural textures, and shaders. Use the Template tool to create custom file templates and share them with your team members.

- File version control (Subversion, Mercurial, and Git) is very well integrated into the SDK. Version control lets your team work in a shared repository that also keeps a history of all changes.

Press *Ctrl + Space bar* to consult Javadoc pop ups for jMonkeyEngine APIs and Java SE APIs.

Click on the editor hints (light bulb symbols) to fix import statements or execute quick fixes.

Open the code palette and drag-and-drop common code snippets into your classes.

The jMonkeyEngine team has put a lot of effort into the creation of the SDK and its tools, and we hope they will make your developer lives easier. Visit `http://jmonkeyengine.org/wiki/doku.php/sdk` to learn more!

# Game-development resources

Do you have questions about Java or game design in general? Explore the following websites with basic game design resources:

## Game-development tips

The jMonkey team recommends the following books and articles:

- Free e-book *The Lucu Guide for Creating Video Games* by *Taksan Tong* (`http://lucu.googlecode.com`) (under **Downloads**)
- The article *Why You Shouldn't Be Making an MMO* (`http://www.gamedev.net/blog/355/entry-2250155-why-you-shouldnt-be-making-an-mmo/`)
- The book *A Theory of Fun for Game Design* by *Raph Koster* (`http://www.theoryoffun.com/`)
- The book *Texturing and Modeling* by *Ebert et al*
- The article *Entity Systems* (`http://entity-systems.wikidot.com/`)

## Game-asset resources

When you search for free media, such as 3D models, include the search term "Commons". You can also be more specific and include "Creative Commons", "Wikimedia Commons", "Flickr Commons", and so on. These keywords help you find free content that allows re-use under the condition that you include the license file and the name of the copyright holder. Remember to check and adhere to the license conditions before using free assets.

Multimedia artwork:

- http://opengameart.org
- http://www.cgtextures.com/
- http://www.sound-effect.com/
- http://beta.freesound.org/
- http://www.planetside.co.uk/
- http://www.angelcode.com/products/bmfont/

3D mesh editors and plugins:

- http://www.ogre3d.org/download/tools
- http://www.blender.org/
- http://www.k-3d.org/wiki/Features
- http://sketchup.google.com
- http://Wings3d.com

Tutorials:

- http://jmonkeyengine.org/wiki/doku.php/jme3
- http://www.theoryoffun.com/
- http://www.photoshoplady.com/
- http://web.media.mit.edu/~jorkin/goap.html
- http://www.pixelprospector.com/the-big-list-of-payment-processors/

# Key input triggers

The following key input triggers are available:

## Mouse

The following mouse triggers are available:

| Trigger | Code |
| --- | --- |
| Mouse button: Left click | MouseButtonTrigger(MouseInput.BUTTON_LEFT) |
| Mouse button: Right click | MouseButtonTrigger(MouseInput.BUTTON_RIGHT) |
| Mouse button: Middle click | MouseButtonTrigger(MouseInput.BUTTON_MIDDLE) |
| Mouse movement: Right | MouseAxisTrigger(MouseInput.AXIS_X, true) |

| Trigger | Code |
| --- | --- |
| Mouse movement: Left | `MouseAxisTrigger(MouseInput.AXIS_X, false)` |
| Mouse movement: Up | `MouseAxisTrigger(MouseInput.AXIS_Y, true)` |
| Mouse movement: Down | `MouseAxisTrigger(MouseInput.AXIS_Y, false)` |
| Mouse wheel: Up | `MouseAxisTrigger(MouseInput.AXIS_WHEEL, false)` |
| Mouse wheel: Down | `MouseAxisTrigger(MouseInput.AXIS_WHEEL,true)` |

# Keyboard

The following key triggers are available:

| Trigger | Code |
| --- | --- |
| NumPad: *1, 2, 3, …* | `KeyTrigger(KeyInput.KEY_NUMPAD1)` … |
| Keyboard: *1, 2 , 3, …* | `KeyTrigger(KeyInput.KEY_1)` … |
| Keyboard: *A, B, C, …* | `KeyTrigger(KeyInput.KEY_A)` … |
| Keyboard: *Space bar* | `KeyTrigger(KeyInput.KEY_SPACE)` |
| Keyboard: *Shift* | `KeyTrigger(KeyInput.KEY_RSHIFT),` `KeyTrigger(KeyInput.KEY_LSHIFT)` |
| Keyboard: *F1, F2, …* | `KeyTrigger(KeyInput.KEY_F1)` … |
| Keyboard: *Return/Enter* | `KeyTrigger(KeyInput.KEY_RETURN),` `KeyTrigger(KeyInput.KEY_NUMPADENTER)` |
| Keyboard: *PageUp* and *PageDown* | `KeyTrigger(KeyInput.KEY_PGUP),` `KeyTrigger(KeyInput.KEY_PGDN)` |
| Keyboard: *Delete* and *Backspace* | `KeyTrigger(KeyInput.KEY_BACK),` `KeyTrigger(KeyInput.KEY_DELETE)` |
| Keyboard: *Esc* | `KeyTrigger(KeyInput.KEY_ESCAPE)` |
| Keyboard: Arrows | `KeyTrigger(KeyInput.KEY_DOWN),` `KeyTrigger(KeyInput.KEY_UP)` `KeyTrigger(KeyInput.KEY_LEFT),` `KeyTrigger(KeyInput.KEY_RIGHT)` |

# Joystick

The following joystick triggers are available:

| Trigger | Code |
|---|---|
| Joystick buttons | `JoyButtonTrigger(0, JoyInput.AXIS_POV_X),` |
| | `JoyButtonTrigger(0, JoyInput.AXIS_POV_Y)` |
| Joystick movement: Right | `JoyAxisTrigger(0, JoyInput.AXIS_POV_X, true)` |
| Joystick movement: Left | `JoyAxisTrigger(0, JoyInput.AXIS_POV_X, false)` |
| Joystick movement: Forward | `JoyAxisTrigger(0, JoyInput.AXIS_POV_Z, true)` |
| Joystick movement: Backward | `JoyAxisTrigger(0, JoyInput.AXIS_POV_Z, false)` |

You can find the most current trigger list at `http://jmonkeyengine.org/wiki/doku.php/jme3:advanced:input_handling`.

# Setting up jMonkeyEngine in Eclipse

For development with the jMonkeyEngine 3, use the jMonkeyEngine SDK that you can download for free from `http://jmonkeyengine.org`.

If you want to use your favorite IDE for coding, you can create a code-less jMonkeyEngine project. This makes it possible to use the asset management tools in the SDK, even if you do not use the SDK's code editor. At the same time, you can manage the source code and build a script in Eclipse (or any other IDE).

Since the SDK is built on top of the NetBeans platform, users of NetBeans IDE should feel right at home. In the following tutorial, we show how to download and set up the latest nightly build of the jMonkeyEngine 3 library for use with the Eclipse IDE.

You can find the most current Eclipse setup tips at `http://jmonkeyengine.org/wiki/doku.php/jme3:setting_up_jme3_in_eclipse`.

# Downloading the software

The currently available JAR binaries are the nightly builds.

1. The nightly build contains the jMonkeyEngine binaries as JAR files. Download the most recent zipped build from `http://nightly.jmonkeyengine.com`.

2. Unzip the file and save the directory as `jME3_2013-xx-xx` in your home directory (`$HOME`).

3. Verify that you have at least the following files and directories:

   ❑ `lib/` and `opt/`: The jMonkeyEngine binaries, and libraries used by the jMonkeyEngine (don't remove)

   ❑ `jMonkeyEngine.jar`: Run this file to see various feature demos (optional)

   ❑ `javadoc/`: jME3 API documentation (optional but useful)

   ❑ `source/`: The jMonkeyEngine library's source code (optional but useful)

# Creating a new game project

Perform the following steps:

1. Open the Eclipse IDE.

2. Choose **File** | **New** | **Java Project**.

3. Enter the **Project Name**; for example, `HelloJME3`.

4. Click on **Finish**.

The new Java project appears in the Eclipse Explorer.

# Setting up dependencies

Your project depends on the jMonkeyEngine libraries, so it needs to know where they are.

1. Right-click on the project in the Eclipse Explorer and choose **Build Path** | **Add External Archives**.

2. In the **JAR selection** dialog, browse to the `$HOME/jME3_2013-xx-xx` directory.

3. Select all JARs in the `lib` directory and click on **Open**.

All necessary JAR libraries are now on the classpath and should appear in the **Referenced Libraries** list.

# Setting up the assets folder

The jMonkeyEngine SDK creates an assets folder for your projects. In Eclipse, perform the following steps manually:

1.  On the top level of your Eclipse project, create a new directory and name it `assets`. Save all your game assets into this folder.

2.  In the jMonkeyEngine SDK, choose **File | Import Project | External Project Assets** from the menu to open the **Import External Project Assets** wizard.

3.  When the wizard asks for a project folder, browse to your Eclipse project's top-level folder.

4.  When the wizard asks for an assets folder, browse to your Eclipse project's assets folder. Click on Next and then on **Finish**.

A so-called codeless jMonkeyEngine project gets saved into your Eclipse project. The project also appears in the jMonkeyEngine's **Projects** window. You use this project to create materials, convert 3D models, and so on.

# Writing a simple application

In the Eclipse IDE, you write your code as you are used to.

1.  From the menu, open **File | New | New Package**. Name the package for example `hello`.

2.  From the menu, open **File | New | Class**.

    1.  Select package `hello`.

    2.  Name the class; for example, `MyGame`.

    3.  Specify the Superclass as `com.jme3.app.SimpleApplication`.

    4.  Activate the checkbox to create the `main()` method if this is the main class of your game.

    5.  Activate the checkbox for **Inheriting Abstract Methods**.

3.  Click on **Finish**.

The new main class based on SimpleApplication opens in the editor. Write your game code, or copy and paste one of the tutorials.

Consult the Eclipse documentation for advice on compiling and deploying your game.

# Best practices for jMonkey networking

Networking is a broad subject that would take more than this chapter to cover in full detail. Since you can learn Java networking from the official Java tutorials, let's focus on jMonkeyEngine-specific networking advice here in this appendix.

## What do the client and server do?

This is a common question asked by developers who design their first network game: How do I best separate the code between client and server?

In general, the server generates game events, such as a swarm of enemy NPCs spawning, random encounters, or quest masters handing out missions. To keep track of the game world, the server centrally maintains all data about objects and characters—these are your game entities. If the game uses JME physics, the server also maintains a master scene graph, but it does not render it. Rendering is the client's job.

The client receives and stores updates from the server. Each client renders its own scene graph from the point of view of its player. Design your game so that the code treats all characters as abstract remote players—this includes the local player too. Some characters are remote-controlled by the server, others by other clients—and one of them happens to be controlled by the local user's input. The only difference between them is that the client's camera follows the player-controlled character.

The server does not care what visual and auditory feedback are like. The server merely broadcasts that a certain event has occurred. It's the client's job to change icons, to play sounds, animations, or particle effects—whatever feedback is needed to convey the event to the player.

Similarly, each client deals with local user options, such as input trigger settings. The client resolves the trigger mapping and sends only the mapping name of the action back to the server. The server does not care at all about the actual input triggers (which depend on the local player's keyboard layout or personal preference).

Each client renders the scene according to their user's settings. This means that different users can play the same game over the same server with different video/audio settings. Remember, the server doesn't care; it only broadcasts the game state—only the client renders the game state from the point of view of its user. For example, you can let users with old hardware switch to the `SimpleWaterProcessor`, instead of using the full-featured `WaterFilter` effect.

Contrast these local settings with global settings such as the selected map, team contest type, or dungeon difficulty. In multiplayer games, game-wide settings are not user options, but server session settings. For example, the player hosting the game server specifies session settings, globally for all clients, before the game starts.

Certain application states are relevant only to the client. For example, when a player toggles to the `SettingsScreenState`, this client is simply idle from the point of view of the server. Application states that manage loading the world and implementing gameplay, on the other hand, are relevant only to the server.

Similarly, some custom controls are relevant only to the client. Think of a `HudControl` or `AnimationControl`. The server must know whether an avatar walks, jumps, or stands—but it does not care what the avatar or HUD looks like while doing that. Other controls may be relevant only to the server. Examples include pathfinding controls for computer-controlled enemies.

# Getting your physics in sync

Imagine a network game where each client runs its own physics simulation. One player jumps and the client broadcasts this action to the server, which passes it on. A few fractions of a second later, other clients begin to calculate the jumper's trajectory. In their copy of the world state, however, this player walked a fraction of a meter farther before jumping. Their trajectories begin at different spots with a different speed. You can easily guess that in such a setting, the clients' states will divert quickly.

There are three ways how you can keep your physics simulation synchronized in a network game:

- **Centralized physics**: The clients send all user input to the server. The server calculates a scene graph with dynamic, static, and kinematic nodes and simulates physics centrally. The server continuously broadcasts new locations to the clients. Each client maintains its own non-physical (kinematic) scene graph to display the state.

- **Decentralized physics**: Server and clients each take on part of the physics simulation.

  - In the client's scene graph, the local player is represented as a dynamic node, and all other players and NPCs are kinematic nodes. The kinematic nodes are controlled by broadcast messages from the server. The client sends the location of its dynamic player to the server, which broadcasts it to all other clients.

  - In the server's scene graph, conversely, NPCs are represented as dynamic nodes, and all players are kinematic nodes. A kinematic player's transformation is updated on the server every time its client sends a new location message.

◆ **Hybrid physics**: Physics run in full mode on both the client and server, and they synchronize every so often. This way you get fast simulations on the client, independent of network lag. The downside of this approach is that you must force regular synchronization to ensure that the server remains authoritative over the player's location. If you don't find a smooth synchronization strategy, this can result in annoying jerks and jumps for player characters.

Decentralized physics has its advantages, but it makes hacking the game very easy, because the server has to trust the clients. If players are authoritative over their location, they can essentially teleport to any location in the world. However, it depends on your game type whether that is an unfair advantage—or an irrelevant fun trick.

## Choosing a server type

Every networked game has one host that runs the server. The host can either be a dedicated public machine, or you can allow players to host games locally. Here are your options:

◆ **Dedicated server**: A company provides a machine or cluster that can handle a large amount of connections. All players play on the same host together. The game world on the central host is typically persisted in an entity database.

◆ **LAN server (also called listen server)**: The player with the fastest hardware and connection volunteers to run a game server in addition to running his game client. In this setup, many smaller groups of players play their own instances of the game in their **LAN (local area network)**. These temporary instances of the game world often last only one round; characters may or may not be persisted.

If you choose to maintain one central server, you can configure each client to connect to the server address directly. Typically, you would implement this as a "Connect" button on the start screen. If your game has several dedicated servers, your user interface should present the player with a list of servers to choose from.

When you write a multiplayer game that lets users run LAN servers, you should design a user interface to negotiate local games. In the typical LAN game, all players first start their clients. One player presses a "Create network game" or "Host multiplayer game" (or similar) button, which starts the server. The others then click on a "Join network game" or "Join multiplayer game" button and connect to this server. It's a nice feature to make the host broadcast its address to the LAN so clients can connect to the server immediately. Alternatively, provide a login screen where players can type in the host's address manually.

Other network games offer a meet-up server. A player's game server connects to the meet-up server and publishes its address and port there. Players start their clients and connect to the meet-up server to get a list of available game servers. Clients pick a host from the meet-up board and the game starts when enough players are present. In this setting, the meet-up server does not simulate any gameplay, it just maintains the list of active game servers.

## Hackers, cheaters, and griefers

Designing a networked game is a lot of work. There will always be hackers who enjoy the challenge of reverse-engineering your client-server communication. The catch is, if you can remote-control the game world by sending messages, then—theoretically—everyone can.

If the message is formed correctly, the server cannot tell whether it was sent by a legal or illegal source. Griefers fabricate messages that waste game resources and disrupt their fellow players. Cheaters fabricate messages that make their own characters rich, strong, invincible, and (of course) handsome.

The most reliable way to prevent cheating and griefing is to centralize all authority. Ideally, the client sends only plain user actions to the server. The server simulates all gameplay and tracks the score. Then, the server broadcasts to all clients what they should see. Even if cheaters send a flood of messages pretending to perform tasks at super-human speed, you can write heuristic tests that detect and ignore messages that are implausible.

## Welcome to MonkeyZone

It is often easier to learn complex concepts such as networking from actual code. This is why the jMonkeyEngine team has created MonkeyZone, a proof-of-concept demo of a network game. MonkeyZone loads a simple wireframe scene where players and NPCs interact. Players can shoot, drive a vehicle, and prompt an NPC to follow or walk away. Several players can connect to the same interactive world. Each player gets paired up with an NPC character.

When a human player presses a button, or an NPC performs a game action, this action is sent to the server. The server calculates the game logic, determines the new state, and broadcasts the results to all clients. The AI code that determines when an NPC acts and where it goes is executed on the client, and the results are sent up to the server. Both clients and server run parts of the physics simulation. The server sends regular authoritative synchronization messages to prevent drifting.

Let's see how much effort is needed. An experienced Java developer wrote this demo in a week using the jMonkeyEngine SDK and the `BasicGame` project template. The open source code follows best practices and showcases synchronization between jBullet Physics and the SpiderMonkey API. The project design makes it possible to edit maps, vehicles, and so on, in the jMonkeyEngine SDK. This allows model designers to contribute artwork more easily without having to change any code.

The MonkeyZone source code is available from our GoogleCode Subversion repository. You can check out a copy using any Subversion client. The following example uses the Subversion integration in the jMonkeyEngine SDK.

1. Choose **Team | Subversion | Checkout** from the menu.

2. Enter the SVN URL `https://monkeyzone.googlecode.com/svn/trunk/`.

3. Wait for the project to download and open it in the SDK when prompted.

4. Right-click the project node to build the project.

5. Run the server first (`com.jme3.monkeyzone.ServerMain`), and then one or more clients (`com.jme3.monkeyzone.ClientMain`).

Feel free to look at the code and re-use it for your own multiplayer games!

# Pop Quiz Answers

## Chapter 2, Creating Your First 3D Scene

### Pop quiz – which way, vector?

| Q1. | 2 |
|-----|---|

## Chapter 3, Interacting with the User

### Pop quiz – input handling

| Q1. | 1 |
|-----|---|

### Pop quiz – how to control game mechanics

| Q1. | a2, a3, b4, b5, c1, c6 |
|-----|------------------------|

# Chapter 4, Adding Character to Your Game

## Pop quiz – managing assets: best practices

| Q1. | 3 |
|-----|---|

## Pop quiz – animating a model

| Q1. | 1b, 2c, 3b, 4c |
|-----|----------------|

# Chapter 5, Creating Materials

## Pop quiz – transparent versus opaque

| Q1. | 1 |
|-----|---|

## Pop quiz – multimapping

| Q1. | 1d, 2e, 3a, 4b, 5c |
|-----|--------------------|

# Chapter 6, Having Fun with Physics

## Pop quiz

| Q1. | 1 |
|-----|---|

# Chapter 8, Creating Landscapes

## Pop quiz

| Q1. | 4 |
|-----|---|

# Chapter 9, Making Yourself Heard

## Pop quiz – audio nodes

| Q1. | 2 |
|-----|---|

# Index

## Thank you for buying
## jMonkeyEngine 3.0 Beginner's Guide

## About Packt Publishing

Packt, pronounced 'packed', published its first book "*Mastering phpMyAdmin for Effective MySQL Management*" in April 2004 and subsequently continued to specialize in publishing highly focused books on specific technologies and solutions.

Our books and publications share the experiences of your fellow IT professionals in adapting and customizing today's systems, applications, and frameworks. Our solution based books give you the knowledge and power to customize the software and technologies you're using to get the job done. Packt books are more specific and less general than the IT books you have seen in the past. Our unique business model allows us to bring you more focused information, giving you more of what you need to know, and less of what you don't.

Packt is a modern, yet unique publishing company, which focuses on producing quality, cutting-edge books for communities of developers, administrators, and newbies alike. For more information, please visit our website: www.packtpub.com.

## About Packt Open Source

In 2010, Packt launched two new brands, Packt Open Source and Packt Enterprise, in order to continue its focus on specialization. This book is part of the Packt Open Source brand, home to books published on software built around Open Source licences, and offering information to anybody from advanced developers to budding web designers. The Open Source brand also runs Packt's Open Source Royalty Scheme, by which Packt gives a royalty to each Open Source project about whose software a book is sold.

## Writing for Packt

We welcome all inquiries from people who are interested in authoring. Book proposals should be sent to author@packtpub.com. If your book idea is still at an early stage and you would like to discuss it first before writing a formal book proposal, contact us; one of our commissioning editors will get in touch with you.

We're not just looking for published authors; if you have strong technical skills but no writing experience, our experienced editors can help you develop a writing career, or simply get some additional reward for your expertise.

## Monkey Game Development: Beginner's Guide

ISBN: 978-1-84969-203-8          Paperback: 402 pages

Create monetized 2D games deployable to almost any platform

1.  Create eight fun 2d games.

2.  Understand how to structure your code, your data structures and how to set up the control flow of a modern 2D game

3.  Learn how to deploy your games to iOS, Android, XNA (Xbox, Windows Phone 7) and desktop platforms (Windows, OSX)

## Corona SDK Mobile Game Development: Beginner's Guide

ISBN: 978-1-84969-188-8          Paperback: 408 pages

An administrator's guide to configuring, securing, customizing, and extending Moodle

1.  Build once and deploy your games to both iOS and Android

2.  Create commercially successful games by applying several monetization techniques and tools

3.  Create three fun games and integrate them with social networks such as Twitter and Facebook

Please check **www.PacktPub.com** for information on our titles

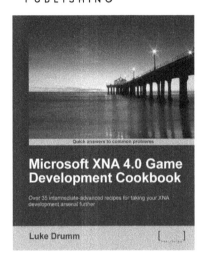

www.ingramcontent.com/pod-product-compliance
Lightning Source LLC
Chambersburg PA
CBHW080151060326
40689CB00018B/3940